Painter 5 Studio Secrets™

PAINTER 5 STUDIO SECRETS™

ADELE DROBLAS GREENBERG & SETH GREENBERG

IDG BOOKS WORLDWIDE, INC.
AN INTERNATIONAL DATA GROUP COMPANY

Foster City, CA ▲ Chicago, IL ◆ Indianapolis, IN ▼ Southlake, TX

Painter 5 Studio Secrets™

Published by
IDG Books Worldwide, Inc.
An International Data Group Company
919 E. Hillsdale Blvd., Suite 400
Foster City, CA 94404
www.idgbooks.com (IDG Books Worldwide Web site)

Copyright © 1998 IDG Books Worldwide, Inc. All rights reserved. No part of this book, including interior design, cover design, and icons, may be reproduced or transmitted in any form, by any means (electronic, photocopying, recording, or otherwise) without the prior written permission of the publisher.

Library of Congress Catalog Card No.: 97-77547

ISBN: 0-7645-4038-6

Printed in the United States of America

10 9 8 7 6 5 4 3 2 1

1K/ST/QS/ZY/FC

Distributed in the United States by IDG Books Worldwide, Inc.

Distributed by Macmillan Canada for Canada; by Transworld Publishers Limited in the United Kingdom; by IDG Norge Books for Norway; by IDG Sweden Books for Sweden; by Woodslane Pty. Ltd. for Australia; by Woodslane Enterprises Ltd. for New Zealand; by Longman Singapore Publishers Ltd. for Singapore, Malaysia, Thailand, and Indonesia; by Simron Pty. Ltd. for South Africa; by Toppan Company Ltd. for Japan; by Distribuidora Cuspide for Argentina; by Livraria Cultura for Brazil; by Ediciencia S.A. for Ecuador; by Addison-Wesley Publishing Company for Korea; by Ediciones ZETA S.C.R. Ltda. for Peru; by WS Computer Publishing Corporation, Inc., for the Philippines; by Unalis Corporation for Taiwan; by Contemporanea de Ediciones for Venezuela; by Computer Book & Magazine Store for Puerto Rico; by Express Computer Distributors for the Caribbean and West Indies. Authorized Sales Agent: Anthony Rudkin Associates for the Middle East and North Africa.

For general information on IDG Books Worldwide's books in the U.S., please call our Consumer Customer Service department at 800-762-2974. For reseller information, including discounts and premium sales, please call our Reseller Customer Service department at 800-434-3422.

For information on where to purchase IDG Books Worldwide's books outside the U.S., please contact our International Sales department at 650-655-3200 or fax 650-655-3295.

For information on foreign language translations, please contact our Foreign & Subsidiary Rights department at 650-655-3021 or fax 650-655-3281.

For sales inquiries and special prices for bulk quantities, please contact our Sales department at 650-655-3200 or write to the address above.

For information on using IDG Books Worldwide's books in the classroom or for ordering examination copies, please contact our Educational Sales department at 800-434-2086 or fax 817-251-8174.

For press review copies, author interviews, or other publicity information, please contact our Public Relations department at 650-655-3000 or fax 650-655-3299.

For authorization to photocopy items for corporate, personal, or educational use, please contact Copyright Clearance Center, 222 Rosewood Drive, Danvers, MA 01923, or fax 978-750-4470.

LIMIT OF LIABILITY/DISCLAIMER OF WARRANTY: AUTHOR AND PUBLISHER HAVE USED THEIR BEST EFFORTS IN PREPARING THIS BOOK. IDG BOOKS WORLDWIDE, INC., AND AUTHOR MAKE NO REPRESENTATIONS OR WARRANTIES WITH RESPECT TO THE ACCURACY OR COMPLETENESS OF THE CONTENTS OF THIS BOOK AND SPECIFICALLY DISCLAIM ANY IMPLIED WARRANTIES OF MERCHANTABILITY OR FITNESS FOR A PARTICULAR PURPOSE. THERE ARE NO WARRANTIES WHICH EXTEND BEYOND THE DESCRIPTIONS CONTAINED IN THIS PARAGRAPH. NO WARRANTY MAY BE CREATED OR EXTENDED BY SALES REPRESENTATIVES OR WRITTEN SALES MATERIALS. THE ACCURACY AND COMPLETENESS OF THE INFORMATION PROVIDED HEREIN AND THE OPINIONS STATED HEREIN ARE NOT GUARANTEED OR WARRANTED TO PRODUCE ANY PARTICULAR RESULTS, AND THE ADVICE AND STRATEGIES CONTAINED HEREIN MAY NOT BE SUITABLE FOR EVERY INDIVIDUAL. NEITHER IDG BOOKS WORLDWIDE, INC., NOR AUTHOR SHALL BE LIABLE FOR ANY LOSS OF PROFIT OR ANY OTHER COMMERCIAL DAMAGES, INCLUDING BUT NOT LIMITED TO SPECIAL, INCIDENTAL, CONSEQUENTIAL, OR OTHER DAMAGES.

Trademarks: All brand names and product names used in this book are trade names, service marks, trademarks, or registered trademarks of their respective owners. IDG Books Worldwide is not associated with any product or vendor mentioned in this book.

 is a trademark under exclusive license to IDG Books Worldwide, Inc., from International Data Group, Inc.

ABOUT IDG BOOKS WORLDWIDE

Welcome to the world of IDG Books Worldwide.

IDG Books Worldwide, Inc., is a subsidiary of International Data Group, the world's largest publisher of computer-related information and the leading global provider of information services on information technology. IDG was founded more than 25 years ago and now employs more than 8,500 people worldwide. IDG publishes more than 275 computer publications in over 75 countries (see listing below). More than 60 million people read one or more IDG publications each month.

Launched in 1990, IDG Books Worldwide is today the #1 publisher of best-selling computer books in the United States. We are proud to have received eight awards from the Computer Press Association in recognition of editorial excellence and three from *Computer Currents'* First Annual Readers' Choice Awards. Our best-selling ...For Dummies® series has more than 30 million copies in print with translations in 30 languages. IDG Books Worldwide, through a joint venture with IDG's Hi-Tech Beijing, became the first U.S. publisher to publish a computer book in the People's Republic of China. In record time, IDG Books Worldwide has become the first choice for millions of readers around the world who want to learn how to better manage their businesses.

Our mission is simple: Every one of our books is designed to bring extra value and skill-building instructions to the reader. Our books are written by experts who understand and care about our readers. The knowledge base of our editorial staff comes from years of experience in publishing, education, and journalism — experience we use to produce books for the '90s. In short, we care about books, so we attract the best people. We devote special attention to details such as audience, interior design, use of icons, and illustrations. And because we use an efficient process of authoring, editing, and desktop publishing our books electronically, we can spend more time ensuring superior content and spend less time on the technicalities of making books.

You can count on our commitment to deliver high-quality books at competitive prices on topics you want to read about. At IDG Books Worldwide, we continue in the IDG tradition of delivering quality for more than 25 years. You'll find no better book on a subject than one from IDG Books Worldwide.

John Kilcullen
CEO
IDG Books Worldwide, Inc.

Steven Berkowitz
President and Publisher
IDG Books Worldwide, Inc.

Eighth Annual
Computer Press
Awards ≥1992

Ninth Annual
Computer Press
Awards ≥1993

Tenth Annual
Computer Press
Awards ≥1994

Eleventh Annual
Computer Press
Awards ≥1995

IDG Books Worldwide, Inc., is a subsidiary of International Data Group, the world's largest publisher of computer-related information and the leading global provider of information services on information technology. International Data Group publishes over 275 computer publications in over 75 countries. Sixty million people read one or more International Data Group's publications each month. International Data Group's publications include: **ARGENTINA:** Buyer's Guide, Computerworld Argentina, PC World Argentina; **AUSTRALIA:** Australian Macworld, Australian PC World, Australian Reseller News, Computerworld, IT Casebook, Network World, Publish, Webmaster; **AUSTRIA:** Computerwelt Österreich, Networks Austria, PC Tip Austria; **BANGLADESH:** PC World Bangladesh; **BELARUS:** PC World Belarus; **BELGIUM:** Data News; **BRAZIL:** Annuário de Informática, Computerworld, Connections, Macworld, PC Player, PC World, Publish, Reseller News, Supergamepower; **BULGARIA:** Computerworld Bulgaria, Network World Bulgaria, PC & MacWorld Bulgaria; **CANADA:** CIO Canada, Client/Server World, ComputerWorld Canada, InfoWorld Canada, Macworld Canada, WebWorld; **CHILE:** Computerworld Chile, PC World Chile; **COLOMBIA:** Computerworld Colombia, PC World Colombia; **COSTA RICA:** PC World Centro America; **THE CZECH AND SLOVAK REPUBLICS:** Computerworld Czechoslovakia, Macworld Czech Republic, PC World Czechoslovakia; **DENMARK:** Communications World Danmark, Computerworld Danmark, Macworld Danmark, PC World Danmark, Techworld Denmark; **DOMINICAN REPUBLIC:** PC World Republica Dominicana; **ECUADOR:** PC World Ecuador; **EGYPT:** Computerworld Middle East, PC World Middle East; **EL SALVADOR:** PC World Centro America; **FINLAND:** MikroPC, Tietoverkko, Tietoviikko; **FRANCE:** Distributique, Hebdo, Info PC, Le Monde Informatique, Macworld, Reseaux & Telecoms, WebMaster France; **GERMANY:** Computer Partner, Computerwoche, Computerwoche Extra, Computerwoche FOCUS, Global Online, Macwelt, PC Welt; **GREECE:** Amiga Computing, GamePro Greece, Multimedia World; **GUATEMALA:** PC World Centro America; **HONDURAS:** PC World Centro America; **HONG KONG:** Computerworld Hong Kong, PC World Hong Kong, Publish in Asia; **HUNGARY:** ABCD CD-ROM, Computerworld Szamitastechnika, Internetto online Magazine, PC World Hungary, PC-X Magazin Hungary; **ICELAND:** Tolvuheimur PC World Island; **INDIA:** Information Communications World, Information Systems Computerworld, PC World India, Publish in Asia; **INDONESIA:** InfoKomputer PC World, Komputek Computerworld, Publish in Asia; **IRELAND:** ComputerScope, PC Live!; **ISRAEL:** Macworld Israel, People & Computers/Computerworld; **ITALY:** Computerworld Italia, Macworld Italia, Networking Italia, PC World Italia; **JAPAN:** DTP World, Macworld Japan, Nikkei Personal Computing, OS/2 World Japan, SunWorld Japan, Windows NT World, Windows World Japan; **KENYA:** PC World East African; **KOREA:** Hi-Tech Information, Macworld Korea, PC World Korea; **MACEDONIA:** PC World Macedonia; **MALAYSIA:** Computerworld Malaysia, PC World Malaysia, Publish in Asia; **MALTA:** PC World Malta; **MEXICO:** Computerworld Mexico, PC World Mexico; **MYANMAR:** PC World Myanmar; **NETHERLANDS:** Computer! Totaal, LAN Internetworking Magazine, LAN World Buyers Guide, Macworld Netherlands, Net, WebWereld; **NEW ZEALAND:** Absolute Beginners Guide and Plain & Simple Series, Computer Buyer, Computer Industry Directory, Computerworld New Zealand, MTB, Network World, PC World New Zealand; **NICARAGUA:** PC World Centro America; **NORWAY:** Computerworld Norge, CW Rapport, Datamagasinet, Financial Rapport, Kursguide Norge, Macworld Norge, Multimediaworld Norge, PC World Ekspress Norge, PC World Nettverk, PC World Norge, PC World ProduktGuide Norge; **PAKISTAN:** Computerworld Pakistan; **PANAMA:** PC World Panama; **PEOPLE'S REPUBLIC OF CHINA:** China Computer Users, China Computerworld, China InfoWorld, China Telecom World Weekly, Computer & Communication, Electronic Design China, Electronics Today, Electronics Weekly, Game Software, PC World China, Popular Computer Week, Software Weekly, Software World, Telecom World; **PERU:** Computerworld Peru, PC World Profesional Peru, PC World SoHo Peru; **PHILIPPINES:** Click!, Computerworld Philippines, PC World Philippines, Publish in Asia; **POLAND:** Computerworld Poland, Computerworld Special Report Poland, Cyber, Macworld Poland, Networld Poland, PC World Komputer; **PORTUGAL:** Cerebro/PC World, Computerworld/Correio Informático, Dealer World Portugal, Mac*In/PC*In Portugal, Multimedia World; **PUERTO RICO:** PC World Puerto Rico; **ROMANIA:** Computerworld Romania, PC World Romania, Telecom Romania; **RUSSIA:** Computerworld Russia, Mir PK, Publish, Seti; **SINGAPORE:** Computerworld Singapore, PC World Singapore, Publish in Asia; **SLOVENIA:** Monitor; **SOUTH AFRICA:** Computing SA, Network World SA, Software World SA; **SPAIN:** Communicaciones World España, Computerworld España, Dealer World España, Macworld España, PC World España; **SRI LANKA:** Infolink PC World; **SWEDEN:** CAP&Design, Computer Sweden, Corporate Computing Sweden, Internetworld Sweden, it.branschen, Macworld Sweden, MaxiData Sweden, MikroDatorn, Nätverk & Kommunikation, PC World Sweden, PCaktiv, Windows World Sweden; **SWITZERLAND:** Computerworld Schweiz, Macworld Schweiz, PCtip; **TAIWAN:** Computerworld Taiwan, Macworld Taiwan, NEW ViSiON/Publish, PC World Taiwan, Windows World Taiwan; **THAILAND:** Publish in Asia, Thai Computerworld; **TURKEY:** Computerworld Turkiye, Macworld Turkiye, Network World Turkiye, PC World Turkiye; **UKRAINE:** Computerworld Kiev, Multimedia World Ukraine, PC World Ukraine; **UNITED KINGDOM:** Acorn User UK, Amiga Action UK, Amiga Computing UK, Apple Talk UK, Computing, Macworld, Parents and Computers UK, PC Advisor, PC Home, PSX Pro, The WEB; **UNITED STATES:** Cable in the Classroom, CIO Magazine, Computerworld, DOS World, Federal Computer Week, GamePro Magazine, InfoWorld, I-Way, Macworld, Network World, PC Games, PC World, Publish, Video Event, THE WEB Magazine, and WebMaster; online webzines: JavaWorld, NetscapeWorld, and SunWorld Online; **URUGUAY:** InfoWorld Uruguay; **VENEZUELA:** Computerworld Venezuela, PC World Venezuela; and **VIETNAM:** PC World Vietnam.

3/24/97

To Angelique, for the joy she brings to us each day.

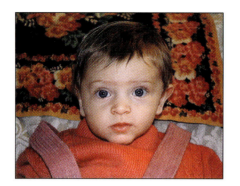

FOREWORD

It takes a long time to bake a new release of Painter. You start with a stock of plug-in brushes, fold in a cup of dynamic floaters, and season with a variety of spicy filter effects. You boil this over the hot minds of a dozen programmers and cook it down to a savory stew of creativity.

As with all culinary creations, you must dip into the broth and sample at all stages of development, delicately adjusting the mix of exotic ingredients. It was over eleven months ago—early into the cooking of Painter 5—when Adele and Seth came to our house to sample a bowl. We laid our best china and ladled out heaping serving of new features. Adele was nine months pregnant, and she could eat, and eat, and eat!

If chefs could be modest, we'd have to say that Painter 5 is our best work to date. It is a perfect mix of innovative new features, like the astounding Liquid Metal dynamic floater, and practical program refinements, like industry-standard masking and super cloning brushes. In this release we redoubled our commitment to Natural-Media with Impasto layer brushes, strengthened the core of the program with hundreds of new brushed effects, and put new looks, new mixing models, and new power in the hands of the artist.

Painter has hundreds, even thousands, of secrets and tricks. One of the key secrets of Painter 5 is that all the new brushes and dynamic floaters use a new extensible architecture. This not only allows new looks to be plugged into the program, but also allows you to combine and recombine the plug-in brushes and floaters in magical ways. The book you're holding will teach you these secrets. Seth and Adele have uncovered the best of the studio secrets. In these pages you'll learn how professional artists are using and taking advantage of Painter 5. You'll learn how to do it, too!

Digital imaging is still expanding, but only Painter continues to explore the territory that lies between digital and traditional art. Our goal is to innovate by combining new technologies with an appreciation for the world of the artist and the designer. Painter 5 is a peek into the future, with its unique looks that can't be created with any other program. We're blazing a new path for the traditional illustrator into the digital medium. Try it. You'll like it.

Jon Bass
Senior Product Manager
MetaCreations

Mark Zimmer
Chief Technical Officer
MetaCreations

PREFACE

Painter is a program bursting at the seams with power and hidden delights. In fact, Painter boasts so many features, we often think it has a life of its own—palettes seem to sprout more palettes, and menu commands seem to sprout more dialog boxes. The more you learn about the program, the more that awaits you.

We realize that most Painter users know how to grab a brush and start painting. But things get a bit tricky when your goal is to complete a complicated project. How do you edit a floater's mask to create a perfect blend between one floater and another? How do you make 3D text pop out of a digital image? How do you animate Painter images to make them come alive? In *Painter 5 Studio Secrets* we answer these questions and focus on topics we feel are the most important to artists.

HOW THIS BOOK IS ORGANIZED

Painter 5 Studio Secrets is divided into two parts. In Part I, "Painter Secrets," we focus on areas many Painter artists often long to know more about—creating masks, floaters, and shapes. Both of us teach Painter classes in New York City; our focus in Part 1 comes from our experience teaching and working with artists.

In Part II, "Studio Secrets," we provide countless examples of amazing and intriguing Painter art grouped according to subject matter. Deciding where to put images was not always easy. If an image was created primarily by painting with brushes, we placed it into Chapter 8, "Painting Techniques." If floaters played the most important role in an image, we placed it in Chapter 9, "Composite Techniques." This means you'll often see work by several artists appearing in different chapters. When possible, we provide step-by-step instructions on how each artist created his or her own work. We also tried to provide an insight into the creative process the artists went through—what their goals were and what they thought about as they approached their artwork.

As we started working on the book and contacting artists, we were amazed at the quality and creativity of the work we received. We're happy and honored to share this with you.

STYLE NOTES

When writing *Painter 5 Studio Secrets*, we were faced with the question of how best to describe the tools artists used in an instructive manner that wouldn't be confusing. For example, an artist might say that he or she used Painter's Scratchboard tool. Where is the

Scratchboard tool? You can click or double-click all day in Painter's tools palette, and you still won't find anything called a Scratchboard tool. This is because the Scratchboard tool is a brush in the Brushes palette. But where in the Brushes palette? It is a Pens brush variant. To help readers find the Scratchboard tool, we describe the tool as the Pens Scratchboard tool. Thus, if you're looking for it in Painter, you know to click the Pens brush in the Brushes palette and select it in the group of Pens brush variants.

We tried to use this naming system whenever a brush variant might be hard to identify. For example, the Distorto brush is a Liquid brush variant. To describe the brush, we write *Liquid Distorto brush variant*. The Big Wet Oils brush is a Brush variant. It is called the *Brush Big Wet Oils variant* in the text.

Usually a brush variant's name provides a hint as to where to look for it. For example, we felt that most readers could guess that the Artist Pastel Chalk brush variant is a Chalk brush variant. Thus, we don't call this brush the Chalk Artist Pastel Chalk variant; nor did we want to bog down the text by calling the 2B Pencil the Pencil 2B Pencil.

Finally, as you read *Painter 5 Studio Secrets*, you'll see many keyboard shortcuts sprinkled about the text. Because Painter is available for both the Mac and PC, we included shortcuts for both platforms. When you see, ⌘/Ctrl, this means Mac users should press the Command Key, and PC users should press Ctrl. Don't be confused if you see Control/Shift (used when cloning). This doesn't mean that Mac and PC users press the Control key and the Shift keys. It simply means Mac users press Control, PC users press Shift.

ACKNOWLEDGMENTS

Painter 5 Studio Secrets couldn't have been written without the help, cooperation, and dedication of numerous people.

We'd like to thank everyone who helped in the creation of this book, especially Mike Roney, who asked us to write the book and helped get this project off the ground and moving.

We'd also like to express our thanks to Development Editors Katharine Dvorak and Amy Thomas for their help and suggestions, and their tireless efforts in shepherding this book on its journey from our Mac and PC to the printed page. Thanks also to Nate Holdread, who diligently copyedited every word of this book. We'd especially like to thank our Technical Editor, Ben Barbante, for his helpful suggestions and comments. (As you read through the book, you'll see several clever and skillful Painter images created by Ben.)

We'd also like to thank Katy German and the rest of the Production staff at IDG Books Worldwide for making the production process go so smoothly.

We also thank everyone at MetaCreations for their support, especially Chief Technical Officer Mark Zimmer and Senior Product Manager Jon Bass for their help—and for writing the Foreword of this book. We'd also like to thank Mark and John Derry for allowing us to intrude on their busy schedules when it came time to answer our interview questions. Thanks also to Kim Kern for helping us get the information we needed in a timely manner.

Others who helped get the product demos for the CD include Sallie Olmsted, Karen Hooten, and Kerry Glassbum.

Thanks also to Terry Campbell, Amy Russell, and Kevin Clark at MetaCreations for helping us extend our list of Painter artists.

Finally, we'd like to thank the many Painter artists who submitted their artwork and enthusiastically offered to share their creative experiences with our readers. They are the true "stars" of this book. We enjoyed working with all of these talented people. If you're an art director looking for some great talent, you can find these artists' e-mail addresses and biographies in the Artist Index in the back of this book.

CONTENTS AT A GLANCE

FOREWORD   vii

PREFACE   ix

ACKNOWLEDGMENTS   xi

PART I: PAINTER SECRETS   1

Chapter 1   Pixel Perfection   3
Chapter 2   The Painter Palettes   13
Chapter 3   The Magic of Masks   39
Chapter 4   Creating Shapes   47
Chapter 5   The Power of Floaters   55
Chapter 6   Startling Effects of the Image Hose   65
Chapter 7   Outputting Your Artwork   75

PART II: STUDIO SECRETS   85

Chapter 8   Painting Techniques   87
Chapter 9   Composite Techniques   111
Chapter 10   Type Effects   141
Chapter 11   Enhancing Digital And Painted Images   153
Chapter 12   Creating Special Effects   169
Chapter 13   Painter, Multimedia, and Web Animation   181
Chapter 14   Using Painter with Other Programs   189
Chapter 15   Painter Gallery   203

APPENDIX   USING THE CD-ROM   219

ARTIST INDEX   221

INDEX   229

ABOUT THE AUTHORS   246

COLOPHON   247

CONTENTS

FOREWORD vii

PREFACE ix

ACKNOWLEDGMENTS xi

PART I: PAINTER SECRETS 1

CHAPTER 1
PIXEL PERFECTION 3

Resolution Secrets 6
    Choosing the proper resolution 6

Resizing Images 9
    Resizing images for print 9
    Resizing images for the Web and multimedia 9
    Reducing images for print, the Web,
        or multimedia 9

Playing Back a Script at a High Resolution 10

CHAPTER 2
THE PAINTER PALETTES 13

The Tools Palette 14

The Controls Palette 15

The Brushes Palette 16

The Art Materials Palette 29
    Art Materials: Color 29
    Art Materials: Paper 29
    Art Materials: Grad 30
    Art Materials: Patterns 32
    Art Materials: Weaves 34

The Objects Palette   34
    The Objects Plugin Floaters   34
    The Objects: Floater List Palette   35
    The Objects: Mask List Palette   35
    The Objects: Network Palette   36

The Color Set Palette   36

Creating A Custom Palette   36
    The Objects: Scripts Palette   36

CHAPTER 3
THE MAGIC OF MASKS   39

Using Selections as Masks   40
    Using the selection mask icons   40
    Saving selections   41

Creating Masks   42
    Creating a mask from a brush stroke   42

Select Menu Secrets   42

Creating Special Effects with Luminance Masks   44

CHAPTER 4
CREATING SHAPES   47

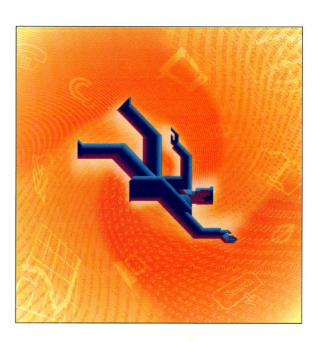

Basic Shapes   48

Using the Pen Tool   48
    Continuing a path   50
    Combining curves and lines   50
    Editing Paths   50
    Ending a path   50

Using the Text Tool   51

Using Duplicate Transform   51

Using Blends   52

Importing and Exporting Shapes from Illustrator   53

Contents   xvii

CHAPTER 5
THE POWER OF FLOATERS   55

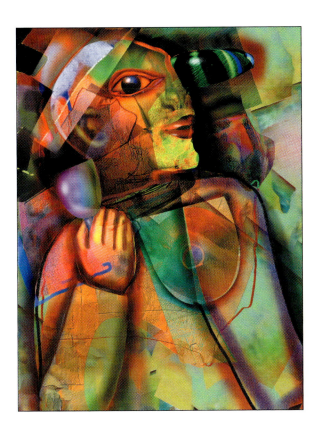

Floaters Examined   56

Creating Floaters   56
    Understanding floater masks   57
    Editing the floater mask   58

Using the Floater List palette   59

Using the floater Composite Methods   59

Creating Transparent Layers   61

Plug-in floaters   62

CHAPTER 6
STARTLING EFFECTS OF THE IMAGE HOSE   65

Loading the Nozzle File   66

Understanding the Nozzle File   66
    Understanding Image Hose ranking   67
    Understanding the Image Hose variants   67
    Using the Nozzle palette sliders   70
    Using the Image Hose and the Controls palette   70

Using Place Elements with the Image Hose   70

Creating An Image Hose Using Floaters   71

CHAPTER 7
OUTPUTTING YOUR ARTWORK   75

The Kodak Color Management System   78
   Implementing KCMS   78
   Using KCMS   79

Printing and Saving Separations with KCMS   80

Outputting Fine Art Prints   80

Using Pantone Colors   81

Outputting to the Web   82
   Saving in JPEG   82
   Saving in GIF   82

Outputting to QuickTime and Video
For Windows   83
   Saving In QuickTime or AVI Format   83

PART II: STUDIO SECRETS   85

CHAPTER 8
PAINTING TECHNIQUES   87

Using the New Paint Tools   87

Using Multiple Brushes   89

Creating a Superhero   90

Taking A Traditional Approach   91

Going Au Naturale   93

Pencil, Chalk, and Water Color   94

Using Mixed Media   94

Ceremony and Cherokee Mist   95

Chao Meng Fu   96

Rooster Genetics   96

Using Wet and Dry Modes   96

Using Paper Textures   98
   Lost toys, Fashion Scents, and Chameleon   98
   Fool and Face   99

Painting with Custom Textures   101

Creating Custom Textures from Photographs   103

More Paintings with Textures   104

Using Cartoon Cell Fill   104
   A friendly dragon   105
   Argon Zark!   106

Customizing Brushes   109

CHAPTER 9
COMPOSITE TECHNIQUES   111

Compositing Images Using Brushes and Photographs   111
   Creating Nostalgia   111
   Creating Tourist   113

Using Cloning and Cloning Brushes to Composite Images   114
   The Blessing   114
   Memory Portrait   115
   Song of Peace   116
   The Owl and the Pussy Cat   118

Using Floaters   120
   Doug Lockyer's floater magic   120

Sword and Butterfly   123
Feast of Fools and The Crack   123
Sky Dream   124
Cosmological Constant   125
Anguish and Coffeehouse/Last Rites   125
Shubat Tulips   126
Cats, dogs, cowboys, and nocturne   126
Sea, Maid, and Landscape   128
Argon Zark!   130
Merlin   134
Vivo   135

Working with Shapes, Floaters, and Selections   135
   Ken's mural   136
   The Transcendentalist   136

Using Selections and Floaters   137
   Flowers and Cats   137
   August Flowers   138
   More Posters   138
   Patrick's computers   139

CHAPTER 10
TYPE EFFECTS   141

Creating Vector Type Effects   141
   Editing vector text   141
   Using Average Points to edit vector text   143

Using Apply Surface Texture to Raise Type   144

Using Apply Surface Texture to Create Chrome Text   145

Raising Text Out of A Digital Image   146

Creating Bevel World Type Effects   146

Using Type and Painting Tools   148

Creating a Mosaic Out of Text   151

CHAPTER 11
ENHANCING DIGITAL AND PAINTED IMAGES   153

CHAPTER 12
CREATING SPECIAL EFFECTS   169

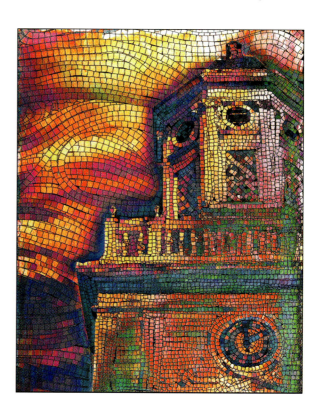

Converting Photographs into Paintings   153
   Painting with Auto Van Gogh   153
   Painting with Auto Clone   154
   Painting with the Van Gogh 2 brush   155
   Tracing over Digital Images   156
   Using the Cloners Brushes   157

Converting Black-and-White Images to Color   158

Adjusting Paintings and Digital Images   160

Working with Glass Distortion   169

Working with Apply Surface Texture   171

Working with Plug-in Floaters   172

Working with Mosaics   176

Contents xxi

CHAPTER 13
PAINTER, MULTIMEDIA,
AND WEB ANIMATION   181

Bangles, Buttons, and Backgrounds   181
    Buttons from Bevel World   181
    Creating an interface   182

Creating and Editing Movies   183

Creating Web Animation   184
    The Animated CD-ROM   185
    Making cats paint…   185
    …and mice jump through hoops   186

CHAPTER 14
USING PAINTER WITH OTHER
PROGRAMS   189

Using Painter with 3D Modeling Programs   189
    Creating Day Dream Charlie   190
    Glowing Buddhas   191
    Blocks of products   191
    The Biker   192
    Robot + Picasso = Robocasso   192

Using Painter with Illustrator and FreeHand   193
    A new look at Lake Tahoe   193
    Flower Seller   193
    Spirit of 'Inde'pendence   193
    Rodney's Japanese playmates   195

Using Painter with Photoshop   196
    Woman, Ship & Pearls   196
    A software package cover   196
    The Buddy System   197

Using Painter with Multiple Programs 197
 Kidstuff 197
 Benevolence and Prophecy 198
 The Age of Aquarius 198
 Dog days 199
 Unicorn Girl 200
 Looking for America 200
 Other worlds 200

CHAPTER 15
PAINTER GALLERY 203

APPENDIX
USING THE CD-ROM 219

ARTIST INDEX 221

INDEX 229

ABOUT THE AUTHORS 246

COLOPHON 247

PART I
PAINTER SECRETS

Pixel Perfection 3
The Painter Palettes 13
The Magic of Masks 39
Creating Shapes 47
The Power of Floaters 55
Startling Effects of the Image Hose 64
Outputting Your Artwork 75

CHAPTER 1
PIXEL PERFECTION

It all starts with pixels...

The digital art that flows from Painter's magical electronic brushes is possible because each Painter image is composed of countless tiny pixels. Painter controls each and every one of them—turning them off, turning them on, coloring them with any one of more than a million different colors.

The pixels that artists transform into Painter art spring from many sources. For many Painter artists, the standard method of creating the pixels that make up a Painter image is to choose File ➤ New in Painter. Next they set the image dimensions and number of pixels per inch. This is how German artist Anton Atzenhofer started *Face* (1.1). He created the image using different papers and brushes and based the image on a pencil sketch. Other artists, who prefer a head start on image creation or wish to give their Wacom tablets a rest, start by digitizing images using scanners, video grabbers, and/or digital cameras.

For example, artist Jack Gold began *Lobster Buoy* (1.2) by sketching a scene of lobster buoys on paper. He turned his sketch into pixels by scanning it. He later created the perspective by choosing the Painter command Effects ➤ Transform.

New Yorker Emily Stedman is another artist who frequently starts her Painter artwork with digitized images. In *Wedding* (1.3) she scanned in marbleized paper to use as the background and then proceeded to paint the flower and wedding ring. To create *The Tied Hands* (1.4), Emily started by scanning a stock photograph of hands and a snake, and then she used

To create* Still Life with Glass and Peaches, *Simon Feldman recorded a script at low resolution and then played it back at a high resolution. While Painter played back the script at a high resolution, Simon went out for sushi.

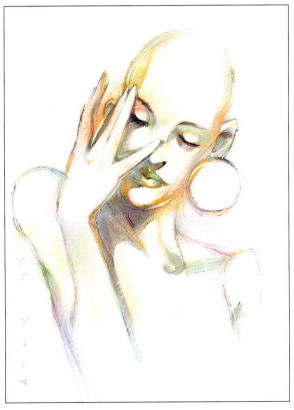

1.1

STILL LIFE WITH GLASS AND PEACHES
Simon Feldman

Painter's cloning tools to composite the images together.

Dennis Orlando's *Summer Flowers Planter* (1.5) started life as a video grab (1.6). Dennis created a freeze frame of the image and then cropped it. Then he used Painter's Tracing Paper feature to sketch the flowers. He used the Water Color brush and Just Add Water brush variant to paint the flowers. When he was finished painting, he applied Adobe's Gallery Effects' Water Color filter.

The descriptions of the elegant artwork that open this chapter should give you an idea of the different

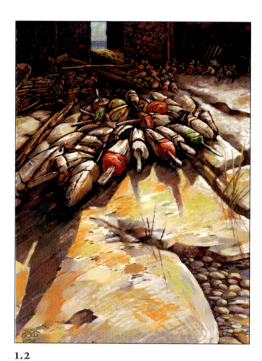

1.2

1.3

THE BEGINNINGS

Interview with Mark Zimmer, Chief Technical Officer at MetaCreations

IT MAY SEEM hard to believe, but Mark Zimmer, Painter's creator, began creating Painter as a program that emulates how a simple lead pencil draws. How did Painter develop into the world's premiere paint program? In the interview found in several of the chapters throughout the book, Mark, MetaCreations Chief Technical Officer, and John Derry, Director of Natural Media Research, share their thoughts on Painter's development and provide insights into the artistic philosophy behind the program.

Mark Zimmer

techniques professional artists use to begin the technical aspects of image creation. However, to output their images successfully, all Painter artists must know the secrets to getting the proper number of pixels into the image they are creating.

Come along as we uncover the hidden world of pixels.

1.5

1.4

1.6

Q: How did Painter get started?

MZ: I started Painter at Fractal Software (partnership with Tom Hedges) in September 1990 by thinking about how I could mimic the effect of a simple lead pencil. I studied paper texture and overlaying of pencil strokes, and did some work studying ink pen as well.

It took some four months of work at home before I showed the work to anyone else (outside Tom Hedges). But the work I had done quickly became a compelling reason to start Fractal Design.

Q: What programming language was used to create Painter?

MZ: Painter was written in C and assembler. In those days, the 68K machines were relatively slow by modern standards, and I had to perk up the program with a small amount of 68K assembler in the tight loops.

Q: How/why did you get started programming?

MZ: A friend in high school named Paul Gootherts was a programming enthusiast. He worked on some code for high-precision numerical calculation, and I helped him apply it to number theory. Among hundreds of other things, we calculated the cube root of two to 2,000 places (I still have the printout!). Later (in 1973) he taught me Basic with the help of after-hours machine time at HP. When I went to CalTech for one year, I began to seriously apply programming to number theory, prime number factoring techniques, and a search for prime quadruplets (which I completed up to 1 billion). But it wasn't until 1974 that I started serious computer graphics programming

RESOLUTION SECRETS

The quality of a digital image is often determined by its resolution. Simply put, an image's resolution is the number of pixels in the image. In Painter you set the number of pixels in an image when you create or resize it. Choosing the proper resolution for an image lays a sturdy foundation for sharpness and color fidelity.

If you choose too low a resolution, you may find that your image prints improperly on a printing press. Choosing too high a resolution may make your image appear too small on a Web page.

In Painter you can set an image's resolution when you first create the image, using the File ➤ New command. In the dialog box that opens, specify the width and height of your image, and the number of pixels per inch (or the number of pixels per centimeter). If you want to start with a digital image, you can scan it directly into Painter using the File ➤ Acquire command.

Although Painter allows you to reduce and increase the number of pixels in an image, it's always safest to start by choosing a resolution based on how you intend to output your image. You can usually remove pixels without fear of impairing image quality, but you can't add pixels to an image without some loss of quality. If you add pixels, Painter must choose painting colors for the pixels that you add, which can result in poorer color quality and a loss of image detail.

UNDERSTANDING SCREEN FREQUENCY

When a digital image is output, the pixels in the image are arranged into a pattern of tiny grids called *halftones*. The overlaying of different colored halftone patterns (of cyan, magenta, yellow, and black ink) produces the illusion of millions of colors when your document is printed. The number of halftones per inch is the screen frequency used to output your image. The greater the screen frequency, the finer the image.

In general, screen frequency is determined by the paper stock and by the printing press used to output your file. The screen frequency used for glossy colored printing is often 150 lines per inch (lpi) or higher. Screen frequency for newspapers can be between 80 and 90 lpi. If you don't know the screen frequency, ask your printer.

CHOOSING THE PROPER RESOLUTION

Most Painter artists output their images to print, to multimedia programs, to the Web, or to fine art substrates such as canvas and rice paper. Each of these specific areas requires different rules for resolution settings.

---

at Calma.

Q: As a successful programmer, what advice do you have for people who want to create their own software? What should they avoid or watch out for?

MZ: The things to do:
- It takes people skills to become successful. Don't just obsess on software—get a life, too!
- Use other activities to enhance your creativity, like Legos and music. Sometimes you get the best ideas in completely different venues.
- Make sure there's a market for something before creating it (unless you have an overriding hunch that a new market can be "plowed").
- Find a good business partner to bounce ideas off of. Two heads are often several times better than one.
- Once a program is out there (in beta or on the market), listen to the users. The users often have something to accomplish. Learn what those things are and learn how to accomplish them yourself.
- Make sure your demo is polished. Try it out on your friends. Do a demo 10 times before doing one that's really important.

Things to avoid and how to avoid them:
- Don't try to do everything yourself. Find people who can help you with marketing, business skills, sales acuity.
- Don't try to build the program to just satisfy yourself — you are inherently biased as its creator! Try to get people from different disciplines to comment on your creation right after the rapid prototyping process, and really listen to their market advice.

Outputting for print

If you are outputting your Painter work to a commercial printing press, the general rule is to set your image resolution at 1½ to 2 times the screen frequency used to output your file.

Using this rule, you can easily determine the resolution you need when you create a file. If your screen frequency is 150 lpi, make your Painter file 300 pixels per inch (ppi). If the screen frequency is 80 lpi, create your new image at 160 ppi.

If you are digitizing an image for print, the same rules hold true. When you use File ➤ Acquire to digitize in Painter (File ➤ Import in Photoshop), set your scanning resolution to twice the screen frequency.

Resolution and digital cameras

As digital cameras grow in popularity and drop in price, you're certain to see more and more Painter artwork first seen through the lens of a digital camera. Stacy A. Hopkins is one Painter artist who is trying out the newest in digital technology. He created *Water Lily Flower* (1.7) by first shooting a picture of a water lily with a digital camera. He then loaded the file into Painter and used it as a clone source. Next he smeared on the colors with small Chalk Cloner brushes and used Painter's Soft Cloner to touch up the image. He completed the image using Alien Skin's Black Box plug-ins to create the round look on the image edges.

Although digital cameras provide artists with more freedom than scanners do, many digital cameras do not provide the resolution necessary for high quality output. Because Stacy used his digital camera image as a clone source, he could clone a low resolution image into a high resolution image. However, if you want to integrate a shot from a digital camera into a Painter image that will be printed on a printing press, you need to ensure that the camera can produce enough pixels for the job.

Unfortunately, trying to determine whether the resolution provided by a digital camera is sufficient can be tricky. Typically, digital camera resolution is measured by width and height in pixels rather than pixels per inch. For example, low-price digital cameras such as Apple Computer's QuickTake camera, as well as cameras manufactured by Agfa, Olympus, Yashica,

TIP

Many artists digitize their work directly in Photoshop and later load it into Painter. Save yourself a few steps by digitizing directly into Painter. This procedure is possible because most Photoshop 3.0 plug-ins are compatible with Painter. The trick to digitizing in Painter is to tell Painter where your digitizing plug-ins are located. To direct Painter to your digitizing plug-ins, choose Edit ➤ Preferences ➤ Raster Plug-ins. Select the directory that contains your plug-in and click OK. (You may want to copy the plug-in to your Painter folder.) After you set the plug-in folder, restart Painter and choose File ➤ Acquire. Your scanning software should appear in the File ➤ Acquire menu.

NOTE

Plug-ins designed for Photoshop 4, such as Alien Skin's Eye Candy, are not compatible with Painter 5. Only plug-ins designed for Photoshop 3 are compatible with Painter 5.

1.7

and Epson, capture images at a resolution of 640 × 480 pixels. The Kodak DC120 camera is a step up—it features a resolution of 765 × 504. The Polaroid PDC 2000/40, which retails for almost $3,000, features a resolution of 1,600 × 2,000.

How do you decide whether a digital camera can capture enough pixels for your artwork? It's easy—let Painter help you out. All you need to do is create a 72 ppi dummy file set to your camera's pixel dimensions, and then use Painter's Resize dialog box to determine if the image contains enough pixels.

For example, assume you are shooting a subject using a digital camera that captures images at a resolution of 1,600 × 1,200. You need the printed image to appear at 4 × 3 inches. Assume you will be printing your image in a magazine that requires output at 150 lpi. The minimum resolution necessary for your Painter image is obtained by multiplying 1½ × 150 (which equals 225 pixels per inch). Can your camera provide an image with 225 pixels per inch that is 4 × 3 inches? Using Painter, follow these steps to find out (This technique works because digital camera files open up in Painter at 72 ppi, regardless of the camera's pixel-capturing capabilities.):

1. Create a new file in Painter and enter the camera's pixel dimensions: **1600** into the width field and **1200** into the height field. In the resolution field, enter **72**. Click OK.

2. Choose Canvas ➤ Resize. Set the width and height measurement units to inches, and make sure the Constrain file size check box is selected. (When this check box is selected, Painter changes image dimensions to compensate for a change in resolution.) Next enter the resolution of the image you need. In this case, you need 225 pixels per inch.

Painter immediately lowers the image's dimensions to compensate for the increase in resolution. Painter indicates that the original 72 ppi image changes to 7.1 × 5.33 inches at 225 ppi. Because this size is larger than the image size you need, the camera should produce an image with enough pixels.

Outputting to the Web

Many digital artists mistakenly assume that the higher the resolution, the better the image quality, no matter whether the image is printed or displayed onscreen. If you are creating Painter images that will be displayed on the Web, you need only create your images at the resolution required to view them on a computer monitor.

Virtually all computer monitors display images at a minimum of 72 ppi (640 × 480 pixels). Typically, Windows 95 and Windows NT users set their monitors' resolutions to 600 × 800, which translates to 96 ppi. Nonetheless, to ensure that all images are displayed properly on as many monitors as possible, many Webmasters recommend creating all images at 72 ppi.

What happens if you create an image at a resolution higher than 72 ppi and output it on the Web? If you create your file at 96 ppi, most PC users will view the image perfectly; however, those users with monitor resolutions of 72 ppi will need to scroll a bit more because the image will appear larger on their screens.

Images appear at different screen sizes because of the difference between the number of pixels your monitor can display per inch and the number of pixels per inch in your image. If you create an image at 72 ppi, and a monitor displays 72 ppi, a 3 × 3 inch Painter image will appear at 3 × 3 inches. However, if you create the image at 96 ppi, only 72 of the 96 pixels appear per inch. The remaining pixels spill over, making the image appear about a half-inch larger. This is obviously not a major problem. But if you create a 3 × 3 inch image at 300 ppi, the image appears approximately four times as large on a 72 ppi monitor.

> **NOTE**
>
> If you attempt the same experiments with a digital camera that captures images at 640 × 480, you find that at 225 ppi, the largest image can be only 2.8 × 2.1 inches. Cameras that feature 640 × 480 resolution are usually best suited for images that will appear on the Web or in multimedia programs.

Choosing resolution for multimedia presentations

Rules for multimedia output are similar to those for outputting to the Web. You need to create your images at the viewing resolution of the computer monitor. If you know that your images will be viewed only on 12– or 13–inch monitors, set your resolution to 72 ppi, and don't set the dimensions larger than 640 × 480 pixels. Otherwise, users will need to scroll to see the entire image. If you're sure that your images will be viewed on PC screens at 96 ppi, you can set your images at 96 ppi with the pixel dimensions no larger than 800 × 600.

RESIZING IMAGES

It's not always possible to predict exactly how large your final image will be if it's going to be output in a book, a magazine, or on the Web. An image often needs to be resized when it appears alongside text in one of these media. When you create or digitize an image, your safest bet is to plan in advance. Many images output to the Web and multimedia are reduced in size. Images scanned from slides most likely will be enlarged. You should plan for these changes when you digitize your images.

Before you resize images, you should be familiar with Painter's Canvas ➢ Resize dialog box, which allows you to change an image's dimensions as well as the number of pixels per inch in the image.

It's important to understand the consequences of resizing an image. When you resize, Painter enables you to add, decrease, or maintain the number of pixels in an image. If you add pixels to an image, you increase its file size and decrease its quality. How do you enlarge the dimensions of an image and preserve quality? Keep the Constrain File Size check box selected.

If you keep the Constrain File Size check box selected, Painter reduces the number of pixels per inch when you increase image dimensions in inches, and it increases the number of pixels per inch when you decrease dimensions in inches. This means that images that will be enlarged must be digitized at a higher resolution than the required output resolution. The following sections provide some typical examples.

RESIZING IMAGES FOR PRINT

To enlarge images that will be printed, you should start by calculating the *scaling factor* of the enlargement using the following formula: Longest side of resized image ratio ÷ longest side of original.

For example, assume that you scan a 3 × 2 inch image, and the image needs to be output at 6 × 4 inches. The scaling formula tells you that your scaling factor is 2.

Assume your printer or prepress house tells you that your final digital image should be 300 ppi. To calculate your scanning resolution, simply multiply the required pixels per inch by the scaling factor: Multiply 300 by 2 and then digitize your image at 600 ppi.

In Painter, choose Canvas ➢ Resize to begin resizing your image. First make sure that the Constrain File Size check box is selected. Then change the longest dimension from 3 inches to 6 inches; Painter immediately drops the resolution from 600 to 300 ppi—your desired resolution.

RESIZING IMAGES FOR THE WEB AND MULTIMEDIA

If you are enlarging images that will appear on the Web or in a multimedia presentation, you must first determine the screen resolution of your viewers' computer displays—typically 72 ppi. (As mentioned earlier, many PC monitors display images at 96 ppi.) Knowing the viewing resolution, you must create or digitize your image at a higher resolution to compensate for the enlargement. (If you don't know the precise scaling factor, simply divide the longest dimension in the final image by the longest dimension in the original image, and then multiply by 72.)

For example, if you are enlarging an image by a factor of three, digitize at 216 ppi (3 × 72). When you resize the image (Canvas ➢ Resize), make sure the Constrain File Size check box is selected. Painter drops the resolution to 72.

REDUCING IMAGES FOR PRINT, THE WEB, OR MULTIMEDIA

Reducing image size is simple. Make sure you create the image at the correct resolution. In Painter's Resize dialog box, uncheck the Constrain File Size check box. When you reduce the image, Painter subtracts pixels from the image but doesn't change the resolution. Don't worry about the missing pixels; when you reduce an image, the missing pixels aren't noticed.

PLAYING BACK A SCRIPT AT A HIGH RESOLUTION

Throughout history, artists have lived with the reputation of being poor and starving. In the digital age, artists never seem to have enough money to purchase the computing power they desire. If your computer system just can't muscle up enough power to produce high-resolution images efficiently, try a time-saving trick used by artist Simon Feldman. To create *Still Life with Glass and Peaches* (1.8), Simon recorded a script at a low resolution and then played it back at a high resolution. While Painter played back the script at a high resolution, Simon went out for sushi.

Although good sushi may not be available in all parts of the country, you can still take advantage of Painter's script-playing capabilities. First plan your image. Simon set up the lighting on a photographic set. He captured his original image (1.9) using a high-resolution Phase One digital camera back (1.10). He lowered the resolution in Photoshop and then opened up the image in Painter to record the script. Simon then used the Select ➤ All command to create a reference rectangle in Painter, and then clicked the record button in the Objects: Script palette to begin the recording.

1.8

1.9

TIP

Before recording a script, open the Script Options dialog box (Script ≻ Script Options) and choose Record Initial State. This ensures that the final playback utilizes the tools chosen when you first recorded your image.

1.10

CHAPTER 2
THE PAINTER PALETTES

Unlocking the secrets of Painter's palettes takes time, but it's time well spent. Once you discover the secrets of Painter's palettes, you gain entry to a world of unlimited digital possibilities. Join us as we take a tour of Painter's palettes, look at some of Painter's underutilized commands, which are easily accessible through palette controls, and explore some of the new features of Painter 5. As you start exploring the palettes, you'll encounter some pleasant surprises. For example, after you open a palette drawer, you can actually click and drag an item out of the drawer to create new palettes, giving you instant access to your favorite brushes, weaves, patterns, gradations, and scripts. Also, if you're hunting for more brushes, more papers, more gradations, and more weaves, look in the pop-up menu in each palette. Select the last menu item, Load Library, and you can load an entire new set of brushes, papers, weaves, and gradations into the appropriate palette. If you want to create your own library of brushes, image hose nozzles, weaves, patterns, and gradations, look in the palette menus for the mover commands. You may even want to create libraries for specific projects. Table 2-1 shows a list of the mover commands and where they're found. In Painter 5 you can actually drag a palette icon directly into a new library. Later you can add, remove, or delete the contents of a library.

As you explore the palettes, don't forget that you can lock your favorite items on palette drawer fronts, and then collapse the palette so that only the drawer

I am used to painting in real oils and watercolors, and would probably not have ever used a computer if I had not found a program like Painter that feels just like the real thing. I'm not much on just applying filters and effects. Even when I do apply filters and effects, I tend to paint into or over them. The real enjoyment for me is using the strokes of the brushes.

MARGARET SWEENEY

front is visible. This procedure not only saves screen space but also helps you avoid wasting time hunting through the palette drawer or pop-up menu for brushes, weaves, patterns, or gradations. To lock the items at the front of the drawer, simply click and hold the mouse button on the icon at the drawer until you see a tiny green dot appear beneath the icon. The green dot indicates that the item is locked. If you want to unlock the icon, click and hold the mouse until the green dot disappears.

ROOT CELLAR
Margaret Sweeney

Table 2-1   Mover Commands

COMMAND	PALETTE	MENU
Brush Mover	Brushes	Brush
Brush Looks Mover	Brushes	Brush
Nozzle Mover	Brushes	Nozzle
Grad Mover	Art Materials: Grad	Grad
Paper Mover	Art Materials: Paper Mover	Paper
Script Mover	Objects: Script	Script

TIP

You can have Painter automatically load your own custom libraries instead of the default libraries. To change default libraries, choose Edit ➢ Preferences ➢ General Preferences. In the Libraries section of the General Preferences dialog box, enter the names of the Libraries that you want Painter to load at start up.

TIP

Stylus users should investigate Painter's Brush Tracking dialog box (Edit ➢ Preferences ➢ Brush Tracking). After you click and drag in the Brush tracking dialog box, Painter uses the brush stroke and the sliders in the dialog box to alter how its own brushes respond to your pressure and velocity. For example, if you click and drag in the Brush Tracking dialog box and barely see a brush stroke, you may wish to raise the Pressure Scale and Pressure Power sliders. This causes Painter to think you are applying more pressure, even though you're not. When using the Brush Tracking dialog box, remember that settings last only for the current Painter session. Each time you use Painter, you need to set the Brush Tracking if you want to take advantage of this feature.

THE TOOLS PALETTE

The Tools palette (2.1) stores 23 tools: Magnifier, Grabber, Rotate Page, Crop, Lasso, Magic Wand, Pen, Quick Curve, Rectangular Shape, Oval Shape, Brush, Paint Bucket, Dropper, Rectangular Selection, Oval Selection, Adjuster, Selection Adjuster, Shape Selection, Text, Scissors, Add Point, Remove Point, and Convert Point. Only 14 tools are displayed at any one time. Where are the other tools? Some reside on flyout menus located on displayed tools. Hidden tools can be displayed by clicking and holding down the mouse on those tools that contain a small black triangle in their tool box location. If you don't know which tool is which, just position the mouse pointer over the tool, wait a second, and the name of the tool appears.

We won't describe how each and every tool works because you see the most important tools in action again and again throughout this book. We will, however, share some handy tool shortcuts:

- Press the spacebar to change any tool to the Grabber hand.
- Double-click the Magnifier tool to set the view to 100%.
- Press Option/Alt and click with the Magnifier tool to zoom out.

2.1

Table 2-2 Tool Keyboard Shortcuts

KEY	TOOL
b	Brush
v	Brush with straight line options selected
r	Rectangular Selection
o	Oval Selection
p	Pen
d	Dropper
f	Adjuster
l	Lasso
k	Paint Bucket
m	Magnifier
q	Quick Curve
w	Magic Wand
e	Rotate Page
t	Text
y	Convert Point
s	Selection Adjuster
g	Grabber
c	Crop

- Press the Shift key while using the rotate page tool to rotate in 90 degree increments.
- Shift+click and drag the Crop tool to constrain your cropping shape into a square. You can also click the aspect ratio check box in the Controls palette while the Crop tool is selected to crop to a specific aspect ratio. For example, a 1:1 aspect ratio is a square.
- Double-click the Brush tool to open and close the Brushes palette.
- Double-click the Paint Bucket tool to set the lock out color to the currently set primary color. After you set the lock color, click the image and the lock out color is not affected.
- Double-click the Floater Adjuster tool to open the Objects: Floater List palette.
- Double-click the Dropper tool to open the Art Materials: Color palette.
- Press ⌘/Alt to access the Dropper tool while any tool is selected.
- Double-click the Rectangular Selection tool to select the entire document.

Have you been wondering whether you can access tools with keyboard commands? Look no further than Table 2-2.

THE CONTROLS PALETTE

The Controls palette (2.2) changes depending on which tool you have selected. For example, when the Brush tool is selected, the Controls palette displays Size, Opacity, and Grain sliders. It also allows you to choose whether to paint in Straight line or Freehand mode. When the Type tool is selected, the Controls palette allows you to pick a point size, tracking, and a font.

2.2

Be sure to take a look at the Controls palette when you use Painter's new Magic Wand tool. By clicking and dragging the Tolerance slider in the palette, you can extend a selection created by the Magic Wand. The Painter 5 Controls palette also allows you to quickly turn a path into a selection. After you create a path, simply click the Make selection button in the palette.

2.3

2.4

2.5

THE BRUSHES PALETTE

The most used and most well-known of Painter's palettes is the Brushes palette (2.3). The painting power packed into this one palette provides more features and controls than several competing painting programs combined. Undoubtedly, the only people who don't like the Brushes palette are those who have a hard time making decisions—in the Brushes palette there's just too much to choose from.

The Painter Brushes palette provides so much depth and utility that many artists create images using virtually nothing but brushes. For example, Margaret Sweeney created *Mooney's Cottage* (2.4), a finalist in Fractal's 1997 digital painting competition, entirely by painting with brushes. No masks, no floaters, no patterns, no weaves. Margaret created *Purple House* (2.5) using the same technique.

The Painter 5 Brushes palette now features 15 brushes: Pencils, Eraser, Water, Chalk, Charcoal, Pens, Image Hose, Felt Pens, Crayons, Airbrush, Liquid, Brush, Artists, Cloners, and Water Color. When you select a brush, the name of the brush appears at the top of the palette, next to the word *Brushes*. You can pick a brush by clicking either the palette pop-up menu or the brush's icon. To see all the brush icons, you may need to click the Brushes palette push bar to open the palette drawer. The five brushes at the top of the drawer are the brushes last selected. When you select another brush inside the drawer, that brush appears at the top of the palette. If you want, you can click and drag a brush icon from within the drawer to the top of the drawer, and then lock the brush in place by clicking and holding the mouse until a tiny green dot appears beneath the brush.

Picking a brush is the easy part. After you select a brush, you need to choose a brush variant. There are so many variants to choose from that we included thumbnail images of each one for easy reference. We've also included samples of the brushes from the Painter New Brushes library. These brushes can be accessed in either of two ways: by choosing Load Library in the Brush palettes menu, or by clicking a brush in the Shortcut to New Brushes palette included with Painter 5. When you click a new brush, its variants load. The array of new brushes and variants is quite impressive. The following sections provide a brief review of these brushes and variants.

Chapter 2 The Painter Palettes

As you examine the thumbnails, don't forget that each brush can be altered by choosing a Method and a Subcategory from the Brushes palette. You can create even more brush effects and vary strokes by choosing commands in the Brushes palette's own menus. If you've never explored these menus, head into the Brushes palette's Controls menu and experiment with the Size, Spacing, and Random commands. Most of the thumbnails you'll see were created using the default Methods and Subcategories.

The thumbnails in this chapter were created in Painter's Brush Look Designer, one of the handiest places to preview brush strokes. To load the Brush Look Designer, choose Brush Looks in the Brushes palette's Brush menu. Then choose Brush Look Designer from the submenu. After the Brush Look Designer loads, preview your stroke by painting in the Brush Look window.

Pencils

  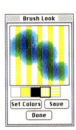   

1 Thick and Thin Pencil   2 2B Pencil   3 500 lb. Pencil   4 Single Pencil Scribbler   5 Sharp Pencil   6 Colored Pencils

Eraser

1 Ultra Fine Eraser   2 Small Eraser   3 Medium Eraser   4 Fat Eraser   5 Single Pixel Bleach   6 Ultra Fine Bleach   7 Small Bleach

  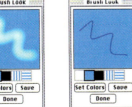 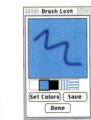   

8 Medium Bleach   9 Fat Bleach   10 Ultrafine Darkener   11 Small Darkener   12 Medium Darkener   13 Fat Darkener   14 Flat Eraser

Water

1 Just Add Water   2 Frosty Water   3 Tiny Frosty Water   4 Single Pixel Water   5 Water Rake   6 Water Spray   7 Big Frosty Water

8 Grainy Water

Chalk

1 Large Chalk   2 Artist Pastel Chalk   3 Oil Pastel   4 Sharp Chalk   5 Square Chalk

Charcoal

 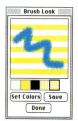 

1 Gritty Charcoal   2 Default   3 Soft Charcoal

Chapter 2   The Painter Palettes

Pen

      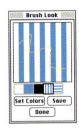

1 Smooth Ink Pen   2 Scratchboard Tool   3 Scratchboard Rake   4 Pixel Dust   5 Calligraphy   6 Leaky Pen   7 Single Pixel

8 Pen and Ink   9 Fine Point   10 Flat Color

Felt Pens

  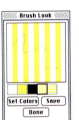  

1 Dirty Marker   2 Medium Tip Felt Pens   3 Single Pixel Marker   4 Felt Marker   5 Fine Tip Felt Pens

Crayons

1 Waxy Crayons   2 Default

Airbrush

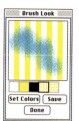
1 Spatter Airbrush

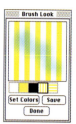
2 Fat Stroke

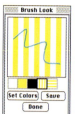
3 Feather Tip

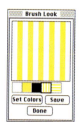
4 Single Pixel Air

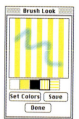
5 Thin Stroke

Liquid

1 Smeary Bristles

2 Total Oil Brush

3 Tiny Smudge

4 Smeary Mover

5 Coarse Smeary Mover

6 Coarse Smeary Bristles

7 Coarse Distorto

8 Thick Oil

9 Distorto

Chapter 2 The Painter Palettes

Brush

1 Penetration Brush

2 Camel Hair Brush

3 Brushy

4 Fine Brush

5 Sable Chisel Tip Water

6 Loaded Oils

7 Big Rough Out

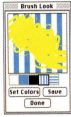
8 Big Dry Ink

9 Huge Rough Out

10 Big Loaded Oils

11 Hairy Brush

12 Big Wet Oils

13 Graduated Brush

14 Smaller Wash Brush

15 Big Wet Ink

16 Cover Brush

17 Rough Out

18 Ultrafine Wash Brush

19 Oil Paint

20 Small Loaded Oils

21 Digital Sumi

22 Coarse Hairs

Artists

1 Van Gogh

2 Impressionist

3 Auto Van Gogh

4 Flemish Rub

5 Van Gogh2

6 Piano Keys

7 Seurat

The Cloners, F/X, Gooey, and Photo examples are based on an image called *Venice* (2.6).

2.6

Cloners

1 Melt Cloner

2 Van Gogh Cloner

3 Felt Pen Cloner

4 Hard Oil Cloner

5 Driving Rain Cloner

6 Soft Cloner

7 Hairy Cloner

8 Oil Brush Cloner

Chapter 2   The Painter Palettes

9 Impressionist Cloner

10 Straight Cloner

11 Pencil Sketch Cloner

12 Chalk Cloner

Water Color

1 Pure Water Brush

2 Broad Water Brush

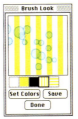
3 Spatter Water

4 Simple Water

5 Large Simple Water

6 Water Brush Stroke

7 Large Water

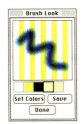
8 Diffuse Water

9 Wet Eraser

The following examples can be loaded from the Shortcut to New Brushes palette. Alternatively, choose Load Library from the Brushes pop-up menu. Then load the library from disk.

F/X

1 Glow

2 Fire

3 Graphic Print

4 Confusion

5 Bubbles

Gooey

1 Bulge

2 Pinch

3 Horizontal Pinch

4 Vertical Pinch

5 Left Twirl

6 Right Twirl

7 Twister

8 Blender

9 Turbulence

10 Diffuse Pull

11 Marbling Rake

12 Runny

Mouse

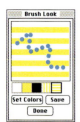 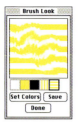   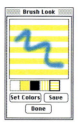 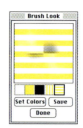 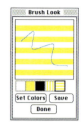

1 Dotted 2 Spirex 3 Line tool 4 Scratchy 5 Brush Dab 6 Rubber Stamp 7 Single Pixel

8 Impressionist 9 Calligraphy

New Paint Tools

1 Palette Knife 2 Dry Brush 3 Sargent Brush 4 Big Wet Luscious 5 Big Wet Turpentine

Photo

1 Dodge 2 Burn 3 Blur 4 Diffuse Blur

Chapter 2   *The Painter Palettes*   27

5 Sharpen

6 Scratch Remover

7 Add Grain

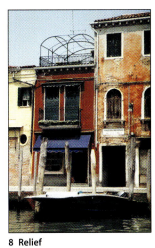
8 Relief

9 Comb

10 Overlay

11 Hue

12 Hue Add

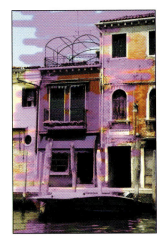
13 Hue Sat

14 Saturation Add

15 Value Add

16 Value Add Sat Subtract

Layer

1 Brush

2 Airbrush

3 Pen

> **NOTE**
>
> To use a Super Cloners brush variant, first create a clone (File ➢ Clone), and then create the points for 2-, 3-, or 4-point Cloners in the original image by pressing Control (on the Mac) or Shift (on the PC) and clicking the mouse. Delete the clone. Next start painting in the blank clone document with a Super Cloners brush. Alternatively, you can open two files and set one to be the clone source of the other (File ➢ Clone Source). In the clone source, set the points by pressing Control/Shift, and then paint with the Super Cloners variant in the other document. The following examples use the Venice original image.

Super Cloners

1 Normal (0 point)

2 Offset (1 point)

3 Rotate & Scale (2 point)

4 Scale (2 point)

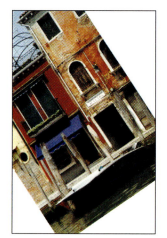
5 Rotate (2 point)

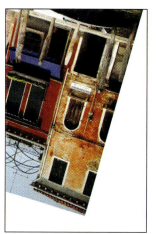
6 Rotate & Mirror (2 point)

7 Rotate, Scale, Shear (3 point)

8 Bilinear (4 point)

9 Perspective (4 point)

10 Perspective Tiling (4 point)

THE ART MATERIALS PALETTE

Exploring the Art Materials palette is like entering a digital art superstore. The Art Materials palette is actually composed of five subpalettes: Color, Paper, Grad, Pattern, and Weave. Clicking one of the icons changes the palette display and the complete functionality of the palette. One valuable but often neglected feature of the Art Materials palette is that you can click and drag a heading, such as Pattern or Papers, to establish another palette onscreen.

The following sections provide a quick review of the Art Materials subpalettes.

ART MATERIALS: COLOR

Clicking the Color icon opens the Art Materials: Color palette (2.7), where you can pick a color by clicking Painter's color wheel and the Saturation/Value triangle. If you use Photoshop and want to see the RGB values, clicking the HSV readouts turns them into RGB readouts. If you don't like using HSV, choose Color Picker from the Color palette's Color menu. In the submenu choose RGB Colors. RGB sliders replace the HSV color wheel. If you don't want to use the sliders, you can enter specific RGB values into the number fields to the right of each RGB slider.

ART MATERIALS: PAPER

Clicking the Paper icon opens the Art Materials: Paper palette (2.8). Using the palette, you can create, choose, and edit textures. Textures can be applied while painting with brushes. Also, several Effects menu commands enable you to apply the selected texture in the Paper palette to your image.

2.7

2.8

Dennis Orlando's *A Play with Light & Shadows* (2.9) provides an excellent example of just what textures can do. As Dennis painted, he picked different textures and edited them by clicking the scale slider in the Paper palette. The scale slider is only visible when the palette drawer is closed and the palette is expanded to full view.

2.9A

2.9B

If you want to create your own paper texture from an image onscreen or a digitized image, simply select the image and choose Capture Texture from the Paper menu. Your texture appears as an icon in the Paper palette, and its name appears in the paper pop-up menu.

To apply a texture to certain areas of your file, you can use a brush. After you pick a brush, make sure the subcategory is set to a grainy option. You can control how much of the texture you paint with by adjusting the Grain slider in the Controls palette. If you want the texture to fill your entire document or a selection or floater, you can use the Effects ➢ Surface Control ➢ Apply Surface Texture command or one of the other Effects ➢ Surface Control submenu commands.

ART MATERIALS: GRAD

Clicking the Grad icon accesses the Art Materials: Grad palette (2.10). In this palette you can pick and edit gradations. The thumbnails show the different gradation styles that can be chosen at a click of the mouse.

> **TIP**
>
> You can create a paper texture from text. First create some text with the Text tool. Click the Drop button in the Floater List palette. Then select the text with the Rectangular Selection tool and choose Capture Paper from the Paper menu. Name and save the texture. Now you're ready to use it.

2.10

Linear

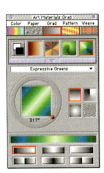 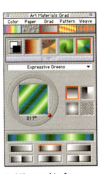  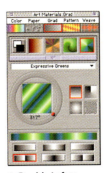  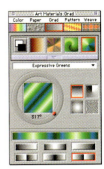

1 Left to Right Grad
2 Mirrored Left to Right Grad
3 Right to Left Grad
4 Double Left to Right Grad
5 Mirrored Right to Left Grad
6 Double Right to Left Grad

Radial

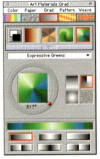   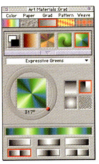 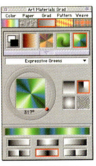 

1 Left to Right Grad
2 Mirrored Left to Right Grad
3 Right to Left Grad
4 Double Left to Right Grad
5 Mirrored Right to Left Grad
6 Double Right to Left Grad

Circular

 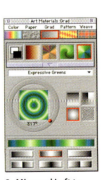 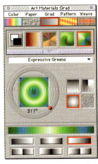 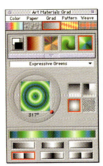  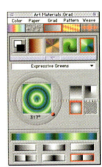

1 Left to Right Grad
2 Mirrored Left to Right Grad
3 Right to Left Grad
4 Double Left to Right Grad
5 Mirrored Right to Left Grad
6 Double Right to Left Grad

Spiral

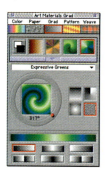 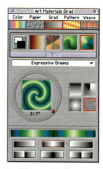 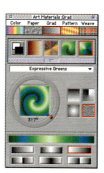   

1 Left to Right Grad
2 Mirrored Left to Right Grad
3 Right to Left Grad
4 Double Left to Right Grad
5 Mirrored Right to Left Grad
6 Double Right to Left Grad

2.11

One of the more unusual commands in the Grad palette is the Express in Image command, which allows you to apply a gradation to an image based on the image's brightness values. With this command you can create some startling and sometimes unusual posterized and psychedelic effects (2.11, 2.12). For a subtle sepia effect, select the Sepia Gradient and choose the Express in Image command. Using this command is simple. First load an image onscreen, and then select a gradation from the Art Materials: Grad palette. Next choose Express in Image from the Grad menu. Use the Bias slider to fine tune the effect.

ART MATERIALS: PATTERNS

Clicking the Pattern icon opens the Art Materials: Pattern palette. Use this palette to create and choose patterns for filling selections. You can use sliders (2.13) to edit any of Painter's preset patterns. You can also select an image onscreen and create a pattern out of it by choosing Capture Pattern from the Pattern menu, which opens the Capture Pattern dialog box (2.14).

2.12

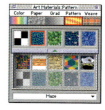

2.13

An excellent example of how patterns can be used in a digital painting is Margaret Sweeney's image *Root Cellar* (2.15). Margaret was inspired to create the image after a trip to Virginia. She created the stone and foreground using patterns and paper textures.

One of the more unusual commands in the Art Materials: Pattern palette is Make Fractal Pattern. In Painter 5, Make Fractal Pattern can be used to create unusual textures. We created this texture (2.16) by choosing Make Fractal Pattern with the Height as Luminance option. We added color with the Express in Image command from the Grads menu. We selected Blue tones grad. We created the second texture (2.17) using Make Fractal Pattern with the dialog box pop-up menu set to the Surface Normal option (2.18).

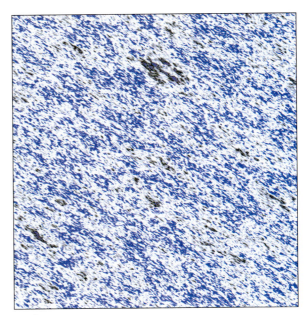

2.16

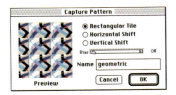

2.14

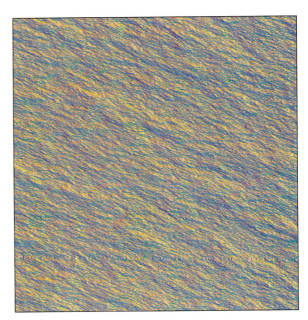

2.17

2.15

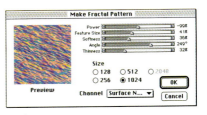

2.18

ART MATERIALS: WEAVES

Clicking the Weave icon opens the Art Materials: Weave palette (2.19). In this palette you can pick a Weave texture with which to paint or fill. Two of the most confusing options available in the Weave palette are the Get Set and Put Set commands. These options enable you to add colors to a weave.

2.19

To add a color to a weave, you must first add to the weave's Color Set. Follow these steps:

1. Open the Color Sets palette by choosing Window ➢ Color Set.
2. In the Art Materials: Weaves palette, click the weave you want to edit.
3. Choose Get Color Set from the Weave menu. The selected weave's color set opens.
4. Choose a primary painting color in the Art Materials: Color Palette. This color is the color you want to add to the color set.
5. Press Option/Alt and click the color in the Color Set palette that you want to replace with the primary color. Painter adds the Color to the color set.
6. In the Art Materials: Weaves palette, choose Put Color Set from the Weave menu. The Weave's color changes.

John Ennis' *Scottish Magic* (2.20) shows how a weave can add style to a Painter image. John started by applying a weave to the background. Next he created the straight pin in a floater over the weave. He erased parts of the straight pin that went under the fabric, and then used the Liquid Distorto brush variant to ripple the fabric to make it look three-dimensional. He added the circular part of the pin as a new floater.

THE OBJECTS PALETTE

The Objects palette contains five subpalettes: P. Float, Floater, Mask, Script, and Net. Each palette also includes its own menu, and each palette can be separated from the others by clicking and dragging the palette's icon.

THE OBJECTS PLUGIN FLOATERS

The Plugin Floaters palette (2.21) enables you to access plug-in floaters—add-ins that extend Painter's capabilities. Most of the plug-ins produce special effects using floaters. They allow you to bevel images, turn them into liquid metal, create kaleidoscope patterns, and singe and tear image edges. To use the palette, click the P. Float icon and select an icon from the top of the palette or the open drawer. As with other palettes, you can also choose a drawer member

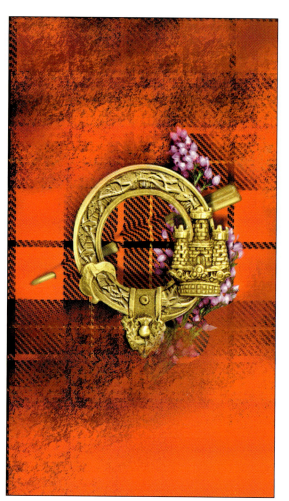

2.20

by name by clicking the palette's pop-up menu. What's not obvious is how to apply the effect.

To use a plug-in floater, first select the plug-in. Then choose Apply from the palette's P. Float menu or click the Apply button (visible when the palette is expanded). (Note that some plug-in floaters can only be applied to selections or floaters.) A dialog box opens that enables you to specify exactly how you want the effect applied. After you've applied the effect, return to the object onscreen and choose Options from the Plugin Floaters palette to alter the effects of the plug-in. After you fine-tune the image to perfection, choose Commit from the P. Float menu to lock down the effect to the background pixels. You'll see examples of plug-in floaters in Chapters 6 and 14.

THE OBJECTS: FLOATER LIST PALETTE

Clicking the Floater icon in the Objects palette opens the Objects: Floater List palette. This palette is the command center for floaters, which are images that float above the background electronic canvas. The Floater List palette can be a bit confusing because it keeps track of all floating objects—not only floaters but also shapes, plug-in floaters, and reference floaters (low-resolution versions of image floaters). The following figure shows each object in the palette (2.22).

Here are a few helpful hints to keep in mind when you're using the Floater List palette:

- To name or rename a floater, double-click it in the palette.
- To rearrange the stacking order of a floater, click and drag to rearrange the floaters in the palette.
- It's often easier to select a floater in the palette rather than to click it onscreen. Press Shift and then click to select more than one floater at a time.

- Even if a floater is selected, changes made to the background canvas do not effect floaters.
- A helpful new Painter 5 feature is the Transparent Layer command found in the palette's Floater menu. This command enables you to create a floater over your entire document, allowing you to use floaters like Photoshop layers. However, be aware that you can paint in a Transparent Layer with only a Transparent Layer brush. Using transparent layers is covered in detail in Chapter 6.
- You can select all floaters in a document by choosing the Select All command in the Floater menu in the Objects: Floater List palette. Painter's standard Select ➢ All command does not select floaters.
- A final floater reminder: Don't forget to activate the Floater Adjuster tool when you want to activate or move a floater.

THE OBJECTS: MASK LIST PALETTE

Clicking the Mask icon opens the Objects: Mask List palette (2.23). This palette is new to Painter 5. Fortunately for Photoshop users, the palette works

2.22

2.21

2.23

similarly to Photoshop's Channels palette. You can use the Mask List palette to save and load selections and edit masks. A helpful feature accessible in the Mask menu is the New Mask command, which creates a mask enabling you to paint and edit masks onscreen with any Painter brush. The command replaces the masking brush found in Painter 3 and Painter 4.

THE OBJECTS: SCRIPTS PALETTE

Clicking the Script icon opens the Objects: Scripts palette (2.24). Use the Scripts palette to record your Painter work and play it back later. As discussed in Chapter 1, you can record a painting session at low resolution and play it back at high resolution. If you want to see your Painter work take shape in a multimedia program such as Adobe Premiere, Adobe After Effects, or Macromedia Director, you can turn your recorded scripts into Painter movies and output them in QuickTime or AVI format.

> **NOTE**
>
> On the Mac, Painter automatically records your work session in a script. The script is automatically named with the date and time you started working.

THE OBJECTS: NETWORK PALETTE

Clicking the Net icon opens the Objects: Network palette (2.25). Using this palette, you can share Painter documents with others on a TCP/IP network. If you're using Painter in an office, talk to your network administrator to see if your local area network allows for communal Painter sessions.

THE COLOR SET PALETTE

The Color Set palette (2.26) allows you to pick colors by clicking color swatches. Color Sets can be handy if you want to store colors that you'll be using again and again. You can also load a library of Pantone Colors into a color set. To load the Pantone set or any other color set, choose Load Color Set in the Art Materials: Color palette's Color menu. You'll find the Pantone Color set in the Extra Art Materials folder in your Painter folder.

If you want to create your own color set, choose Adjust Color Set from the Color menu. This opens the Art Materials: Color Set palette. Next click the New Set button and add colors to your color set by selecting them from the Art Materials palette and clicking the Add Color button.

CREATING A CUSTOM PALETTE

What's the most valuable Painter palette? Probably the one you create yourself.

If you find that your screen is too cluttered with palettes because you need to constantly access different brushes and art materials, create your own palette as we did (2.27). Our palette includes not only brushes and patterns but also the handy Apply Surface Texture command.

2.24

2.25

2.26

2.27

Here's how to create your own custom palette. Open the palette that contains the item or items that you want to add to your custom palette. Click and drag the icon of the item from its original palette to your canvas. When you release the mouse, Painter places the item in a new custom palette. To add other items, simply drag them to the newly created custom palette. To add brush variants to the custom palette, choose the variant and then click and drag the icon to the palette.

Here are several tips for creating custom palettes:

- To rearrange the icons on a custom palette, press Control+Shift/Ctrl+Shift. Then click and drag the icon to the desired location.
- To delete an icon in a custom palette, press Control+Shift+Option/Ctrl+Shift+Alt and position the mouse over the icon you want to delete. When you see the trash can icon, click.
- To add a menu item to your custom palette, choose Window ➢ Custom Palettes ➢ Add Command. In the dialog box that appears, select your custom palette in the pop-up menu. Choose the menu item that you want to add to the palette from the appropriate Painter menu. In the add command dialog box, click OK.
- To rename, delete, or export your custom palette to disk, choose Window ➢ Custom Palette ➢ Organizer. In the organizer dialog box, select your palette by name, and then choose whether to load, rename, or delete a palette.

CHAPTER 3
THE MAGIC OF MASKS

Masks are undoubtedly one of the most confusing features in Painter. Masks are confusing because they serve many functions. In Painter (as in Adobe Photoshop), a mask can be used to protect an area you want to avoid painting over. Thus, a mask can be something as simple as a selection created by one of Painter's selection tools. Masks can also be used to create special effects that involve blending one image into another. This type of mask is often called an *8 bit mask* because it is actually an object with 256 possible gray levels. When the mask is applied, the gray levels control the transparency when one image is composited with another.

Andrew Faulkner's image, *Bodyclock* (3.1), shows how masks can be used to create transparency blending effects. The blend between the clock and the statue was created from masks in floaters that were overlaid at different opacities. Andrew controlled exactly which parts of the images would appear by editing the floater masks. He created the image for a *Los Angeles Times* story on how medications tend to be more or less effective during certain times of the day. Andrew started by scanning the images and then copying and pasting them into one file.

John Ennis' image, *Waking Beauty* (3.2), which he created for a romance novel published by HarperCollins, shows an example of another mask at work. John created the white stripe effect by transforming a brush stroke into a mask. To create the image, John digitized a photograph of a model's hands, and then digitized a photograph of rope. (The model wouldn't let him tie the rope around her hands—

> **Painter is very helpful at the beginning stages of my artwork. It allows me to quickly create compositions that look like traditional medium. Then I use these ideas when I paint with oils on canvas or on wood (to create woodscreens).**
>
> BEA DROBLAS

3.1

imagine that.) He composited the two together in Adobe Photoshop, and then he turned to Painter to create the masking strokes. Later in this chapter, you see how a brush stroke can be used to create a mask using the Objects: Mask palette's New Mask command.

> **NOTE**
>
> If you use Adobe Photoshop, you'll be ecstatic over the new Painter 5 masking features because many of them now work like Photoshop's. For example, saved selections now appear listed in Painter's Objects: Mask palette. The setup is quite similar to saving a selection in Photoshop's Channels palette.

USING SELECTIONS AS MASKS

The simplest mask in Painter is a selection. If you've never seen how a selection can be used as a mask, simply create a selection with the Rectangular selection tool, the Oval selection tool, or the Lasso tool. After you create the selection, try painting inside and outside the selection area. By default, Painter allows you to paint within the selection because the selection acts as a mask. The mask protects areas outside of the selection from being affected.

Artist Stacy A. Hopkins used selections as masks to create *Catch of the Day* (3.3). Stacy started by sketching the fish using the Pencil brush variant. He used the Lasso tool to make a small selection, and then he filled it with a gradient. He used the Just Add Water and Airbrush brush variants to add the colors. He repeated this selection and coloring process until he completed the fish. The background (which started as a gradient) and the fish were composited together in Photoshop, where Stacy used Alien Skin's Eye Candy plug-in filter to make the bubbles.

USING THE SELECTION MASK ICONS

After you create a mask, you generally want to edit the area within the mask by painting within the selection or by applying a special effect to the selected area. However, if necessary you can reverse the protected and non-protected areas of the mask. When you do this, the areas within the mask are protected and the areas outside the mask are unprotected.

To change mask functionality, use the *mask drawing* icons at the bottom-left corner of the Painter window (3.4). The first mask icon, Draw Anywhere, turns off

3.2

3.3

the mask completely. If you select this icon, any onscreen selection will not function as a mask; in other words, Painter ignores the selection onscreen, no matter where you paint.

The second mask icon, Draw Outside, protects the area within the selection. Painting affects only areas outside the selection. The third mask icon, Draw Inside, protects areas outside the selection, allowing you to paint only within the mask.

SAVING SELECTIONS

Selections are so handy that you may want to use them again and again. Fortunately, Painter allows you to save your selections, an extremely useful feature. For example, you may create an intricate selection onscreen and then apply an effect to the selection. After you save the image, you may wish to use the selection again to make more changes to the previously selected area. Using Painter 5's new Mask List palette, you can easily save and load a selection. When you save a selection, it is stored with the file as a permanent mask—unless you delete it in the Mask List palette.

To save a selection, follow these steps:

1. Create a selection onscreen.
2. Open the Objects palette by choosing Window ➤ Show Objects.
3. Open the Mask List palette and then click the Mask icon in the Objects palette.
4. In the Objects: Mask List palette, click Save Selection.
5. In the Save Selection dialog box that appears, make sure the pop-up menu is set to New, and then click OK. After you click OK, the mask is listed in the Objects: Mask List palette.
6. If you wish to assign the mask a name, double-click the default name (for example, Mask 1, Mask 2, and so on) and type a name in the Mask Attributes dialog box. Click OK. Your selection is now saved.

After you save your selection, the selection marquee disappears from the screen. To load the selection back onto the screen, click the Load Selection button in the Mask List palette. The Load Selection dialog box appears. The options in this dialog box allow you to perform the following actions:

- Load the selection as a new selection onscreen, removing all others from the screen
- Add to the selection
- Create a new selection from the intersection of the current onscreen selection and the loaded selection
- Subtract the loaded selection

Here are several other helpful hints and suggestions regarding working with selections:

- Selections that you want to access in different Painter documents can be saved in the Selections palette. The Selections palette stores paths created with the Oval tool and Lasso tool. Paths converted from the Pen tool can also be saved in the Selections palette. Choose Select ➤ Selection Portfolio. Use the Selection Adjuster tool to drag the selection into the Selections palette. Then name the selection in the Save Selection dialog box.
- If you load a Photoshop file with an alpha channel into Painter, the alpha channel appears in the Objects: Mask List palette.
- Use the Selection Adjuster tool to move and adjust selections. If you want to rotate a selection, ⌘/Ctrl+drag a handle with the Selection Adjuster tool.

3.4

- You can transform selections into path selections so they can be edited with the Selection Adjuster tool. To transform a selection into a path selection, activate the selection and then choose Select ➤ Transform Selection.
- You can save and load selections by choosing Select ➤ Save Selection and Select ➤ Load Selection.

SELECT MENU SECRETS

After you create, save, or load a selection, Painter provides many controls for changing it. Most of these controls are found in the Select menu. For example, you can use the Select ➤ Invert command as an alternative to switching mask drawing icons. Choosing Select ➤ Invert selects everything onscreen except the selected area.

You can modify an existing selection with the Select ➤ Modify submenu. The commands in this submenu enable you to widen or contract a selection by entering pixel values in a dialog box. Choose Select ➤ Modify ➤ Border to add a border to a selection. Choose Select ➤ Modify ➤ Smooth to smooth a selection.

> **NOTE**
>
> Even if the Draw Anywhere or Draw Outside icons are selected, the Effects ➤ Fill command always fills a selection.

One of the more interesting features of the Select menu is the Select ➤ Stroke Selection command, which strokes a selection with the current brush variant's stroke. This means that you can even stroke a selection with digital images by executing Stroke Selection after choosing the Image Hose brush (3.5). The elements used to make the nozzle file for the Image Hose were created from a selection taken from Painter's Selections palette. We created the balloon (which was also part of the Image Hose nozzle) from a Lasso tool selection that was filled with color.

CREATING MASKS

Painter is packed with mask-creation features. You can create masks from a brush or from the color or paper texture in an image. After you create the mask, you can apply a brush to the mask and edit it to create special effects.

CREATING A MASK FROM A BRUSH STROKE

If you want to gain more control or create special effects from a selection, you may wish to create a mask from a brush stroke. When you create a mask from a brush stroke, you can control its opacity by painting with shades of gray. Painting with gray creates a mask with 50 percent opacity. The closer the color is to white, the lower the opacity; the closer the

> **TIP**
>
> You can also create selections (which can be used as masks) from the brightness values, paper texture, and color in an image. These features are found in the Select ➤ Auto Select and Select ➤ Color Select dialog boxes. The options are similar to the Auto Mask and Mask Color commands accessed in the Objects palette's Mask menu. The mask commands are most helpful when you want to edit the mask with a brush.

3.5

color is to black, the higher the opacity. After you create the mask, you can choose the Load Selection icon to create a selection from the mask. If you copy and paste the selection over another selection, you'll see a blend onscreen between the selection and the background. The blend between the two images results from the mask's opacity. We used this technique to create the effect in the fairy and flower figure (3.6). The original images of the flowers (3.7) and the fairy (3.8) were created by artist Bea Droblas. The mask overlay (created by a brush) is also shown (3.9). After we created the mask, we turned it into a selection and pasted it into the flowers image.

To turn a brush stroke into a mask, first select the Brush tool and then choose the brush variant that you wish to use to create the mask. To create a soft edge effect, try the Charcoal or Airbrush variant. To create a transparent effect in your mask, set the primary painting color to gray. (You can also change the opacity of the brush stroke by clicking and dragging the opacity slider in the Controls palette.) Start by opening the Objects palette by choosing Window ➢ Objects. Click the Mask icon in the palette to view the Objects: Mask List palette. Choose New Mask from the palette's Mask menu, and then begin to paint. Try painting using different shades of gray.

As you paint, you see the mask-colored overlay appear onscreen. When you finish creating your mask, click the Load Selection button in the Mask List palette. Copy and paste the selection into another image. The image you pasted onscreen (which is now

> **NOTE**
>
> **Previous versions of Painter required you to switch to a masking brush variant to edit masks with a brush. Because you can now edit a mask with a brush by clicking the Mask in the Objects: Mask List palette, brush variants have been eliminated in Painter 5.**

3.6

3.7

3.8

3.9

a floater) is transparent in areas that you painted in lighter shades of gray, and is more opaque in areas that you painted in darker shades of gray. One of the great benefits of using this technique is that you can reselect the mask in Painter's Objects: Mask List palette and edit the mask. As you edit the mask, the composite effect changes based on the changes you make to the mask. To turn off mask editing, simply click the words *RGB-Canvas* in the Mask List palette. When the mask editing mode is turned off, you can paint over your image once again.

CREATING SPECIAL EFFECTS WITH LUMINANCE MASKS

Few digital imaging programs can match Painter's capability to create different types of masks. For example, using the Color Mask command, you can create a mask based on the color in an image. Using the Auto Mask command, you can create a mask based on the luminance (brightness values) or paper texture in an image. You can even create masks based on the brightness values in a clone image.

The following example illustrates the power of the luminance mask, which is a mask based on the brightness value of an image. We used a luminance mask to create a flower with brick textures (3.10). We created the luminance mask in Bea Droblas' *Flower* image (3.11), and then we pasted the image in a new file. We then filled the background canvas with Painter's brick pattern in the Art Materials color palette.

> **TIP**
>
> You can also view the mask onscreen without the image. To do this, click the RGB Canvas Mask eye icon to close it, and click the eye icon of the mask you want to view. The mask appears as a grayscale entity, and the rest of the image is hidden.

Chapter 3 The Magic of Masks

To create a similar effect using a luminance mask, follow these steps:

1. Open an image onscreen.
2. Open the Objects palette by choosing Window ➢ Objects, and select the Mask icon. The Objects: Mask palette appears.
3. In the Objects: Mask palette, choose Mask ➢ Auto Mask. In the pop-up menu, choose Image Luminance. (This creates a mask from the brightness value of your image.) Click OK.
4. In the Objects: Mask palette, click the Load Selection button to load the selection created from the mask onscreen. After the Load Selection dialog box opens, click OK.
5. Choose Edit ➢ Copy.
6. Close the file onscreen.
7. Load an image onscreen that you want to blend with the original file.
8. Choose Edit ➢ Paste. Painter pastes the copied image's brightness values into the image onscreen. The result is a blend between the two images.
9. Now fine tune the effect by editing the mask. Select the mask in the Objects: Mask List Palette, and then paint in your image using a shade of gray. Painting with black adds to the mask and hides the background image; painting with white subtracts from the mask and reveals more of the background image.
10. When you finish editing the mask, turn off mask editing by clicking RGB in the Mask List palette.

> **NOTE**
>
> Copying and pasting creates a floater with a mask in it. To learn more about floaters, see Chapter 6.

3.10

3.11

CHAPTER 4
CREATING SHAPES

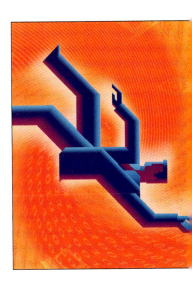

Perhaps the most underused feature of Painter is *shapes*. Many people think of Painter's shapes as simply a means of using vector-based graphics in a painting program. In other words, with shapes you can draw and move objects just as you can in a drawing program. But the real power of Painter's shapes is not your ability to draw objects, but your ability to add effects that are not possible in most drawing programs. Because shapes can be used to create selections and floaters, you can eventually apply blending effects to them and even create soft-edged feathering effects—try that in your drawing program. An added benefit of shapes: Because text in Painter is created from shapes, Painter allows you to manipulate text in ways not possible in other programs.

Shapes can also be a bit confusing because they appear as objects in the Floater List palette. Although this may seem illogical, it actually isn't; like floaters, shapes float above the background canvas and share several of the same properties. You can easily convert a shape into a floater (Shapes ➢ Convert to Floater). Once converted, you can apply drop shadows and composite effects to the converted floater. Adele Droblas Greenberg's *Girl of My Heart* (4.1) provides an example of how Painter can turn simple flat shapes into a textured 3D image. To create the image, Adele used the Pen, Quick Curve, and Oval Shape tools to build the basic underlying shapes of the figure. She edited the shapes using the Scissors, Add Point and Remove Point, and Shape Selection tools. After the shapes were created, Adele converted them into floaters and then filled some of the floaters with

Painter combines vector-based shapes with pixel-based images into an integrated working environment.

BEN BARBANTE

4.1

gradients. To create the 3D textured effects, she applied Painter's Effects ➢ Surface Control ➢ Apply Surface Texture command.

Because many Painter artists are not familiar with the Pen tool—Painter's most versatile shape-creating tool—this chapter concentrates on Pen tool techniques and then provides an overview of shape tricks that can be generated with the Text tool. However, before embarking on a look at the Pen and Text tools, you should become familiar with some of the basic features of shapes.

BASIC SHAPES

Shapes can be created with the Rectangular and Oval Shape tools, and the Pen, Quick Curve, and Text tool. You can resize, move, or transform shapes with the Adjuster tools. Shapes created with the Pen and Quick Curve tools can be edited with the Add Point and Remove Point Scissors and Corner/Smooth point tools.

When you create a shape using the Pen, Oval, or Rectangular Shape or Text tool, Painter can stroke the shape (outline it with a color) or fill the shape with a color. To set the default stroke, fill, and other attributes of Shapes, choose Edit ➢ Preferences ➢ Shapes. Once you change these settings, they are applied to every shape you create—as soon as you create them. To edit the attributes of individual shapes, first select them and then choose Shapes ➢ Set Shapes Attributes, or double-click the shape's name in the Objects: Floater List palette.

USING THE PEN TOOL

For even the most talented artists, drawing a perfect curve can be a challenge. After you create the perfect curve, editing it is even harder. The Pen tool enables you to precisely draw and control curves. Anton Atzenhofer's *Train* (4.2, 4.3) is an example of the Pen tool at work. To create the outline of the train and the windows on the train, Anton turned to the Pen tool. In creating the train, he also used brushes to paint in the masks created with the Pen tool. This image is only part of a series he created for Siemens, a German multi-national company. Other images in the series include other parts of the train as well as its interior.

Ben Barbante's *Information Anxiety* (4.4), which won second place in the MetaCreations' 1997 Beyond the Canvas competition, provides another example of the Pen tool in action. Ben used the Pen tool to create the figure floating in a swirl of anxiety, and he used masking techniques and gradients to create the background.

4.2

> **NOTE**
>
> Shapes created with the Pen and Quick Curve tools are also called *paths*. Creating paths in Painter is quite similar to drawing them in Adobe Illustrator, Macromedia Freehand, and CorelDRAW. Painter's paths can also be converted into selections (like Photoshop) and thus can be used to create masks. To turn a selected closed pen path into a selection, click the Make Selection button in the Controls palette or choose Shapes ➢ Convert to Selection. To turn a path created from the Rectangular and Oval Shape tools into a selection, first select the shape and then choose Shapes ➢ Convert to Selection.

Chapter 4   Creating Shapes

Unfortunately, using the Pen tool takes some getting used to, particularly for artists whose primary artistic tools are brush variants. The Pen tool doesn't create curves along a brush stroke. Instead, the Pen tool creates curves by connecting points. The secret of pointing yourself in the right direction with the Pen tool curve is to start by clicking and dragging in the direction you want the curve to face. To connect a few curves together, follow these steps:

1. Select the Pen tool from the toolbox. Click and drag down, and then release the mouse. This sets the direction of the first curve.
2. Move the Pen point to the right about an inch, and then click and drag up. The curve starts to take shape (4.5).
3. Create another curve by moving to the right, and then click and drag down (4.6).
4. End the curve by pressing ⌘/Ctrl and clicking onscreen. This prevents the curve from continuing the next time you click the Pen tool.

> **TIP**
>
> If you need help drawing more precisely, Painter's grid can help you judge distances. You can place Painter's grid onscreen by clicking the Grid icon in the upper-right corner of the document window.

4.3

4.4

4.5

4.6

One of the most important features of the Pen tool is that it enables you to easily edit the curve to fine-tune it. To edit a curve, click and drag the control points of the wing. If you want to stretch out the points, click the anchor point with the Direct Selection tool and drag.

ENDING A PATH

If you keep clicking and dragging, your Pen path will never end. If you want to stop one path and create another, you must either close the path or deselect the last end point.

To close a path, simply move the Pen tool over the path's starting point and click. You can also close the currently selected path by clicking the Close button in the Controls palette. If you create a path that isn't closed and then wish to create another path, deselect the last point in the path by pressing ⌘/Ctrl and clicking away from the path you created.

CONTINUING A PATH

If you've created an open path and want to add to it, you must first select the last point of the path. To do this, select the Shape Selection tool and click and drag over the end point. As you click and drag, a box appears onscreen. After the box surrounds the end-point, release the mouse. The last anchor will be selected. You can then continue using the Pen tool to finish your curve.

COMBINING CURVES AND LINES

One of the trickiest techniques to master when creating shapes with the Pen tool is how to connect curves to lines and lines to curves (4.7). To attach a curve to a straight line, follow these steps:

1. Click to establish the anchor point.
2. To create the straight line, move the mouse about an inch to the right and click.
3. To create the curve, move the mouse point over the last anchor point (a corner icon appears indicating that you can add a corner point), and then click the last anchor point and drag down. This tells Painter that you want to create a curve that points downward.
4. Move the mouse to the right and click and drag up to end the curve.

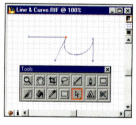

4.7

4.8

EDITING PATHS

When you know the basics of creating curves, you can edit shapes by adding and subtracting anchor points. We created *Broken Heart* (4.8) by creating a simple shape with the Pen tool and then editing it with the Scissors and Shape Selection tools. After snipping the heart with the Scissors tool, we rejoined the path by clicking one end of one path with the Pen tool and then clicking the end of another path.

We also used the Pen tool to create a curved shape (4.9) by adding an anchor point to a rectangle. We started by creating a rectangle, and then we clicked both sides of the rectangle with the Add Point tool to add an anchor point to the rectangle. Next we clicked and dragged the direction lines with the Shape Selection tool to create the curve in the middle of the rectangle.

Chapter 4   Creating Shapes

The following steps illustrate how to instantly transform a square into a triangle by removing an anchor point with the Scissors tool:

1. Create a rectangle with the Rectangular Shape tool.
2. Select the Remove Point tool.
3. Click any corner anchor point of the rectangle. The corner is subtracted and transformed into a triangle.

USING THE TEXT TOOL

When shapes came along, the power of Painter's Text tool increased dramatically. In Painter 5, text you create becomes individual objects and appears in the Objects: Floater List palette (4.10). Because all letters you create are shapes, you can drag letters onscreen with the Floater Adjuster tool, and you can easily scale text without affecting the quality of the text. The following steps illustrate how to scale text. In Chapter 10 you learn how to create many different special effects using text.

1. Select the Text tool.
2. In the Controls palette, choose a font and use the Type Size slider to choose a type size.
3. Click the screen and type some text.
4. Select the Floater Adjuster tool. To select all the text, click and drag over the text with the Floater Adjuster tool. (Alternatively, you can press Shift and click each letter individually in the Objects: Floater List palette with the Floater Adjuster tool.)
5. When each letter is selected, use the Floater Adjuster tool to click and drag any one of the handles. As you drag, the text is scaled. Hold the Shift key before you drag to constrain proportions.

If you click text with the Shape Selection tool, anchor points appear. You can then edit the text as you would edit any path. We created the text shown in Figure 4.11 by selecting the top part of the letter T with the Shape Selection tool. Then we simply dragged the top of the T to the right.

USING DUPLICATE TRANSFORM

A handy utility for creating shapes automatically is Painter's Shapes ➤ Automatic Transform command. With this command you can transform the size, location, rotation, and scale of a shape. By repeating the transformation, you can instruct Painter to take the last transformed object and transform it again. Although you can use Automatic Transform to alter any shape, manipulating text often produces interesting effects (4.12).

4.10

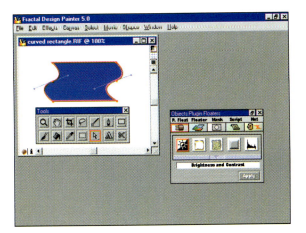

4.9

4.11

To create the twirled type, we first typed the word Art onscreen. We used the Shapes ➢ Attributes command to set the colors and the fill of the letters. Next we chose Shapes ➢ Set Duplicate Transform. In the Duplicate Transform dialog box, we set the Horizontal and Vertical Offset to 10 pixels, Scaling to 80 percent, and Rotation to 10 degrees. After setting the transformation options, we created the text effect by executing Shapes ➢ Duplicate. To create many transformations, we used the keyboard shortcut ⌘-]/Ctrl-].

To create the cutout effect, we used another under-used Shapes feature—Make Compound. This command enables you to select two objects and cut the foremost object out of the back object. The result is a transparent hole. We selected several pairs of letters and applied the Shapes ➢ Make Compound command several times.

After creating the effect, we selected all the objects and clicked the Group button in the Objects: Floater List palette. We then created a drop shadow by choosing Effects ➢ Objects ➢ Create Drop Shadow. This turned the objects into floaters. We then lowered the opacity for all letters in the Controls palette. To help make the letters stand out more, we selected the first and last letters and raised the opacity in the Controls palette. Next we used Effects ➢ Fill to fill the screen with Painter's Quilt pattern, which is found in the Art Materials: Pattern palette. To complete the image, we applied the Effects ➢ Esoterica ➢ Custom Tile command to achieve the brick effect.

USING BLENDS

Many artists confuse blends with gradations. Because gradations are easy to use, many artists assume they don't need to use blends. But blends are actually quite different from gradations. Like Illustrator, Painter blends are actually a series of objects that transform shape and color from one object to another. This means that you can actually use a blend to automatically create artwork for you—artwork that might be time-consuming to create by hand. We created the effect in the next figure by simply typing numbers on the screen with the Text tool (4.13). We then used the Floater Adjuster tool to resize the shapes. We set the Fill and Stroke for each number using the Shapes ➢ Set Attributes commands.

Next we selected each of the images by pressing Shift and clicking each number. Finally we executed the Blend Command by choosing Shapes ➢ Blend. We specified how many objects we wanted to create by choosing a setting of 10 in the Number of Steps field in the Blend dialog box.

> **TIP**
>
> You can use the Effects ➢ Rotate and Effects ➢ Orientation Distort menu with shapes. You can quickly rotate a shape by pressing ⌘/Ctrl and then clicking and dragging a corner handle. You can skew (slant) a shape by pressing ⌘/Ctrl and clicking and dragging the middle handle of the shape.

4.12

4.13

For the finishing touches, we selected each group and then applied a drop shadow by choosing Effects ➢ Objects ➢ Create Drop Shadow. Next we added a background by choosing Effects ➢ Fill to fill the image with Painter's Wavy Water pattern. To create the frame around the image, we also used a blend. We created a circle in each corner and then chose the Hue CCW (Counter Clockwise) option in the Blend dialog box to create a series of colored ovals that frame the image.

IMPORTING AND EXPORTING SHAPES FROM ILLUSTRATOR

Although Painter shapes provide the basic tools for using shapes in a painting program, Adobe Illustrator users may want to take full advantage of their favorite drawing program by importing shapes from Illustrator directly into Painter. To import shapes from Adobe Illustrator, choose File ➢ Acquire ➢ Adobe Illustrator file. If you want to export your shapes to Adobe Illustrator, choose File ➢ Export ➢ Adobe Illustrator file.

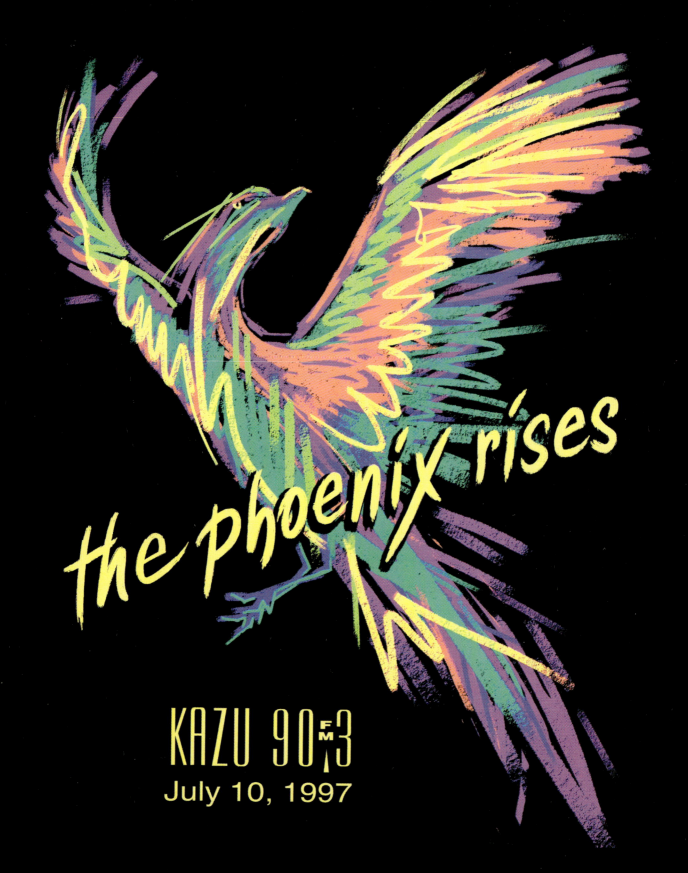

CHAPTER 5
THE POWER OF FLOATERS

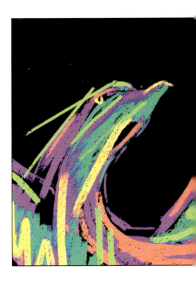

If you see a piece of digital art that features layers and layers of images seamlessly blended into another, chances are the artist used *floaters*. The more you use floaters, the more you see how this Painter feature can add amazing digital effects to traditional painting.

Unfortunately, floaters have long been considered confusing and complicated because they require a knowledge of selections and masking and layering, and because there are so many different ways artists can use the features and benefits of floaters. Nonetheless, any Painter artist who wishes to expand his or her horizons beyond the basics of digital brush strokes should begin to explore the magical world of floaters. You'll be amazed at what you can do.

Andrew Faulkner is a Painter artist who frequently turns to floaters when creating his art. Andrew used floaters to create the superimposition effect in the image *Lit* (5.1), which was used for the cover for the literary insert of the weekly Bay Area newspaper, the *San Francisco Bay Guardian*. In *Lit*, Andrew made use of both masks and floaters. Newspaper clippings were scanned and pasted in at different opacities with the Hard and Soft Light composite methods—commands only available when working with floaters. Andrew integrated the photos of the people by first scanning them and then colorizing them using the Effects ➢ Tonal Control ➢ Adjust Color command. The magazines and type were created in Painter using selections and the Text tool.

What is the secret to using floaters? First you must gain an understanding of exactly what a floater is and how it is created. Next you need to start turning selec-

Any Painter artist who wishes to expand his or her horizons beyond the basics of digital brush strokes should begin to explore the magical world of floaters!
ADELE DROBLAS GREENBERG AND SETH GREENBERG

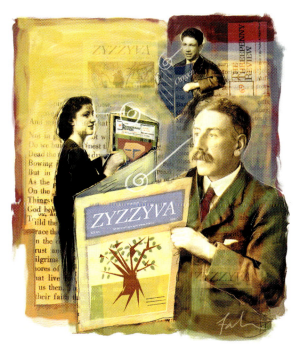

5.1

Chelsea Sammel

tions and shapes into floaters to see how they magically blend image areas together.

Adam Sadigursky created *I Like Vino* (5.2) with a variety of floaters. Adam started his image by using Painter's Pen tool to create the basic shapes of the face (he did not use any scanned images). He then turned the shapes into floaters by choosing Shapes ➢ Convert to Floaters. To give his image a 3D look, he painted with textures, applied the Effects ➢ Surface Control ➢ Apply Surface Texture command, used the Effects ➢ Objects ➢ Create Drop Shadow command, and layered the floaters with Painter's Composite Methods (discussed in detail later in this chapter).

FLOATERS EXAMINED

In many respects a floater is like an image painted on a rectangular acetate sheet that is just a little bigger than the image. Like a small sheet of acetate, a floater can easily be moved around over a background image or moved on top of other floaters. The power of floaters doesn't become apparent until you start blending a floater over its background. When you work with floaters, Painter enables you to change the opacity of the floater, access special digital effects, and use a brush variant to create even more effects.

CREATING FLOATERS

Perhaps the simplest way to create a floater is to select an area in your image and then click it with the Floater Adjuster tool. After you click, a yellow rectangle surrounds the selected area, indicating that it is a floater. After a floater is created, it can be moved around onscreen as if it were a layer floating above the background pixels.

When you deselect a floater, its yellow rectangle disappears, but the image area is still a floater. Click the floater again (to re-select it) and the rectangle reappears, and you can drag the floater around onscreen or apply different composite effects that blend the floater and the area beneath.

> **NOTE**
>
> When you create a selection with the Lasso or Oval Selection tool and turn the selection into a floater, the selection becomes a mask in a floater. (Using floater masks is discussed later in this chapter.)

> **TIP**
>
> If you are going to move a floater after you create it, it's often a good idea to copy it first. Otherwise, when you move the floater, it will leave a white hole in its place. This is because the first time you move a floater, Painter assumes you are trying to cut the floater's mask out of the background canvas. To copy a floater, press Option/Alt and then click and drag the floater to the new location.

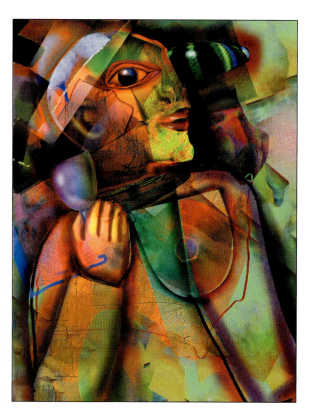

5.2

Chapter 5 The Power of Floaters

Floaters can also be created when you copy and paste a selection from one area onscreen to another area or to another image. This technique is often used by artists creating a Painter image from various digitized elements.

UNDERSTANDING FLOATER MASKS

The key to harnessing the power of floaters is understanding how floaters and masks are interrelated. When you first create a floater, Painter plays a clever trick. Painter uses a mask to hide the part of the floater it thinks you're not interested in viewing. When you create a floater out of a selection, Painter reveals the area within the selection (using the selection as a mask) and hides the rectangular area outside of the selection—but the hidden area is still part of the selection.

Adele Droblas Greenberg's *Golden Statue* (5.3) illustrates the Painter mask at work. The image was created by combining an image of a statue (5.4) with a background image (5.5) created from a custom gradient and by applying the Apply Surface Texture and Quick Warp commands. The background figure shows the floater used to create the blending effect. Notice that the floater is rectangular and includes more than just the statue's face. However, only the statue's face appears in the final image.

To produce this effect, Adele created a mask with a brush stroke. As she painted over the face, she created a soft edge oval mask (5.6). (Chapter 3 describes how to create a mask out of a brush stroke.) Next, Adele turned the mask into a selection by choosing Select ➤ Load Selection and then copying and pasting the mask into the background image. When the image appeared in the background file, Painter automatically created the floater and showed only the masked area of the statue.

To turn the statue's face gold, Adele selected the Luminosity composite method in the Controls palette. The Luminosity composite method kept the brightness values of the statue but used the color values of the background image.

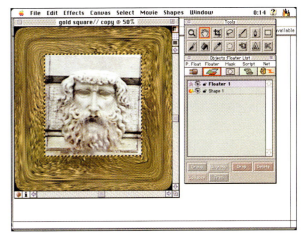

5.4

5.3

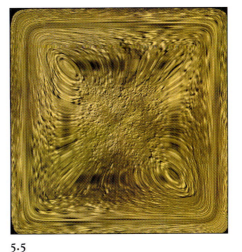

5.5

Although Painter displays only the masked area of the floater, the floater remains a rectangle and includes areas that extend beyond the mask. You can easily see the areas not shown in the floater by double-clicking the floater's name in the Objects Floater List palette. In the Floater Attributes dialog box, set the Floater Visibility Mask section to Inverted. This shows the floater without the image within the mask.

EDITING THE FLOATER MASK

A floater's mask can be turned on and off, and its edges and opacity can be edited. This feature provides you with endless possibilities for image alteration.

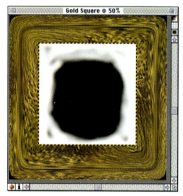

5.6

> **NOTE**
>
> Photoshop users: The technique of editing a floater mask technique is similar to using a layer mask in Photoshop. However, in Painter the layer mask is automatically added when the floater is created.

Here's how to edit a floater mask using a brush variant:

1. Create a floater by making a selection using the Oval, Lasso, or Pen tool. If you use the Pen tool, turn the pen path into a selection by clicking the Make Selection button in the Controls palette.
2. Copy and paste the selection into another image. Painter creates a floater and transforms your selection into the floater's mask.
3. Select the brush variant you wish to use to blend your image. (Use the Airbrush to create a soft-edge blending effect.)
4. To tell Painter you want to edit the mask, select the mask in the Objects: Mask List palette. To open the palette, choose Windows ➢ Objects and click the Mask icon in the palette. In the palette, click the floater mask.

If you don't see the mask for your floater in the Objects: Mask List palette, chances are the floater is not selected. Select the floater by clicking it with the Floater Adjuster tool, or select it in the Objects: Floater List palette.

To reveal more of the background image, Paint with white. To add more of the floater to the image, paint with black. To change the opacity of the top floater, paint with a shade of gray. As you paint, you'll see how editing the mask changes the appearance of the image.

You can also edit the floater by creating a selection onscreen. If you want the selection to cut a hole out of the floater, double-click the floater's name in the Floater Object: List palette, and then choose the Selection Conceals Floater option.

USING THE FLOATER LIST PALETTE

When you're using floaters, the Objects: Floater List palette becomes an essential tool. You may want to drag the Floater List palette onscreen as a separate palette so that you can view the Objects: Mask List and Objects: Floater List at the same time. Another handy trick for quickly accessing the Floater List palette is to double-click the Floater Adjuster tool.

After you've placed the Objects: Floater List palette onscreen, manipulating floaters is just a few clicks away:

- To hide the floater or make it visible, click the eye column.
- To lock or unlock the floater in the image to prevent it from moving, click the lock icon.
- To rename a floater, double-click the name of the floater and enter a name in the Name field.
- To change the order of floaters, click and drag the floater up or down in the palette. Doing so changes the stacking order of the floaters.
- To place several floaters in a group to either move them together as one unit or apply an effect to the entire group, you must first select all the floaters you want to add to the group. To select the floaters, press Shift and click each floater you want to include. After you select the floaters, click the Group button at the bottom of the palette. (You can also choose Group from the Floater menu in the Objects: Floater List palette.)

TIP

To edit a floater mask without seeing the floater image, click the floater mask in the Objects: Mask List palette and deselect the RGB Canvas mask. Then you're able to edit a grayscale version of the mask.

When you're finished working on your floaters, you can integrate your floaters into the background canvas by clicking the Drop Floater icon in the Objects: Floater List palette. Be aware, however, that after you drop a floater, it no longer floats. If you need to save your file in TIFF or another file format besides RIFF or Photoshop 3, Painter warns you that you must first drop the floaters before saving because other file formats do not support floating objects.

USING THE FLOATER COMPOSITE METHODS

Painter's Composite Method enables you to create fascinating blending effects between a floater and the background canvas or between one floater and another floater. To use the Composite Methods, you only have to select a floater and choose the Composite Method in the Controls palette. The thumbnail images on the following page summarize the effects of the Composite Methods.

TIP

Painter's Select ➢ All command does not select floaters. Select floaters by clicking the floaters or by selecting them in the Objects: Floater List palette.

NOTE

Composite Methods in Painter correspond with Photoshop's blending modes. Many have identical names and produce similar results.

Composite Modes

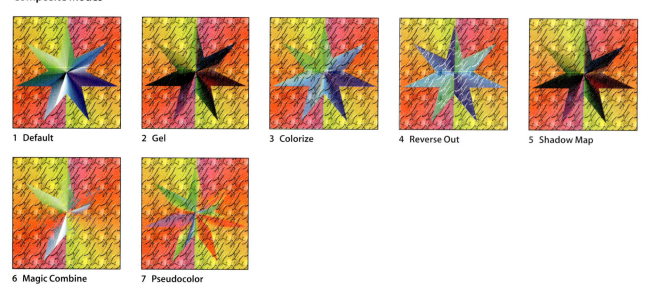

1 Default
2 Gel
3 Colorize
4 Reverse Out
5 Shadow Map
6 Magic Combine
7 Pseudocolor

Photoshop-compatible Modes

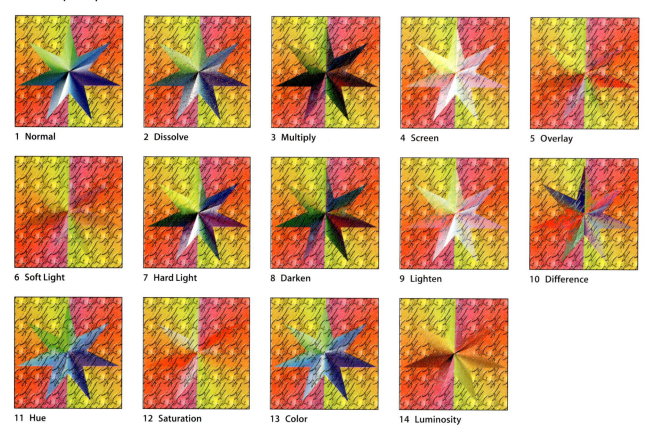

1 Normal
2 Dissolve
3 Multiply
4 Screen
5 Overlay
6 Soft Light
7 Hard Light
8 Darken
9 Lighten
10 Difference
11 Hue
12 Saturation
13 Color
14 Luminosity

CREATING TRANSPARENT LAYERS

From time to time you may want to create a floater to cover the entire background canvas—much the same way a layer works in Adobe Photoshop. To create this floater, you need to create a transparent layer and paint within it using Painter's Transparent Layer brush, a plug-in brush accessible from the Brushes palette. When you paint in a transparent layer, it's as though you are painting on a sheet of acetate that covers the entire canvas. As in Photoshop, you can paint in overlapping layers, hide layers, and reorder layers. When you paint in one layer, your work does not affect other layers.

Artist Chelsea Sammel found Painter's Transparent Layers feature to be perfectly suited for an image she created for a T-shirt design for a radio station (5.7). Transparent layers proved to be the most efficient way to create the image because the T-shirts were going to be silk-screened. In the silk-screen process, each color is applied separately, somewhat like spot colors in printing. When creating the image, Chelsea chose a brush variant and then chose the Transparent Layer Brush plug-in Method Category before painting in a transparent layer. After she created the artwork, each of the six layers were output separately for use in the etching process prior to the actual silk-screening.

Here's how to use a Transparent Layer brush in a transparent layer:

1. Choose a brush variant from the Brushes palette.
2. Choose Plug-in from the Method pop-up menu in the Brushes palette. In the Subcategory pop-up menu, choose Transparent Layer Brush.
3. Choose Transparent Layer from the Floater menu in the Floater's List palette to create the transparent layer.
4. Start painting.

As you paint, you are painting in a layer above the background. Because you are painting in a floater, you can turn the opacity on and off and change the Composite Methods in the Controls palette. You can also use the Adjust Color command to change the color of the painted area of the floater and apply various effects. (Be aware that a low Saturation value in the Adjust Color dialog box produces gray.) For example, you can use the Effects ➢ Apply Surface texture to apply paper grain to the area you are painting over.

If desired, add another transparent layer. You can then hide a layer by clicking the layer's open-eye icon in the Objects: Floater List palette. After you click, the eye closes. To make the layer visible again, click the closed-eye icon. You can also rearrange layers by dragging one transparent layer over the other in the palette.

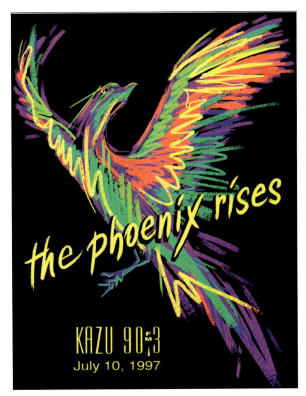

5.7

PLUG-IN FLOATERS

Plug-in floaters add an abundance of special effects to Painter images. Many of the effects generated by plug-in floaters are similar to special effects provided by Painter and Photoshop plug-ins. For example, Painter's plug-in floaters can bevel an image, turn it into liquid metal, and create burning and singed-edge effects. But why use a plug-in floater effect rather than a third-party plug-in? Perhaps the primary advantage is that the altered image floats above the background canvas, enabling you to experiment to your heart's content without affecting the background pixels.

To apply a plug-in floater, select part of an image onscreen. Open the Objects palette by choosing Window ➢ Objects. To open the Plug-in floaters palette, click the P.Float icon. To view all the available plug-ins, click the palette drawer to open it, or click the pop-up menu to see a list of the plug-ins. Next choose a plug-in by clicking the icon of the plug-in you want to use or by selecting a plug-in by name in the pop-up menu.

To apply the plug-in, click the Apply button in the Objects Plug-in Floaters palette, or choose Apply in the palette's plug-in menu. This opens the plug-in dialog box (5.8). You can edit the plug-in effect by clicking and dragging the slider to the desired effect and then clicking OK.

If you want to reopen the dialog box and change the effect, make sure the plug-in floater is selected onscreen. Then choose Options in the P.Float menu at the top of the palette.

You can also reapply the effect by first opening the Objects: Floater List palette. In the lists, you'll see the plug-in name. Double-click the floater name. This opens the plug-in's dialog box. In the dialog box, you can edit the effect. When you're satisfied with the plug-in floater's effect, you can *commit* the floater by clicking the commit button in the P.List palette. This converts the plug-in floater to a standard Painter floater. After you commit the plug-in, you no longer can change the dialog box settings for that floater.

Various plug-in effects are shown in the following thumbnail figures.

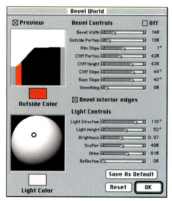

5.8

> **TIP**
>
> When using a plug-in floater, don't forget that the Composite Methods are available in the Controls palette.

> **NOTE**
>
> The Impasto and Bevel World plug-in floaters are discussed in Chapter 12. Many examples of the Bevel World plug-in are discussed in Chapter 10.

Plug-in Effects

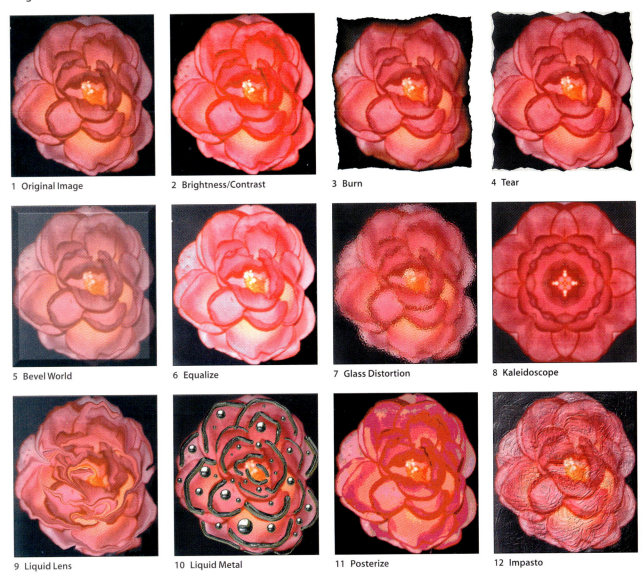

CHAPTER 6
STARTLING EFFECTS OF THE IMAGE HOSE

Painter's Image Hose is probably the program's most amazing brush. Unlike most Painter brushes that emulate traditional characteristics, Painter's Image Hose is a twentieth-century artistic tool that sprays the screen with digital images. Using the Image Hose, you can quickly create startling effects with a few clicks and drags of a brush.

Because the Image Hose sprays digital images rather than paint, the brush doesn't use Painter's primary painting color. Instead, the secret behind the Image Hose's brush strokes is the contents of its nozzle file. Painter includes a number of nozzle files that enable you to paint your screen with such diverse objects as ivy, poppies, stones, clouds, insects, sushi, and even the contents of a Mediterranean village. We created *Insects* (6.1) by painting with the Image Hose brush using Painter's Insect Library nozzles.

The Image Hose brush can also be used to quickly add a background to an image. The clouds in the background of Patrick Lichty's *Have a Prozac Day* (6.2) were painted with the Image Hose brush with Painter's Clouds nozzle file. Patrick created the landscape by creating a KPT Gradient Designer sky with two applications of radial fills with varying degrees of opacity. He created the lower landscape with the Chalk brush and the Distorto brush variant. He then applied the KPT filter. He drew the face in CorelDRAW and applied KPT Gradient Designer ➢ Gradients on Paths to the eyes and mouth. Patrick created and rendered the pills in 3D Studio Max.

I enjoy Painter because of its interface logic. I was originally trained as a fine artist and worked with oil paints, so with Painter I feel right at home.

GEORGE KRAUTER

6.1

LOADING THE NOZZLE FILE

The Image Hose brush is accessed like any other brush—from Painter's Brushes palette. (The Image Hose brush can be identified by the garden hose icon with the shamrocks spraying from the hose.) However, unlike Painter's other brushes, you don't click the brush, pick a color, and start to paint. With the Image Hose you must pick a nozzle file to paint with. A nozzle contains a grid of digital images. As the Image Hose paints, it pours one digital image after another onto the Painter canvas.

Two primary techniques are used to load a nozzle file. The simplest is to load a nozzle from Painter's default library of nozzles in the Brush Controls: Nozzles palette. To open the Nozzles palette, choose Nozzles from the Nozzle menu in the Brushes palette. In the Nozzles palette, you can pick a nozzle simply by clicking any of the nozzles at the top of the palette. You can also open the palette drawer and choose a nozzle by clicking its icon or by clicking its name in the pop-up menu in the palette.

Extra nozzles can also be loaded directly from disk. For example, the Sample Nozzle Files from the *Painter 5 Studio Secrets* CD-ROM must be loaded directly from the CD-ROM or from your computer's hard disk. To load a nozzle file from disk, choose Load Nozzle from the Nozzle menu in the Brushes palette. Select the file in the dialog box, and then click OK to load the nozzle file. After you load the nozzle file, the Image Hose paints with the contents of the file.

UNDERSTANDING THE NOZZLE FILE

If you want to see the contents of the loaded nozzle file, choose Check Out Nozzle from the Nozzle menu in the Brushes palette (the same menu item appears in the Brush Controls: Nozzle palette).

We created a nozzle file using images from the MetaCreations PowerPhotos stock photo CD-ROM (6.3). Notice that the elements are arranged in rows and columns. As the Image Hose paints, it picks elements from the columns and rows of the nozzle file (6.4). What appears on the screen depends not only on the contents of the nozzle file but also on the chosen Image Hose variant in the Brushes palette.

6.3

6.2

6.4

UNDERSTANDING IMAGE HOSE RANKING

Undoubtedly, the most confusing aspect of the Image Hose nozzle files is the concept of rank. *Rank* is a sophisticated factor in determining exactly which nozzle element appears onscreen. Painter accommodates three levels of Image Hose ranking. The simplest nozzle files are 1-Rank; the most sophisticated are 3-Rank.

The ranking system was created to allow the Image Hose to respond to various users controls, such as the variants in the Brushes palette and sliders in the Brush Controls Nozzle palette.

The Image Hose ranking means that Image Hose elements are not necessarily sprayed indiscriminately onscreen. For example, in a 2-Rank nozzle file, the nozzle designer can cause the direction of the brush stroke to control the size of the element painted, and the speed of the stroke to control the angle of the element painted.

A 2-Rank nozzle may have two rows of shapes in which the shapes in row 1 are smaller than the shapes in row 2. Within each row, each shape appears at a different angle. In this nozzle file, size is 1-Rank and angle is 2-Rank. Because the nozzle was set up as a 2-Rank file, image elements can be controlled with the 2-Rank brush variants (2-Rank R-P and 2-Rank P-D) and by using the 1-Rank and 2-Rank sliders in the Brush Controls: Nozzle palette.

UNDERSTANDING THE IMAGE HOSE VARIANTS

Image Hose brush variants determine the size and placement of elements sprayed from the Image Hose brush. Deciphering the words used in the variants listing can help you predict how the Image Hose will paint. For example, the words *Small*, *Medium*, and *Large* indicate the amount of spacing when the stroke is applied—not the size of the brush stroke.

Linear variants (such as Small Random Linear) paint the Image Hose nozzle elements directly on the brush path. Spray variants (such as Small Random Spray) spray the images on the screen. *Random*, *Sequential Directional*, and *Pressure* refer to how the various elements in the nozzle file are chosen. Random chooses the images randomly; Sequential chooses elements in the Nozzle file one after another; Directional varies the brush depending on the direction of the stroke; and Pressure varies the images based on pressure applied to a stylus tablet.

The Small Luminance Cloner is the most unusual of the variants. It chooses the images from the nozzle file based upon the brightness values of a clone source. For example, assume you are painting with a nozzle file composed of small to large meatballs. If the clone source is dark on the left and white on the right, the Image Hose might paint small meatballs to large meatballs. If the clone source is white on the left and dark on the right, the Image Hose paints the contents of the nozzle file by placing the larger meatballs onscreen first.

Several of the variants only affect 2- and 3-Rank nozzle files. In the Rank variants, *R*, *P*, *D* stand for Random, Pressure, and Direction, respectively. For example, in 2-Rank R-P, the elements in columns of the nozzle file may be sprayed out randomly while the row elements are sprayed according to pressure.

Image Hose Brush Variants

1 Small Random Linear

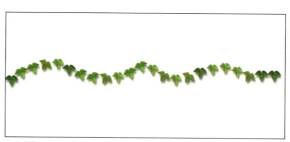
2 Medium Random Linear

3 Large Random Linear

4 Small Random Spray

5 Medium Random Spray

6 Large Random Spray

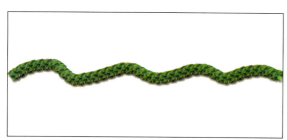
7 Small Sequential Linear

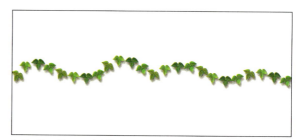
8 Medium Sequential Linear

9 Large Sequential Linear

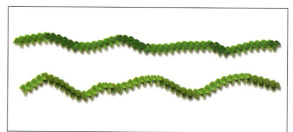
10 Small Directional

Chapter 6 *Startling Effects of the Image Hose*   69

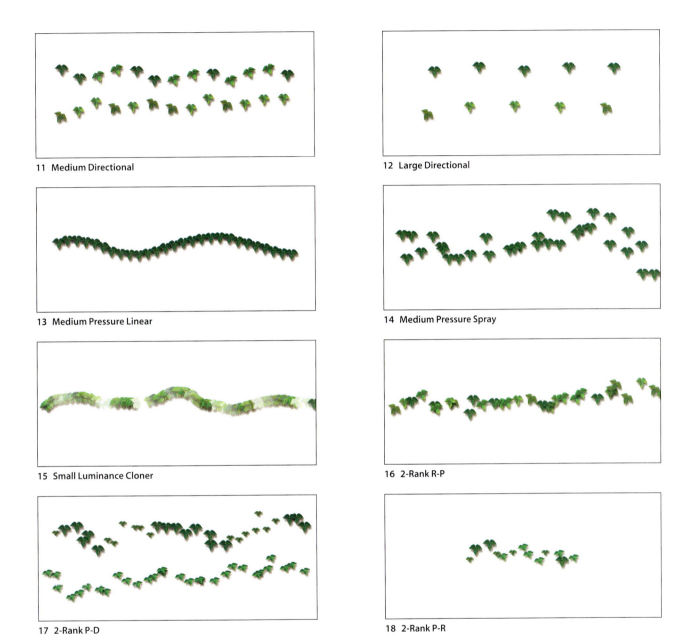

11 Medium Directional

12 Large Directional

13 Medium Pressure Linear

14 Medium Pressure Spray

15 Small Luminance Cloner

16 2-Rank R-P

17 2-Rank P-D

18 2-Rank P-R

USING THE NOZZLE PALETTE SLIDERS

As you choose brush variants, the Rank vertical sliders in the Brush Controls Nozzle palette automatically change. These sliders can be manually adjusted to further alter how an Image Hose brush variant paints. If you have a multiranked nozzle file, you can specify how each individual element in the rank appears onscreen.

For example, if you want the Image Hose to spray its contents sequentially, click the 1-Rank slider and drag to Sequential. If you want the contents sprayed according to the direction the brush is dragged, choose Directional. When you choose Directional, painting left to right only produces the first element in the nozzle file. Moving counter-clockwise paints the next image in the nozzle files rank. When you choose Random, the elements from the Image Hose rank are sprayed onscreen randomly. When you choose Pressure, elements are placed based upon pressure applied to the stylus. Thus, when painting with a 2-Rank nozzle file, you can set Rank 1 to Random and Rank 2 to Directional (6.5).

If you choose Source, the images are placed according to the brightness values of the clone source. If no clone source is designated, the brightness values of the current pattern are used.

6.5

6.6

USING THE IMAGE HOSE AND THE CONTROLS PALETTE

Although the effect of the Image Hose is primarily determined by the brush variants and the nozzle file, other palettes can also effect the Image Hose output. As with other brushes, the Controls palette enables you to control opacity. If you lower the opacity, you can make your Image Hose paint with a transparent effect. Unlike other brushes, the Grain slider provides a surprising effect. If you drag the Grain slider to the left, more of the secondary painting color is added to the color of the images from the Image Hose's nozzle file.

USING PLACE ELEMENTS WITH THE IMAGE HOSE

Although Image Hose controls have changed little since Painter 3, owners of the latest version of Painter can use the Image Hose in conjunction with the Place Elements command. *Sushi* (6.6), by Seth Greenberg, was created solely by using the Place Elements commands—clicking and dragging was not used. When you use Place Elements, Painter piles Image Hose nozzle elements on top and around a center spherical shape based on what Painter's programmers call a *virtual sphere*.

Place Elements paints the Image Hose's nozzle file into a *virtual* sphere based upon randomly automated brush strokes. To use Place Elements with the Image Hose, select the nozzle file you want to apply. Then create a rectangular or elliptical selection onscreen. Next choose Effects ➢ Esoterica ➢ Place Elements.

> **NOTE**
>
> The Size slider in the Brush Controls Size palette does not affect the size of the Image Hose brush stroke. (Use the Size slider in the Brush Controls: Nozzle palette instead.) However, the Placement slider in the Advanced Controls Random palette does alter placement of nozzle file elements.

In the Place Elements dialog box, use the Points slider to specify how many Image Hose elements you want placed on the virtual sphere. When the points are placed, they are randomly dispersed. The points begin to move away from each other based on the Iteration setting in the dialog box. A low Iteration setting results in randomly placed elements; higher iteration settings result in more constant spacing.

The complexity of the final image can be controlled by the Number of Levels radio button. For example, choosing Level 2 results in each element used as the reference point of another virtual sphere. Level 3 adds another level of sphere creation. Level 1 leaves each place element along its original virtual sphere. The Radius Fraction slider controls the size of the second and third levels. Numbers above 1 increase overlapping. Numbers below 1 decrease overlapping. *Sushi* has an iteration setting of 200 and was set at Level 2 with the radius slider set to 1.05.

The Ambient slider can be used to create more depth in the edges of the virtual sphere. Increasing the Ambient slider adds more of the secondary color to the edges of the virtual sphere.

CREATING AN IMAGE HOSE USING FLOATERS

After you experiment with the Image Hose and its variants, you'll soon want to create your own nozzle files. One of the easiest ways to create a simple 1-Rank nozzle file is from a group of floaters. We used floaters to create the nozzle file shown in an image earlier in the chapter (6.3).

The secret to creating an elegant-looking nozzle file is to create a mask around items in the file. If you don't create a mask, your image hose elements appear with a rectangular border around them. Another useful technique when creating an image hose nozzle is to use Painter's Objects ➢ Create Drop shadow command. This can help add a 3D effect to your image hose.

Follow these steps to create a nozzle file:

1. Create a new blank file in Painter large enough to hold all Image Hose elements. For example, if you are going to put six 1-inch square elements in a nozzle file, you probably want to line up the elements in two rows, with three images in each row. Thus you may want to make the file's dimensions approximately 5 in. × 4 in. This blank file eventually becomes the nozzle file that contains all your image hose elements.

2. Scan or create each element you want to appear in your nozzle file. (You may want to create these in different files.)

3. After you've created all the elements, open the first image you wish to place in your nozzle file. Select the portion you want to place in the nozzle file. (Even if you've created the image on a white background, you still need to select or silhouette the outlines of the image.)

4. After you've created the selection, copy and paste the selection into the original blank file. This creates a floater in the nozzle file. Do this for each element you want to have in your image hose. Position all the elements in a grid of rows and columns.

5. To create a drop shadow in your floater, select the floater in your nozzle file. Then select Objects ➢ Create Drop Shadow. In the Drop Shadow dialog box, choose the Collapse to one layer option (so that another floater isn't created).

6. Before turning the floaters into a nozzle file, you must *group* them. Select all floaters in the file by clicking and dragging over them with the Floater Adjuster tool or by pressing Shift and clicking the different floaters in the Objects: Floater List palette. (You can also choose Select All in the Floater menu.) After selecting the floaters, click the Group button in the Objects: Floaters List palette.

7. Trim the edges of the floater by choosing Trim from the Floater List palette.

8. To create the nozzle file, select the Nozzle menu in the Brushes palette, and then choose Make Nozzle From Group. In the dialog box that opens, name the file and save it.

9. To use the nozzle, choose Nozzle ➢ Load Nozzle in the Brushes palette.

10. To add the nozzle to the current nozzle library, choose Nozzle ➢ Add Nozzle to Library in the Brushes palette.

6.7

6.8

Experiment and have fun. Before you start, you may want to look at artwork created from custom nozzle files. For example, Chelsea Sammel created *Garden* (6.7, 6.8) from an Image Hose of painted flowers. To create the Nozzle file, Chelsea painted a series of flowers and leaves on a plain white background using the Water Color brush. When she finished painting, she dried the canvas by choosing Canvas ➢ Dry.

To create a nozzle file from floaters, she needed to select each element. Because she had painted the elements on a white background, Chelsea chose Auto Select ➢ Current Color, which was white.

Next she floated the images individually and created a drop shadow for each element (Effects ➢ Esoterica ➢ Create Drop shadow). Then she grouped the floaters together and created the nozzle by choosing Make Nozzle From Group in the Nozzle Menu in the Brushes palette.

Before using the nozzle, Chelsea added it to Painter's Nozzles library by choosing Add Nozzle to Library from the Nozzle menu. After the nozzle was in the Library, she could choose it and use the Scale command in the Brush Controls: Nozzle palette, as well as use the Grain slider in the Controls palette, which enables you to add the Secondary color when painting.

George Krauter created *Digital Junk* (6.9) using a nozzle file he created from 3D objects. George created the 3D objects in Strata StudioPro and rendered most of them using textures he created in Painter. Each 3D object was rendered with an alpha channel and then opened in Adobe Photoshop. The alpha channel enabled George to select each image easily. To create the drop shadows, George offset and feathered the selections around the objects six pixels down and to the right. Then he arranged all the images in a grid

> **NOTE**
>
> **If you are using a file that already contains a mask of the image area that you want to place in your nozzle file, select the mask in the Objects: Mask List palette and then click the Load selection button to create the selection.**

three columns wide by 10 rows deep. Each cell was 360×300 pixels. After creating the nozzle file, he loaded it and started painting with his stunning digital junk.

Dennis Berkla created *Impressionism* (6.10), *Birch* (6.11), and *Sonoma* (6.12) using nozzles from *The Garden Hose* CD-ROM. For tips on how to use the nozzles from the CD-ROM or for information about how to order *The Garden Hose* CD-ROM, see `http://www.gardenhose.com`.

6.11

6.9

6.12

6.10

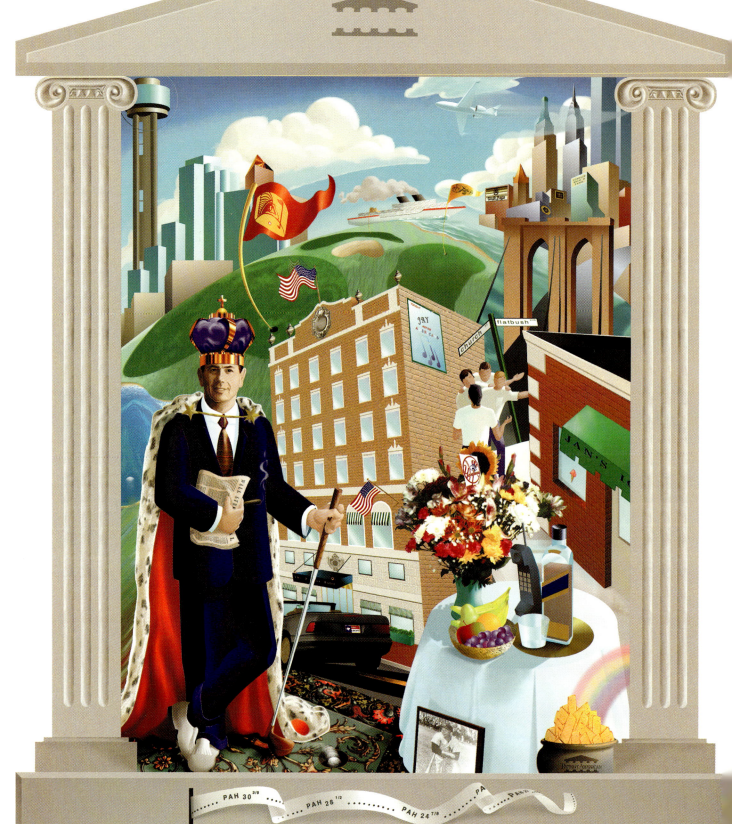

CHAPTER 7
OUTPUTTING YOUR ARTWORK

Art knows no boundaries. Artists create their work on paper, canvas, sidewalks—even on the sides of buildings. Although you can't create your Painter artwork on the side of a building, you can output it to canvas and have your mural stretched across the side of your apartment or house.

Looking Back (7.1), by Dorothy Simpson Krause, is another image outputted in an unusual manner. Dorothy printed the image onto fabric, and on the back of a jacket. The original image is 40 × 50 inches printed on spunbonded polyester that is heavily textured with molding paste and pearl pigment. Dorothy created the image in Painter and Photoshop using layers. The image is based on a photograph by Viola Kaumlen.

If you're skeptical that an image created on a 21-inch computer screen can be outputted on such a large canvas, take a look at Kenneth Gore's *Love of Labor, Gift of Health*, a mural created for the Shriners Children's Hospital in Salt Lake City, Utah. Kenneth created the image in Painter and output it on four 22¼- × 9-foot canvases (7.2, 7.3, 7.4, 7.5).

James Dowlen's *Incredible Sign* (7.6), created for Jonathan Lipson's new record store and rock-n-roll museum in Sebastopol, California, is another example of large-format outputting. James created the sign in CorelDRAW and colored it in Painter. After creating the image, James output it to slide film using his 35mm film recorder. He then projected the image onto a 13-foot board and traced and airbrushed the image in sign painter's enamels.

Digital files on canvas can be retouched by hand with real oil paints.

KENNETH GORE

7.1

CEO PARODY
Kenneth Gore

7.2

7.3

Chapter 7 Outputting Your Artwork

7.4

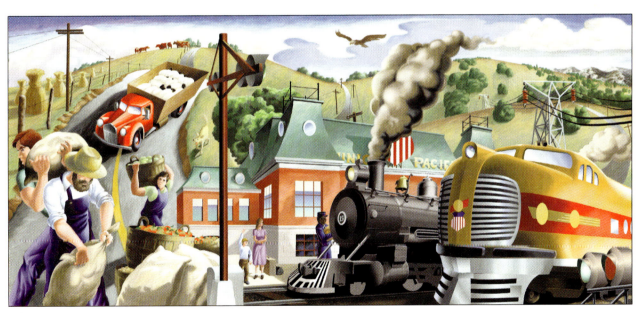

7.5

How do you output your Painter artwork from your Macintosh or PC onto a mural, or to a printing press, or to the Web? And how can you ensure that the colors will be correct? This chapter unlocks those secrets.

THE KODAK COLOR MANAGEMENT SYSTEM

Whether outputting to paper, canvas, or a sheet of vinyl or plastic, all Painter artists are faced with a common problem—predicting how their images will look when printed. Printed output never exactly matches screen output.

If you're not familiar with the problem of matching screen colors to printed colors, here's a brief review of the problem. Your computer generates colors by combining different proportions of red, green, and blue light. By emitting different combinations of red, green, and blue (RGB), your computer gives Painter the capability to display over 16 million different colors.

When you see color on a printed image, the page or canvas obviously doesn't emit light. Instead, color is created when light is absorbed and reflected off the page. To create the illusion of countless colors, different percentages of cyan, magenta, yellow, and black (CMYK) ink are combined on the printing press, a process simulated by many Postscript color printers. During the commercial printing process, the cyan, magenta, yellow, and black inks are applied by separate printing plates. The overlaying of tiny dots of the four inks provides the color you see on a printed page.

To print your Painter file using CMYK colors, the file first must be separated to a file that can handle four channels of colors. During the separation process, the colors are converted from RGB to their CMYK equivalents. This process usually results in a darkening or dulling of colors. Sometimes the process produces unforeseen results because the artist's color monitor provides a misleading indication of the actual colors generated by the computer file. The process can also provide misleading results because computer painting programs enable you to create colors onscreen that fall beyond the spectrum (or gamut) of printable colors.

Although Painter does not allow you to choose your colors with a CMYK color model, Painter 5 comes a long way in addressing the needs of users who are outputting their images to paper and canvas.

IMPLEMENTING KCMS

Painter 5 is the first version of Painter to provide a CMYK preview option based upon the monitor you are using and your output device. Painter 5 also features a gamut warning feature—a means of showing you what parts of the images fall beyond the printable color spectrum.

To implement these important outputting additions, Painter programmers turned to Kodak to help provide a solution. Painter makes use of a digital color matching system created by Kodak called the Kodak Color Management System (KCMS)—a utility automatically installed when you install Painter. When you turn on your computer, the KCMS files are automatically loaded into your system.

Incredible Records and CDs Dowlen ArtWorks © 1997

7.6

The secret behind the accuracy of KCMS is a set of *device profiles*, programs specifically designed to alter the screen colors based on the characteristics of your monitor. When a device profile is used, screen colors should better approximate printed output.

USING KCMS

The first step in using KCMS is to set up the default settings for a CMYK preview. Start by choosing Canvas ➢ Output Preview ➢ Kodak Color Correction. The first time you execute this command, Painter opens the Select Profiles dialog box.

In the Select Profiles dialog box, specify an Input Profile, an Output Profile, and a Monitor Profile. If your image was created in Painter, you don't need to specify an Input Profile. If you are outputting to a color printer, click in the Output Profile. If you see your output device listed, choose it from the pop-up menu. Then choose a monitor profile in the Monitor Profile pop-up menu.

If a profile doesn't exist for your printer or monitor, contact the manufacturer. If you want to add more profiles and use a Macintosh, copy the profiles into the ColorSync Profiles folder in the System Preferences Folder. If you use Windows, copy the profiles into the Windows\System\Color directory. If you can't obtain a Monitor Profile, use the Generic P22 1.8.

> **NOTE**
>
> During the Painter installation process, you can choose not to have the KCMS system installed. If you don't install it, you cannot preview your files for print.

Your next step is to enable the Show Gamut warning check box. The gamut warning works by covering all non-printable colors in your image with a color. (If you want to change the gamut warning color, click the color swatch and change it with the Apple or Windows color picker.) After you select the Show Gamut Warning check box and choose a profile, you can see how your image should actually appear when printed. To view the CMYK preview, choose Canvas ➢ Output Preview ➢ Kodak Color Correction. The preview generally dulls bright colors, and you'll see that any out-of-gamut colors are covered with the gamut warning color.

> **TIP**
>
> If you will be importing your Painter file into Photoshop and using Photoshop's RGB to CMYK color table, choose Photoshop RGB to CMYK in the Output Profile menu. This profile is designed to match Adobe Photoshop's default RGB to CMYK color table.

> **TIP**
>
> If colors are out-of-gamut, try painting over them with colors lower in saturation. To do this, set the primary painting color to the out-of-gamut color by clicking the color with the Eyedropper tool. Then reduce the saturation percentage of the primary painting color by clicking and dragging the Hue Saturation Value color wheel in the Art Materials: Color palette.

PRINTING AND SAVING SEPARATIONS WITH KCMS

Because Painter does not allow you to edit colors in a CMYK file, many users assume Painter cannot create or output color separations. Thus they load their files into another program such as Photoshop to create the separations there.

In fact, Painter can output separations to a printer and/or create a CMYK file. However, Painter does not provide as many separation controls as do some programs such as Photoshop. If you are outputting directly from Painter and want Painter to use the output profile when it creates the separation, select the Use Output Preview in the Print dialog box.

If you want to create a color-separated file in Painter and send it to your prepress house, you must save the file in EPS (Encapsulated PostScript) format by Choosing File ➤ Save. In the Save As dialog box, choose the EPS option. Painter creates a file for each CMYK color and a preview file, if the preview option is selected in the EPS dialog box. If the Kodak Output preview is selected when creating the EPS file, Painter creates the separation with the KCMS information in an attempt to match the preview as closely as possible.

After you save the file in EPS format, Painter creates five files. One file is a low-resolution preview that is assigned the filename of your original file. The other files include the original filename with a letter indicating which CMYK plate the file is designed for.

OUTPUTTING FINE ART PRINTS

Years ago, if you wanted to output your Painter artwork to canvas, you had to search around the country for an output house specializing in fine art printing. Today, many service bureaus provide the service. The output is often very true to the screen colors. For example, *Bouquet*, by Adele Droblas Greenberg (7.7), was created in Painter and then outputted to canvas on a LaserMaster printer. She was so happy with the "printed" version that she had it framed and hung it in her dining room.

Digital printers can output not only to canvas but also on rice paper and even vinyl sheets. For large-format printing, many service bureaus use Encad Novajet printers. (For information about these printers, see the Encad Web site at www.encad.com.) For smaller canvases, service bureaus often use Scitex Iris. (For information about the Scitex Iris system, see the Scitex Web site at www.scitex.com.) Using a process called Iris Giclee, service bureaus can output canvas sheets as large as 30 inches to 46 inches.

During the printing process, most fine art printers spray more than four million drops of ink on canvas and archival papers. Kenneth Gore's *CEO Parody* poster (7.8), created for R. Jones and Associates and hanging at American Patriot Headquarters in Dallas, Texas, was output to an IRIS printer.

Kenneth, who frequently outputs his Painter work to canvas, advises Painter users to carefully shop around for a service bureau that can handle the job you want. Prepress houses should be able to provide you with Pantone and Iris color charts that indicate how your digital colors will print on a specific printer.

Kenneth suggests that you inquire about what type of files the prepress house requires. Many houses require you to convert your files to TIFF and won't accept files in Painter's standard RIFF format.

7.7

Chapter 7 Outputting Your Artwork

Before sending files to a prepress house, Kenneth suggests using the Painter 5 KCMS system to preview the files. He also suggests that you output a few test proofs to see exactly how the final colors match the screen colors. You may even want to create your own color charts and have them output to see how closely the output color matches your screen colors. Kenneth also recommends that you stick with one service bureau. When you're happy with the results it provides, you can be pretty confident that the job will be output satisfactorily the next time. Ask other artists in your area to recommend venders if you are having a difficult time finding one you are happy with. Kenneth also notes that digital files on canvas can be retouched by hand with real oil paints.

USING PANTONE COLORS

Using the Pantone Color system is another approach some artists take to ensure they know exactly how their printed work will be output. As she works, New York-based artist Emily Stedman uses a Pantone color swatch book to pick her colors. After she finds the colors she wants, she loads Painter's Pantone color set. To load the Pantone color set, Emily chooses Load Color Set from the Color menu in the Art Materials palette. Then she chooses the Pantone color set from the Colors, Weaves Grads folder. With the color set onscreen, Emily can simply click a Pantone color to choose it as her painting color. When the image prints, the colors match the colors in her swatch book.

Emily Stedman's *Landscape* (7.9) and *Wine Country* (7.10) both use colors Emily chose in a Pantone color swatch book.

7.9

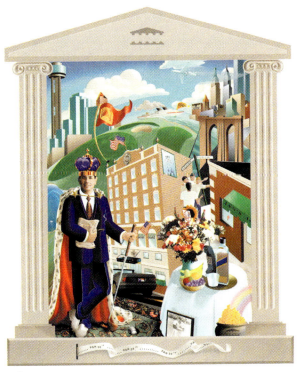

7.8

OUTPUTTING TO THE WEB

If you want to showcase your Painter art, you can't get a wider audience then that provided by the World Wide Web. Fortunately for Painter artists, outputting a file to the Web is an easy affair. First you need to save your image in either JPEG or GIF format. If you've created a Painter movie, you can save your file as an animated GIF file. The animation can then be placed on your Web page.

7.10

SAVING IN JPEG

When outputting for the Web, Most Painter artists will probably want to save their files in JPEG because JPEG does not reduce the number of colors in an image.

Because Painter files are often quite large, your best bet is to use Painter's JPEG compression options to reduce your image's file size. When saving in JPEG, Painter provides four quality settings: Excellent, High, Good, and Fair. The higher the quality, the larger your file, thus the slower the file will download to a user's computer. Try starting at Good and viewing the results. If the file looks fine, try dropping the quality to Fair. To give you an idea of the different degrees of compression these settings produce, we created a 500K painter file and saved it as a JPEG file in Good format. The resulting file was about 60K. Saving the file using the Fair option produced a 53.7K file. Saving the same file as High quality resulted in a 71.5K file.

SAVING IN GIF

The GIF file format is probably the most popular file format used for simple Web graphics. However, Painter artists should be wary of saving files in GIF format because the format reduces the colors in an image to 256 colors or fewer.

Why would anyone want to use GIF file format if the color restriction is so great? There are several reasons why GIF is attractive. Perhaps the most important reason is that many Web surfers can view only 256 colors at a time on their screens. If you save your Web files as JPEG instead of GIF, visitors to your Web page may not view the page as you intended. The decision is up to you. If you think clients, artists, and art directors will be heading to your Web page with powerful computers, you're probably better off with JPEG images.

Painter's GIF file format also enables you to use a mask to create a transparent area in your image. The transparent area can allow the background color of a Web page to show through the mask in your image.

OUTPUTTING TO QUICKTIME AND VIDEO FOR WINDOWS

Painter's animation capabilities go largely overlooked by most computer artists. Many artists wonder exactly what they can do with a movie they've created in Painter. Obviously, you can't play the movie in a magazine or hang it on a wall in a traditional art gallery. So how do you gather an audience for a movie you've created in Painter? Output your movie in QuickTime or AVI format or as an animated GIF file.

If you want people to view your movie or a multimedia presentation, you need to save your movie in either QuickTime or AVI format. QuickTime and AVI are standard digital video formats used by many different multimedia programs. For example, you can load a Painter movie saved in QuickTime or AVI format to programs such as Macromedia Director, Adobe Premiere, and Adobe After Effects. The Painter movie found on our CD-ROM, *The Ultimate Interactive Guide to Painter 5*, was created in Macromedia director and features several painter movies saved in QuickTime format (7.11). (More information about this CD-ROM is available on the CD-ROM that accompanies this book and at our Web site at www2.infohouse.com/~addesign.)

> **NOTE**
>
> To learn about creating animated GIF files, see Chapter 13.

> **NOTE**
>
> Because QuickTime is a standard digital video format used on the Web, QuickTime can be used on both PCs and Macintosh platforms. Thus it is often the preferred format for cross-platform multimedia. If your audience is strictly PC, Windows users can save their Painter movies in AVI format (Video for Windows format).

SAVING IN QUICKTIME OR AVI FORMAT

Only Painter's frame stack movies can be saved in QuickTime or AVI format. After you've created your movie and fine-tuned the artwork, choose Save As from the file menu. The dialog box that opens allows Macintosh users to save their movies in QuickTime format; PC users can save their files in AVI format (Video for Windows format). After you name your file, another dialog box appears with compression choices for your movie.

The pop-up menu enables you to save your file using a variety of different compression schemes. Rather than analyze all the formats, we discuss only the most popular for Painter artwork. Most Macintosh Painter artists choose the Animation compression scheme, which enables them to create a movie in millions, thousands, 256, 16, or 4 colors, and which enables them to specify the quality of the final movie. The higher the quality, the larger the file size. PC users normally choose the Full Frames AVI option, which provides no compression and thus no loss in quality.

7.11

If you want to compress the file but retain quality, choose Cinepak. This compression scheme is primarily used when outputting to CD-ROM. With Cinepak you can limit the output data rate so that it is slow enough for double speed CD-ROMs to handle the information. If you want to limit the data rate for two speed CD-ROMs, enter **180** in the Limit data rate to field.

> **NOTE**
>
> QuickTime and AVI movies can also be opened from Adobe Acrobat PDF files. To create the link between a PDF file and a QuickTime or AVI movie, use Acrobat Exchange.

For both Animation and Cinepak, you can add to the compression by changing the number of frames per second. Thirty frames per second provides the highest quality. Animation that does not display a lot of movement often can look good when output at 15 frames per second.

After you save your file, you can load it into a multimedia program, or you can store it on your Web server and allow users to download the file from your Web page.

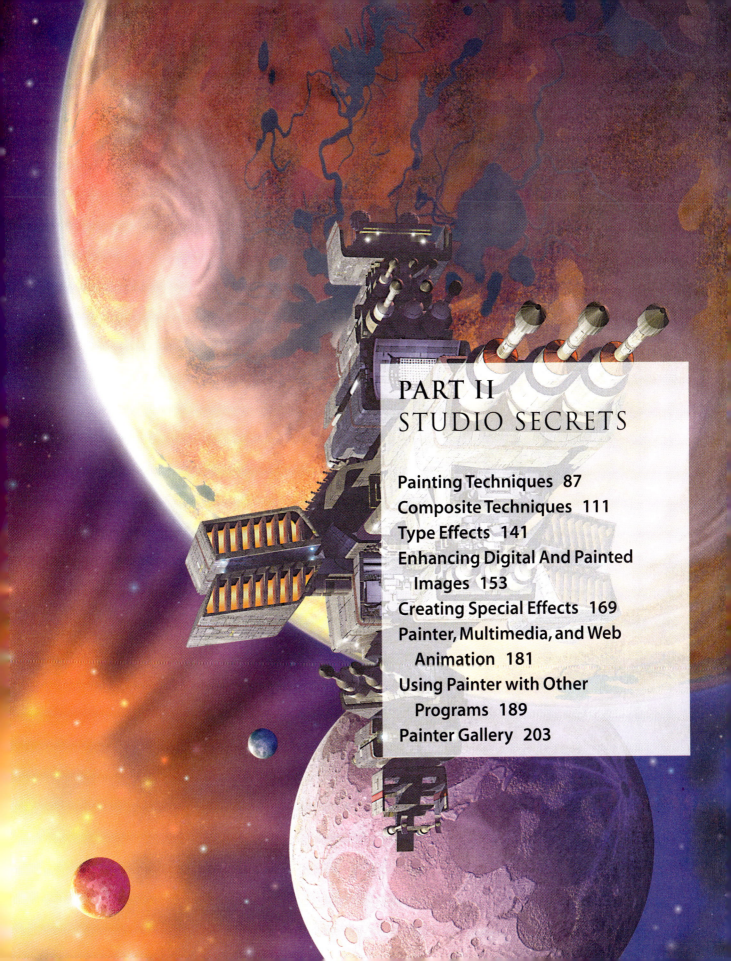

PART II
STUDIO SECRETS

Painting Techniques 87
Composite Techniques 111
Type Effects 141
Enhancing Digital And Painted Images 153
Creating Special Effects 169
Painter, Multimedia, and Web Animation 181
Using Painter with Other Programs 189
Painter Gallery 203

CHAPTER 8
PAINTING TECHNIQUES

The styles, tools, and techniques used by Painter artists are many and diverse. To start an image, some artists simply pick up a Painter brush and start painting. Others sketch with Painter's Pencil brush, and then paint over the sketch with a variety of brushes. Still others create sketches on paper, scan the sketches, and paint.

This chapter examines the techniques, styles, and tools used by a variety of professional Painter artists. As you'll see, not all artists use the same tools and strategies.

When I discovered Painter, it coaxed me from the traditional world of creating artwork and, to date, I have no intention of going back.

CHET PHILLIPS

USING THE NEW PAINT TOOLS

Margaret Sweeney created *Cracker House* (8.1) using several brushes from the Painter 5 New Paint Tools brush library, such as the Sargent and Dry brushes. Margaret likes to use these brushes because they provide a more painterly look than many of the brushes in previous versions of Painter. If you ask Margaret, the new brushes take a little more practice to control, but they're worth it.

Margaret started *Cracker House* by creating a rough onscreen sketch with the Loaded Oils brush variant. Then she selected the Shortcut to New Brushes palette so that she could access Painter's new brushes. In the palette she clicked the Spatula icon. (To load the Shortcut to New Brushes palette, choose Window ➢ Custom Palette ➢ Shortcut to New Brushes. You can also load this new library of brushes by choosing Load Library in the Brushes pop-up menu. Then select

8.1

FASHION SCENTS
Chet Phillips

8.2

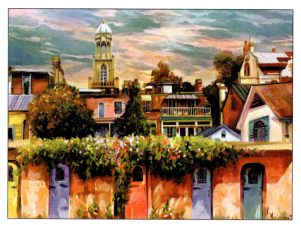

8.3

New Brushes from the Painter 5 folder. In the New Brushes folder, choose New Paint Tools.)

Margaret then chose colors and painted primarily with the Sargent brush variant (named after John Singer Sargent), which she likes because it enables her to achieve a fluid, painterly look. The trick to getting this painterly look is to raise the opacity in the Controls palette. In addition to the Sargent brush variant, Margaret also used the New Paint Tools variant, Dry brush.

To create a second version of *Cracker House* (8.2), Margaret made a clone of the first image and applied Effects ➢ Surface Control ➢ Apply Surface Texture. In the Apply Surface Texture dialog box, she set the Using pop-up menu to Image Luminance to add a raised look to the image. She set the shine to a low setting so the image wouldn't look too metallic.

Margaret created *Alley Doors* (8.3) primarily using various Brush variants, especially the Loaded Oil and the Hairy brush. *Alley Doors* is a composite of different sketches of buildings she created while in Savannah, Georgia. She created the doors by creating and selecting one door and then copying it. Next she applied Effects ➢ Tonal Control ➢ Adjust Colors and reset the Hue slider to create the different colors.

THE BEGINNINGS

Interview with Mark Zimmer, Chief Technical Officer at MetaCreations, and John Derry, Director of Natural Media Research

Q: How, when, and why did you start painting?

JD: I was always the artist of the class from first grade onwards. I knew from an early age that I'd be involved in art in some form or another. My first formal introduction to painting was in high school. I became more interested in manipulating images than just painting, though.

MZ: I was an artist in class as well. But, unlike John, I applied my drawing to visualization of mathematical creations, like polyhedra or geodesic domes. I did my best to learn artisan skills, both in basic drawing and in 3D construction of models. In high school I started working in oils and colored felt pens. I found these media very difficult to master. So when the computer came along, it promised to

Mark Zimmer   *John Derry*

USING MULTIPLE BRUSHES

New York-based artist Doug Lockyer painted the image *Clone of Charlie Runs* (8.4) with a variety of brushes. Here's how he created the image:

1. Doug started by creating a tightly rendered pencil sketch and scanning it. Then he broke up the piece into sets of component characters and a background.

2. Doug cloned the pencil sketch (File ➢ Clone) and used Painter's Tracing Paper function to block in and paint the background details around the outlines that designate where the characters are going to be dropped in.

3. He painted in the characters using various textures, chalks, and watercolor brushes, as well as fine-tipped felt pens, in Cover Method mode rather than the Buildup Method Subcategory.

4. Doug dipped into Live Picture for a few moments to composite the 10 or so files together.

5. Finally Doug reopened the file in TIFF format in Painter and applied a subtle texture throughout. He chalked over the shadows and highlights where characters interplay with the background, especially over the border areas.

8.4

solve some of the problems with the immutability of a completed work.

Q: John, as a successful creative director, what advice do you have for someone who is interested in being an art or creative director?

JD: First, be open-minded. You often have to work with ideas which are not of your own invention and be willing to rely on others' creativity besides your own. For me, it's important that an art director have some basic level of artistic skill. One reason for this is that it helps you understand the mind of the artists you work with. Secondly, it's often important that you can communicate an idea you have to others. Basic drawing skills tremendously facilitate this.

Q: John, where did you go to school for art, and what is your philosophy on art?

JD: Cranbrook Academy of Art, Bloomfield Hills, MI; MFA, Painting 1981

I consider art to be a personal expressive statement based upon one's own life experiences. The artist is responsible for communicating a message, emotion, or point of view to an audience. Art is ultimately a reflection of the times in which it was created.

Q: How did you go about translating traditional painting techniques to digital painting techniques?

MZ & JD: We actually re-acquainted ourselves with the traditional media in our "wet lab." There we worked in silk screens, inks, acrylic paint, airbrush, scratchboard, and linoleum block.

Once we understood the techniques, we used that information to help us to create software that simulated or at least approximated the looks we were able to get traditionally. The experience in

CREATING A SUPERHERO

Doug created *Axis Superheroes* (8.5) as an advertising illustration celebrating the merger of two of Manhattan's premier design and illustration studios. Doug explains, "We chose superheroes because Image Axis and Studio Designs, the companies concerned, are frequently called on to work day and night at short notice on emergency, last-minute campaigns, and literally come to the rescue of their clients frequently."

When creating *Axis Superheroes*, Doug made extensive use of the Pens Scratchboard tool. Doug considers the tool to be "one of the specialized and unique brushes in the Painter toolbox. With this pen you can render long, fast-tapering lines and hatching, which is how I created the comic book inking effect for the outlines of Captain Axis and Design Man."

After creating the sketch with the Scratchboard tool variant, Doug simply blocked in colors with the flat color variant of the Chalk Brush. Using the Airbrush, he highlighted and shaded the muscle tones. He drew a mask selection with the Lasso tool and used the mask as he airbrushed in some mist.

To make Design Man pop out while Captain Axis faded back, he drew a Pen tool mask around Design Man to conceal him before airbrushing the mist.

8.5

graphics and image processing helped a lot here.

Q: Mark, can you tell us more about your wet lab?

MZ: The wet lab is a place where we go to experience the natural media tools in their "real" incarnations. We use real airbrush, real water colors, real acrylics. We do silk-screen work. There are tables with drop-cloths. An unlimited supply of papers and paints. But most of all, it's a place we can go that has no phones or computers. We can sit and talk and draw out our ideas without distractions for hours.

Q: John, can you tell us more about your wet lab?

JD: The wet lab is an off-site location we have used to play around with traditional media. We have stocked it with a wide variety of tools and supplies. Whenever we want to try something out, the way paint splatters for example, we can use the wet lab to play with paint to observe exactly how paint tends to splatter. We can then use these observations and experiments to create software that simulates this. Many of Painter's tools have evolved this way.

The wet lab, among other places, has been the site of our "idea sessions" (other locations include airports, airplanes, automobiles, bars, and beaches). We don't use anything other than notebooks and pens to jot down and diagram our ideas. We use a fairly freewheeling approach to coming up with ideas. We have created several notebooks of ideas over the years. Sometimes we pull the old notebooks out and revisit our thoughts and check off the ideas that have been implemented. Much of the work we are currently working on comes from these notebooks.

Chapter 8 Painting Techniques

TAKING A TRADITIONAL APPROACH

Artist Dennis Orlando uses a traditional painter's approach to creating digital art. Dennis usually begins his paintings by drawing the composition with Pencil brush variants or the Artist Pastel Chalk variant. Then he paints into and over the top of the drawings, building up the image as he refines it in each step, as shown in *The Welder* (8.6–8.13). He uses reference photos to work out compositions, sliding them under the clear acetate layer on his Wacom tablet. Dennis doesn't scan photos and rarely uses a video grab. Any effect filters are always painted into and never used just for an easy effect. If an effect, such as a lighting transition or flare on a subject, works with his other techniques and blends seamlessly, he tests the effect first and then considers whether he could paint it better himself.

To create *The Welder* (8.13), Dennis started with a drawing created in Painter with the Pencil brush. Next he blocked colors with the Artist Pastel Chalk variant, and then he painted with oil brushes. When using the oil brushes, he set the Hue slider in the Color Variability sliders (in the Art Materials: Color palette) to 7%, the S slider to 2%, and the V slider to 7%. Dennis then used the Liquid brush to mix colors together—which gives a painterly look and feel. Finally he applied a KPT filter to produce the spherical pearl on the welder's shoulder. He imported the image into Photoshop and applied the Lens Flare filter to produce the flare over the welder's shoulder and goggles.

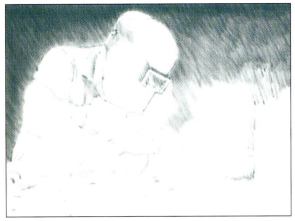

8.7

8.8

8.6

8.9

8.10

8.11

8.12

To create *Pink Rhody's* (8.14), Dennis Orlando used just a few Painter brushes. Dennis brought home some pink Rhododendrons and loaded Painter. He started painting using the Artist Pastel Chalk brush variant with the Method pop-up set to Cover and the Subcategory set to Grainy Soft Cover. Next he used the Liquid Total Oil brush variant with the Method set to Drip and the Subcategory set to Grainy Drip, to shape the flowers.

Dennis used three different paintings to create *Shoreline at Sam Lord's Castle* (8.15). He created the sky from one painting and the shoreline from another. The steps in *Sam Lord's Castle Steps* (8.16) are from another painting he created. If you look closely at the bottom-left side of the steps, you can see the Ghost of Sam Lord.

Dennis created the sky using the Liquid Total Oil brush variant and the Just Add Water brush variant. He applied large blocks of color to create the shoreline. To create the steps, he drew them with the Pencil brush and painted over the area with the Artist Pastel Chalk variant with the Method pop-up menu set to Cover and the Subcategory set to Grainy Soft Cover. He also adjusted the Color Variability slider in the Color palette. To fill in the areas, he used the Liquid Total Oil brush variant with the Method set to Drip and the Subcategory set to Grainy Drip to smear color back and forth.

8.13

Chapter 8   Painting Techniques

GOING AU NATURALE

To create *The Cat Who Walked By Himself* (8.17), which is based on a Rudyard Kipling story, Emily Stedman turned to Painter's Nature brushes, using brushes from the Nature library: Ivy Cluster, Fern, Leaf Stencil, Leaves, and Complex Fern. Emily also used some of the brushes from the Fun Brush library, such as Treey2 and Leafy. While she worked, Emily used paper textures to add texture to the trees and some of the animals.

8.16

8.14

8.15

8.17

PENCIL, CHALK, AND WATER COLOR

Patrick Lichty started *Green Nude* (8.18) by creating a rough sketch. After scanning the sketch and loading it into Painter, Patrick cloned the image. He set up the clone so he could sketch on tracing paper and rough in the undertones with Chalk and Charcoal brush variants. He flipped fluidly through the types, depending on how he felt at the moment. When the image was sufficiently blocked in, Patrick built up the image in a fairly straightforward manner, using Chalk variants for detail and texture and Water Color variants for blocking in the green color.

> **NOTE**
>
> Hidden away in your Painter folder, in the Extra Brushes folder, are some unusual Brush libraries: Nature Brushes, Fun Brushes, and String Library. (These brushes are on the Painter installation CD-ROM.)

USING MIXED MEDIA

Susan LeVan used various brushes to create *The Garden Within* (8.19) for *Boston Globe Home & Garden* and *Outlook* (8.20) for the cover of *CPA* magazine. Susan says that all her images are built virtually the same way: all are mixed media, which is exactly how she worked in conventional media. Susan says that one reason she took to Painter so easily is because it afforded her the opportunity to work as she always had but with even greater ease and flexibility.

Typically, Susan uses the following brushes: Chalk (Square especially), Water Color (Simple Water variant), Brush (Camel Hair, Big Wet Oils, Big Dry Ink, and a variant of her own), Default Crayon, and Airbrush (Spatter and Fat variants). She often uses all these brushes in a single image. Susan likes a little bit of mystery. She says an image may look at first glance like a chalk drawing, but there are other marks. For Susan, the other marks are part of the magic of digital painting. Every now and then she tries some brush she's never used before and incorporates it into her

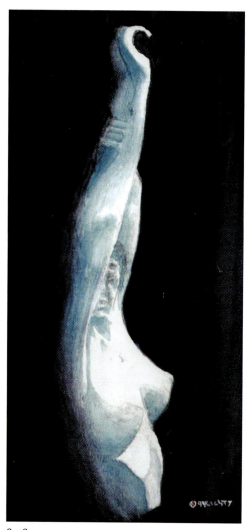

8.18

8.19

style. Doing so keeps her work looking fresh and allows a constant fluid change.

Susan rarely starts her images by scanning anything. Ninety-nine percent of the time she sketches her roughs in Painter, sometimes in black and white and sometimes in color. After a sketch is approved by a client or changes are made to the rough, Susan uses tracing paper to go to final. The rough becomes a template for the finished image. Susan also often uses the trace function when she wants to create the image in pieces. She draws something on the clone, masks and floats it, and drops it back into the original image.

Susan also uses masks in her images. She creates masks using the Auto Mask command, Magic Wand, and floaters, which she also uses to create drop shadows.

CEREMONY AND CHEROKEE MIST

Dan Crowe, a San Francisco artist, created *Ceremony* (8.21) and *Cherokee Mist* (8.22) using Painter brushes. Both images, in different years, were finalists in Fractal Design's (now MetaCreations) annual art expo. Both images were created much the same way. However, to create *Ceremony*, Dan integrated four sketches: the village, the people, the ground, and the crow. Next he used the Pencil, Airbrush, and Chalk brushes to turn the sketches into a single, seamless piece. To create *Cherokee Mist*, Dan used the Airbrush and Chalk brushes. To both images Dan applied Effects ➢ Focus ➢ Glass Distortion.

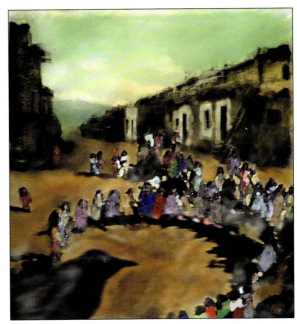

8.21

8.22

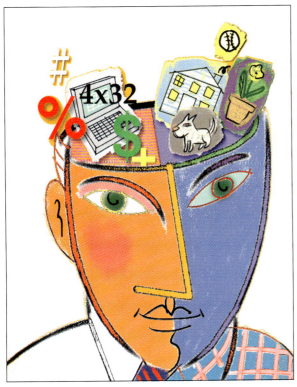

8.20

CHAO MENG FU

George Krauter, a San Francisco artist, created *Chao Meng Fu* (8.23) for an issue of *Analog* magazine. He painted the image almost entirely in a freehand fashion over a pencil drawing. The mountains were painted using a Charcoal brush variant. The only things George didn't paint were the astronauts' helmets, which were rendered in Macromedia Extreme 3D. The 3D file was saved in PICT format and opened in Painter. George pasted the image into the painting as a floater so that he could move it into the right position.

ROOSTER GENETICS

Stacy A. Hopkins created *Rooster* (8.24) by first drawing a rooster using the Chalk brush on a black canvas. After the rooster chalk drawing was complete, Stacy cloned the image, selected the Impressionist Cloner brush variant, and chose Effects ➤ Esoterica ➤ Auto Clone. Stacy also did a little cloning by hand to finish the painting.

USING WET AND DRY MODES

To the amazement of many artists, Painter can simulate both wet and dry watercolor painting over pencil and pen sketches.

When you paint with the Water Color brush, you paint in a wet layer above the background canvas. Artists often create a rough sketch on the background canvas using a Pen brush variant, and then paint over it with a watercolor brush. As you paint with the Water Color brush variant, you can see the pencil sketch in the dry layer. If you switch the method category to Erase, you erase your wet brush strokes but not the background sketch. If you wish to delete the background sketch, simply choose Select ➤ All and then press Delete/Backspace. Choosing Select ➤ All only selects the background layer, so pressing Delete/Backspace does not delete the wet layer. When you finish painting, you can lock all your painting down to the dry layer by choosing Canvas ➤ Dry.

Margaret Sweeney's *Storm* (8.25) was created using wet and dry brushes. Margaret started the image by creating an ink sketch in Painter using a Pen brush variant. Then she applied large areas of color with the Water Color Large Simple Water brush variant. Next she added details and darker areas using the Loaded Oils variant. She smoothed these with the Sable Chisel Tip Water brush variant. Margaret often uses the

8.23

8.24

8.25

Chapter 8 Painting Techniques

Sable Chisel Tip Water brush variant to add a watercolor look to her artwork. Because she tends to switch back and forth between wet and dry brushes, she recommends saving in RIFF format—"When you reopen the image, you can keep the wet areas wet."

Montana artist Dorothy "Pat" Erickson also uses Painter's wet and dry modes when creating many of her paintings. In *Apples* (8.26), Pat created a new canvas and began using the Pencils 2B variant brush to sketch some apples. Pat likes to use Painter's tracing paper option over her sketches so that she has a reference image on which to base her painting. To use the tracing paper option, Pat cloned the sketch of the apples using the File ➤ Clone command, and selected the entire clone content with the Edit ➤ Select All command. With the entire content selected, Pat deleted it by pressing Delete/Backspace. Next she clicked the Tracing Paper icon in the top right-hand corner of the window.

After Pat set her sketch over some tracing paper, she painted the apple shapes using the Water Color Simple Water variant. She used a combination of wet and dry modes, drying the wet modes (by choosing Canvas ➤ Dry) as needed. Next Pat used the Lasso tool to create the shape of the apple stems. After creating the stem shapes, she used the Artist Pastel Chalk variant for color and the Eraser Ultrafine Darkener and Medium Bleach variants for the finishing touches and highlights.

After the apples where completed, Pat selected them with the Lasso tool to isolate them from the background. Then she used a paper texture to simulate a cold press watercolor paper texture. Next she selected the Airbrush Fat Stroke brush variant and painted the plate, reflections, and background. She used the Water Color Simple Water brush variant to add the finishing touches in the background area. To use the paper texture she had selected with the Simple Water brush variant, she set the Method to Grainy Soft Cover. To finish the painting, Pat used the Small Eraser and Small Darkener Eraser to create the design in the plate rim.

James Dowlen used Water Color brushes to create the image *Tibetan Girl At Yamdrak Tso* (8.27) and *Tibetan Ceremony* (8.28). James started each image by scanning photographs he took during his travels in the Orient. After scanning the photographs, he touched them up in Painter. James used some cloning techniques and Water Color brushes to turn the image into a watercolor painting.

James met the little girl in *Tibetan Girl at Yamdrak Tso* at the top of a windy pass called Yamdrak Tso. She and her little brother were watching over a yak herd and living in a house made of stacked stones.

8.26

8.27

Tibetan Ceremony depicts two monks playing ceremonial horns, cymbals, and drums in a Buddhist dedication for a recent death at the Jokong temple in Lhasa, Tibet.

USING PAPER TEXTURES

Without texture, paintings would be flat and certainly less interesting. Fortunately, Painter arrives packed with textures that you can apply with a brush or with several commands in the Effects menu. Painter also enables you to create your own textures from scanned images or other paintings. This section reveals how several artists add texture to their digital images.

LOST TOYS, FASHION SCENTS, AND CHAMELEON

Chet Phillips created *Raiders of the Lost Toys* (8.29) primarily with the Airbrush. He used masks with paper textures added to "document a discovery very much repressed from the media."

Chet created *Fashion Scents* (8.30) for an article in the *Dallas Morning News* House and Garden section. The article discussed how Texans can coordinate their gardens much the same way they can accessorize their wardrobes. Chet used pastels, the Airbrush, and several paper textures for the shrubbery and trees. Some of the flowers, such as the passion flower and buttons, were saved as floaters and duplicated. He also duplicated the bottom half of the foreground figure, flipped it, and lowered the opacity slightly to create a reflection in the pond. He created one side of the vine with masks and the Airbrush variants, and then he duplicated and flipped accordingly to create all four sides of the border.

8.28

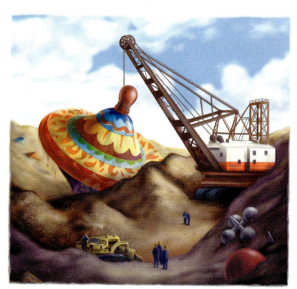

8.29

8.30

Chapter 8 Painting Techniques

Chet created *Chameleon* (8.31) for a local service bureau to use for print and Web page design. Chet used the Pencil brush to simulate sketching in the far left of the image. He added color chips and the pencil using the Airbrush and masks. He created the middle section exclusively with the Pastel brush variant—with the exception of the Photoshop palette, of course. He pasted in the palette as a floater from a screen shot of the Photoshop interface. In the right section Chet used a combination of the Airbrush and Pastel brushes. Then he drew irregular mask shapes following the contours of the chameleon's body and applied the Applied Surface Texture command with a lizard skin texture. He then varied the size of the texture in places to give it more depth.

FOOL AND FACE

German artist Anton Atzenhofer's *Fool* (8.32, 8.33, 8.34) shows the progression of a sketch from inception to finished image and illustrates how textures truly enhance a finished piece. Anton likes to start his images by creating a simple pen and ink sketch on paper and scanning it. Anton used this technique to create *Fool*. After he digitized his sketch, he colored it with solid colors and added some paper textures to the image. Finally Anton added more textures and the finishing touches.

Anton also used paper textures to create *Face* (8.35). Again, he started by scanning a simple pen and ink sketch (8.36) and adding color to it (8.37, 8.38). Next Anton added textures to the image (8.39). Finally he added more textures and the finishing touches.

8.32

8.33

8.31

8.34

8.35

8.37

8.36

8.38

PAINTING WITH CUSTOM TEXTURES

In the award-winning image *Back Alley Blues* (8.40), Margaret Sweeney created her own custom textures. To create the image, she started by drawing a black-and-white sketch of a wall using the Pens Scratchboard tool and the Charcoal brush set to Grainy Soft Cover. The paper textures she used were created from photographs of old bricks found in Savannah, Georgia. After she scanned the photographs, she selected them with the Rectangular Selection tool and turned them into paper textures by choosing Capture from the Paper menu in the Art Materials: Paper palette. You can clearly see this pattern in the front sidewalk area.

The street musician was created from a sketch Margaret made when she was in Savannah. She cut the archway out of the sketch and added the bricks in perspective. She added the color for the wall and bricks by applying the Effects ➢ Surface Control ➢ Apply Lighting command and then painting into it and applying lighting. The sketch and the neon lights were then added, and the lighting was tweaked again to adjust for the neon. Margaret added the windows in the front last. The diners in the window on the left were added after their shapes suggested themselves when Margaret was applying all those lights and textures.

Margaret created *Stocking Up* (8.41) starting with a paper sketch of the building. She painted the buggies from sketches taken in the area. Although she created the sketch in October, Margaret thought it would be interesting to create a snow scene since the building was white and the buggies were black. The snow was applied with paper textures made from scanned pieces of lace.

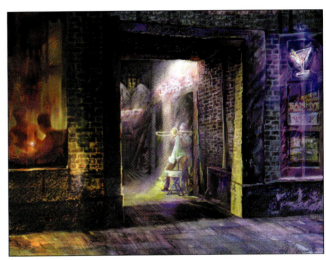

8.40

8.39

8.41

In *North Jetty* (8.42) Margaret Sweeney used many paper textures, patterns, and brushes. Margaret couldn't list, or even remember, all the papers, patterns, and brushes she used, because this image is like a kitchen sink worth of stuff thrown onto the screen. The image started out as an exercise; Margaret was just fooling around with different brushes and papers. The image started looking like water and rocks and developed from there. The patterns were selected and brushed in with the Cloners Straight Cloner brush variant with opacity set low in the Controls palette.

Sheriann Ki-Sun Burnham is another Painter artist who makes extensive use of Painter's paper textures. She even created a huge library of her own custom textures to draw from. Sheriann says that she scanned in all kinds of things, from rice paper to photos taken out of airplane windows to photos taken off the screen of images created with an Atari 1200XL computer. She usually paints using Painter's Charcoal brush with these paper textures to build up layers of form and texture. She also creates masked areas to draw into, both geometric and freeform. She frequently uses the Airbrush, the Liquid Distorto brush variant, and various pens. Along with drawing, Sheriann utilizes paper textures with water distortion, Dye Concentration, and Apply Surface Texture. She also uses various focus distortions, such as blurring areas.

Sheriann's *Space Tango* (8.43) was built by mirroring and altering areas (blocks) as she went along. She copied and pasted the blocks, which created a floater. She then flipped the block to match it to the original block. Next she "dropped" the floater and continued painting. Sheri did this over and over again until the image was complete.

Space Tango has about an equal mix of Painter-supplied textures and custom textures. The custom textures include the blue areas that show part of a boat railing and areas peeking through that are from a photo of ferns. The shape with bubbly texture in the lower middle is from a stone lithograph she made in college.

All the textured areas in Sheriann's *Sonata* (8.44) are custom Paper Textures. These textures were created from scanned photographs of designs programmed in BASIC and shot off the monitor from an Atari 1200XL computer.

Sheriann's *Nomad* (8.45) uses the Liquid Distorto brush variant and Airbrush extensively. The lacy areas are custom paper textures from some stone lithography images she created in college.

8.42

8.43 ©1996 Sheriann Ki-Sun Burnham

8.44 ©1996 Sheriann Ki-Sun Burnham

Adam Sadigursky is a Russian artist who now lives in Palo Alto, California. Adam created *Otilio* (8.46) using various paper textures. He applied paper textures with Painter's brushes, with the Apply Surface Texture command, and with the Apply Lighting command. While painting, Adam adjusted the colors in *Otilio* to his liking by using the Effects ➢ Tonal Control ➢ Correct Colors command. Adam does not use scanned images; instead, he paints with brushes and uses shapes and floaters to create his images.

CREATING CUSTOM TEXTURES FROM PHOTOGRAPHS

Gary Clark, Assistant Professor of Art at Bloomsburg University in Bloomsburg, Pennsylvania, uses an interesting technique to create textures. Gary creates textures from photographs he takes with a digital camera.

Gary created *Spring Flood* (8.47) starting with a digital photograph of a sculpture. He used the Liquid Brush Coarse Smeary Bristles and Square Chalk brush variants to paint over the sculpture. He created the water with KPT and the Photoshop Zig Zag filter. Gary frequently changes textures as he paints. He likes to clone textures from original photographs into his paintings using the Cloners brushes. He also likes to add different textures by photographing real dyes, inks, waterpaint paper, and glass photo plates. He scans them in and uses them as textures as he paints.

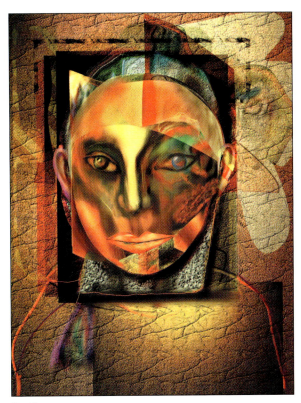

8.46

©1996 Sheriann Ki-Sun Burnham

8.45

8.47

Gary started *Susquehanna* (8.48) by making a traditional pencil drawing at a site above the Susquehanna River. He also used a digital camera to take a picture of the area for reference. He started blocking in the image using the Liquid Distorto brush variant with a flat-chisel square point. He also set the color variability for variation in color. He built up the color using the Chalk brush with a flat-square tip and a rough paper. (Gary likes to use the flat-square tip because he feels it gives a nice flat edge.) He used the digital camera image and the Straight Cloner brush variant with a low opacity to bring some textures from the photograph to the painting. He also used the Water brush to smudge colors together. At the end, Gary used a Coarse Distorto brush variant and one of the Eraser Bleach variants to create edges and more textures.

8.48

MORE PAINTINGS WITH TEXTURES

Steve Campbell is an award-winning Painter artist. Steve started *Puppet Fall Down* (8.49) by scanning a pencil sketch. He then created and filled selections with color, textures, and lighting. In addition, he applied distortions using some of the Effects commands.

Doug Lockyer created this promotional image for Chesterfield cigarettes (8.50) by painting with the Chalk brush over a rougher watercolor paper. Doug used the Artist Pastel Chalk variant and a scaled up texture, starting with a dark sepia background. He then built up lighter and brighter colors over the dark background.

Dan Crowe created *Ghostdance* (8.51), a finalist in Fractal Design's (now MetaCreations) annual art expo, by using the Pencil, Airbrush, and Chalk brushes. He also used the Glass Distortion command and applied paper textures. The paper textures were added to the background using the Charcoal brush. Dan used the Paper library "Navajo" from Fractal Design's (now MetaCreations) "Miles Of Tiles."

USING CARTOON CELL FILL

Painter has already convinced many painters that the computer provides many advantages to traditional paper, canvas, and oils. As Painter grows in power and popularity, more and more cartoonists are joining the Painter fold. One of Painter's handiest features for

8.50

8.49

cartoon artists is its Cartoon Cell fill. Cartoon Cell fill is particularly useful for filling color in shapes created with solid lines. When you fill a selection, the solid lines are not affected.

The secret to using Cartoon Cell fill is to create a selection from your drawing using Painter's Select ➢ Auto Select command. When you apply the Auto Select command, choose the Image Luminance option in the Using pop-up menu. This automatically selects the outlines of your image.

Before filling the selection with the Paint Bucket, double-click the Paint Bucket icon. This opens the Mask Threshold dialog box. The Mask Threshold slider is necessary to compensate for the anti-aliasing (blurring), which eliminates the jagged edges in your lines. Set the Mask Threshold to about 14% for lines drawn with the Pens Scratchboard tool variant. If you leave the setting at 0%, the boundaries of your artwork are ignored. To fill with the Cartoon Cell, make sure the Paint Bucket is selected and choose Cartoon Cell from the What to Fill pop-up menu in the Controls palette. Then choose whether you wish to fill the selection with the Current Color, Grad, Clone Source (the currently selected Pattern), or a Weave. Finally, click within the outlines of your cartoon to fill with color.

A FRIENDLY DRAGON

James Dowlen, a Santa Rosa, California, artist, created the amusing dragon in the following figure using the Painter Pens brush variants (8.52). The black and white drawing was created for a T-shirt silk screen print for an advertisement for the Ronald the Dragon children's CD-ROM story. James, who has always loved traditional pen and ink work, finds that the Pens brush in Painter is especially effective when he needs an expressive thick or thin line.

James used the Pens Scratchboard tool brush variant to draw this line drawing. He used a smooth, thick black line for most of the drawing. In shaded or dark areas, he created a solid black line and then "scratched out" white lines. Working back and forth like this, he was able to keep a balance of light and dark and not overwork any area with too much detail or produce clutter with too much cross hatching. Later, to add color to the dragon, James floated the

8.51

8.52

black line drawing and created color plates under the black plate.

For the color version of the dragon, James scanned a pencil sketch (8.53). In Painter he painted over the original scan drawing using the Tracing Paper option. For the most part, he filled each section of the dragon with a solid color of green, and then he shaded each part with the Airbrush to add the bumps and scales. When painting, he set the Method Subcategory to Grainy Soft Cover, with a paper texture from the "Wild textures" library. James created a floater out of the finished dragon, floated the image over the green graduated background, and added text. The dragon can be seen again on the cover of the children's story (8.54).

James used Painter's Auto Mask command often in this project. As mentioned earlier, he drew the image with the Pens Scratchboard tool to outline the image in black. In the Auto Mask dialog box, he chose the Image Luminance option to create the mask. (In Painter 5, Auto Mask can be found in the Mask menu in the Objects palette.) Choosing Image Luminance created a good anti-aliased mask. James then filled in the shapes with a solid color or gradation using the Paint Bucket tool with Cartoon Cell chosen in the Controls palette. If there were broken lines that didn't quite complete a shape, he closed the lines by painting with the Masking Method category while the mask was visible. He then filled the shape with no leaks. Although he closed the broken lines in the mask, he left the actual painted lines onscreen broken.

Sometimes James uses a slightly different technique. He starts by creating a mask with the Auto Mask's Image Luminance option. Then he floats the outline so that it remains a separate layer. Next he colors the canvas layer below with the Airbrush, textures, and so on. This creates a softer look.

ARGON ZARK!

Charley Parker is a freelance cartoonist, illustrator, and Web designer living in the Philadelphia area. His online "virtual comic book," *Argon Zark!* (at www.zark.com), has received numerous awards since its inception in 1995. The comic strip has been featured in newspaper articles in the United States and abroad.

8.53

8.54

Charley created *Argon Zark!* (8.55) using the Cartoon Cell fill and other techniques. In this page, Argon "hotwires a search engine" as he, Zeta, and Cybert attempt to find the hideous Badnasty Jumpjump.

Charley started by sketching out a rough version of the image with Painter's 2B Pencil set to a low opacity, and a light neutral color to keep the feel of sketching freely in pencil (8.56). He then raised the brush's opacity and refined the drawing. When the pencil drawing was firmed up, he drew the inks on a full-size floater filled with white and lowered the opacity to about 80% (which acts as adjustable tracing paper).

In an attempt to match the action of a traditional flexible steel nib (like the Hunt 108), Charley created a customized inking pen by using the Pens Scratchboard tool variant with the Brush Controls: Size palette set to Size: 2.4, +/-Size: 2.00, and Size Step: 1%. This enabled Charley to create a springy, flexible, thin-to-thick line ideal for his inking style.

The finished inks floater was then dropped. He made a mask of the black lines using Edit ➤ Mask ➤ Auto Mask and chose the Image Luminance option in the auto mask pop-up menu.

Charley opened the image in Photoshop and used the Photoshop Magic Wand tool to select all the panel backgrounds (isolating the backgrounds from the figures) and saved the selection as a channel.

Charley's *Search Engine* was constructed (8.57) and rendered in KPT Bryce 2 (8.58). It was then composited into the selected background of panel 1 in Photoshop using the Paste Into command.

Returning to Painter, Charley colored the figures with gradations using the Paint Bucket tool with the Mask Threshold set to 75% (accessed by double clicking the Paint Bucket tool) and Controls palette set to Cartoon Cell fill with Gradation. Charley then used the Airbrush set to a low opacity (8% or so) and modeled the figures in more detail. He also used the

8.55

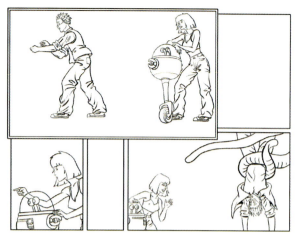

8.56

Cover Brush at 6% to 8% Opacity (for sharper edges) and the Dodge and Burn brushes. He filled Argon's vest using the KPT 3.0 Texture Explorer texture, modified with Dodge and Burn.

Charley created the electric blue halos using Painter's Pen tool to cover the figure and then painting in the halo with the Airbrush set to a low opacity.

Charley created the lettering in a transparent layer in Photoshop. The word balloons were made on a white-filled reduced opacity layer with Photoshop's Oval Marquee tool and Bezier pen tool. When the balloons were finished, Charley returned the layer to 100% opacity. He selected the background with the Magic Wand and deleted it, leaving the word balloons floating on a transparent layer, which was then dropped onto the image (8.59).

Charley used the KPT twirl filter to help create the background in panel 3. For the background of panel 4, Charlie created abstract shapes filled with KPT textures and modeled with Photoshop's Dodge and Burn tools.

Charley copied and saved the final image as a medium-quality JPEG file for use on the Web as a page in the *Argon Zark* virtual comic book.

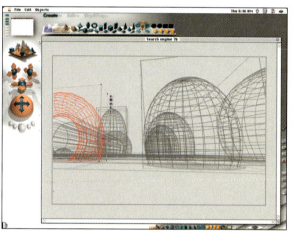

8.57

8.59

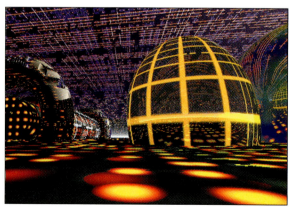

8.58

CUSTOMIZING BRUSHES

In addition to providing dozens of brush variants, Painter allows you to fine tune virtually every aspect of a brush stroke. Most of the commands for customizing brush variants are found in the Brushes palette's Control menu. After using these commands, you can create your own brush variant by choosing Save Variant in the Brush palette's Variant menu.

Jay Paul Bell, an artist and art professor in Illinois, often turns to the Brushes palette's Control menu to customize brushes. In creating images for the series *Homage to Constable* (8.60, 8.61, 8.62), Jay first worked in a traditional manner by creating a contour drawing of the landscape. The contour was then scanned at the size and resolution of the final image.

Jay created the color in the landscape area using the Airbrush Feather Tip variant with the Size slider set at 3.2 and 2.0. He also used the Airbrush Thin Stroke variant with the Size slider set to 3, 6, 11, and 22, and saved each Size slider change as a new variant. The new variants appeared in the Variant pop-up menu on the Brushes palette.

In addition, Jay adjusted the Color Variability: HSV sliders while using the Airbrush. This allowed him to paint with noise when creating a particular textural area in the landscape.

Jay modulated the sky by filling with a custom fill he created out of a gradation. He added clouds using the Image Hose and then manipulated them with the Airbrush variants at various sizes.

This technique gave him an initial representational landscape image. He used the same approach for developing the various textures he blended with the representational landscape to create the final landscape image.

> **NOTE**
>
> To alter the size of a brush stroke, choose Size from the Control menu in the Brushes palette. Then drag the Size slider in the Brush Controls: Size palette.

8.60

8.61

8.62

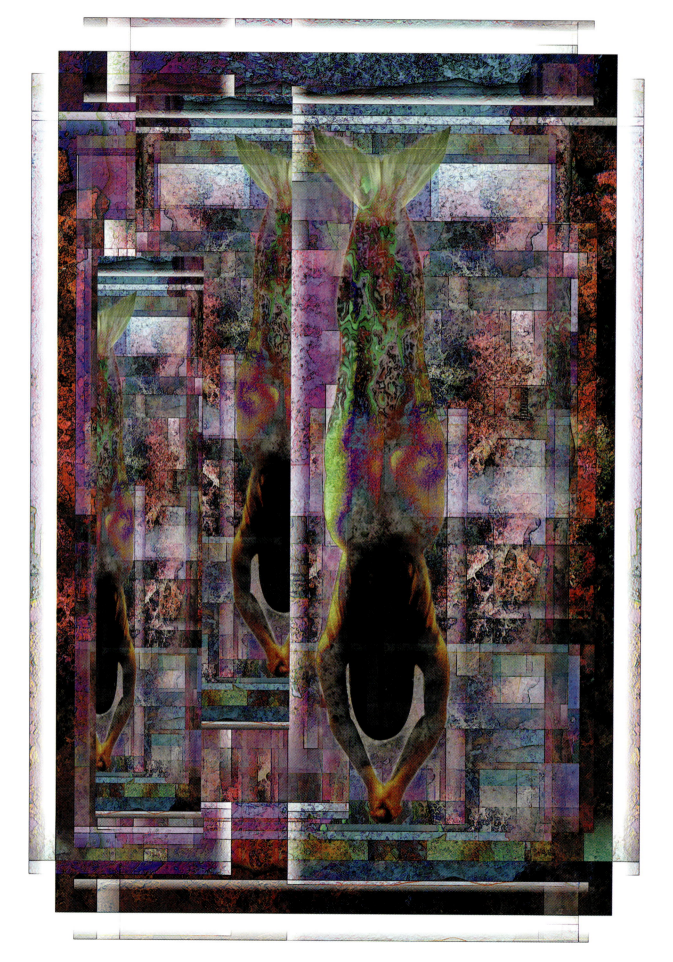

CHAPTER 9
COMPOSITE TECHNIQUES

Many digital artists use Painter to paint much the way a traditional artist paints. They pick a brush and a color and start painting. But Painter is not only a powerful painting program; it is a remarkable image editing program as well.

Digital artists combine Painter's painting power and its robust cloning and floaters features to composite different images and image elements together. In this chapter you will see how many professional artists use these features to create their artwork.

The total freedom of manipulation and experimentation the computer offers has made the creative process more spontaneous than with many traditional disciplines.

JAY PAUL BELL

COMPOSITING IMAGES USING BRUSHES AND PHOTOGRAPHS

Sometimes the secret behind a beguiling work of Painter art is a combination of both paintings and photographs. Pat Watson is an example of an artist who integrates photographs into his paintings. One of the most interesting facets of his work is his technique of painting over photographs to give them a painterly look. The result is often surrealistic.

Pat tries to keep his range of technical approaches limited so that a certain series of work has a unified look. He feels that Painter has so many technical possibilities that to explore each possibility would seriously distort his image making. Pat feels that using Painter is like having the materials of an entire art warehouse at your disposal; yet he doesn't want to use every tool available to make a single image. Pat feels that the work would then become more about the materials and not about the content. Pat much prefers Painter's own set of tools, and he rarely uses any third-party filters.

CREATING NOSTALGIA

When originally thinking about creating *Nostalgia* (9.1), Pat Watson knew he wanted to create a cowboy. He wanted the cowboy to convey the feel of old Hollywood westerns—the ones with caricatured heroes. Pat latched onto the notion of a hero caricature. While he had this idea in mind, the image of a faceless hero came to him. He thinks that the idea probably came from some "Lone Ranger meets Rene Magritte" synthesis.

Next Pat went looking for a picture of a Hollywood cowboy with a big Tom Mix-type ten-gallon cowboy hat. After much searching, Pat found a suitable picture

MAID...
Jay Paul Bell

to scan. The top of the hat was cut off, so he drew in that part. Pat found another cowboy image to use for the shirt and scanned it in, but to make the shirt match the look and feel of the hat, he had to extensively redraw it.

In Painter, Pat Watson likes to use the Just Add Water brush variant to soften and flatten the tones. Pat then usually uses the Airbrush to highlight and shadow the areas. Pat avoids strict realism. The slightly abstract look of what many would call *Social Realism* appeals to him. Pat said that people who see his images frequently mention Rene Magritte's work, but he would rather have his work remind people of Edward Hopper.

In creating a background, if Pat sets the Just Add Water variant a bit thicker than the default and then always strokes in the same direction, the brush blocks in an area while flattening and blending color. By putting spaces between the strokes, and using a consistent angle of stroke, Pat can get some interesting abstract color structures. With the right touch Pat can get the tool to suggest a flattened plane with a hint of highlight on the leading edge, and a darkening as the plane moves away. That was the effect he was after in the treatment of the rocks in *Nostalgia*. To get the striation and *gopher hole* effect in the rock background, Pat used the Liquid Smeary Mover brush variant after adding a drop of black paint. The resulting effect has a small highlight on the edge of the rock. Pat then drew the grassy foreground from scratch. He stroked in color with the Water Color brush while trying to ensure a suggestion of perspective.

The clouds came from an old photograph Pat scanned. When working with clouds, Pat likes to paint over areas with the Airbrush, soften dark areas with the Just Add Water variant, and then use the Liquid Smeary Mover variant to hold the bushy portions of the cloud together. After working the area, the clouds usually begin to get muddier than he would like. To resolve this, Pat uses the Chalk brush to add back the color he wants—either in the highlights or in the shadows. The texture of the Chalk brush helps Pat avoid getting blobs of identical color shapes. He likes to add color to the lightest or darkest areas and then work the color into the other areas. Pat also prefers to get the color adjustment of the image set to his satisfaction and then take color samples from the image, rather than have a set color palette.

The title of the work comes from the idea that "Our nostalgia for the past clouds our vision of it." The cowboy's face is blank because, according to Pat, "We wouldn't recognize a legitimate hero anyway."

9.1

CREATING TOURIST

Pat Watson's *Tourist* (9.2) is a partner piece to *Nostalgia*. Pat felt that the first image—*Nostalgia*—turned out a bit more frivolous than he intended. So he thought about ways to make the idea a bit more pointed. To Pat, replacing the cowboy with an Indian would have a similar, but more political, message.

In *Tourist*, Pat again started from a photograph. After scanning it, he had to redraw substantial portions of the background and foreground to convincingly portray a landscape without distracting from the primary figure. The redraw included adding colors that would fit with painterly conventions, such as atmospheric perspective. Also, Pat needed to present the sagebrush as a consistent, easily recognized landscape. The real landscape is not so cooperative. Using the Chalk brush, he could get a passable highlight on the top of the brush. Using conventional brushes, he stroked the darker shadow area and obtained an agreeable illusion of sagebrush. Then, using the Just Add Water brush variant, Pat blended the two areas and made a softened, slightly out-of-focus background.

Pat intentionally avoided many postmodern stylistic tendencies to "confound the common perception of digital imaging." The image of the Indian came from an old postcard from his family archives. The original image used a buckskin suit (or the appearance of one) with a great deal of bead work. Pat simplified the suit and changed it to white to make the idea more direct. Pat learned that the most effective way to simplify the suit was to use the Just Add Water variant to smear and push the image in the areas he wanted simplified. Pat then painted over the area with the Airbrush set to semi-transparent (the level of transparency depends on the effect he wants) to eliminate the unwanted bead work. As the highlights took shape and became believable, the places that needed more shading became evident.

To create *Suitable Salesman* (9.3), Pat Watson started with a photo he took of his son while they were driving in the California foothills. To Pat, the curve of the road and the grasslands ended up being the most interesting parts of the photograph. (He already had numerous images of his son, so he edited him out of this one.)

When thinking about the photo, Pat began associating it with the image of a traveling salesman. He associates salesmen with suits, so he thought a traveling suit would be a good idea. He took a photo of his only suit and scanned it. He changed its color and painted it with the Straight Cloner brush variant set at reduced opacity. He then put the suit in the sky, adding the shadow and working the grass to obtain the effect he wanted.

Pat used the Pencil brush to perfect the grass by starting with dark colors and moving to lighter colors. The image seemed to need a good front-to-back contrast device, or maybe two. With that in mind, he decided that the best solution to get the right front-to-back contrast was to have the road actually go

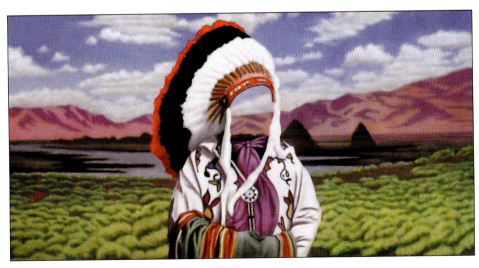

9.2

somewhere, and have a point of interest along the way to the destination. Because Pat likes old cars, he thought a new suit, an old car, and an old castle were a pretty good *here-to-there* transition. He found the image of the car in an old Main Street panorama photograph, and he drew the hatted figure as well as the castle in the distance.

> **NOTE**
>
> Pat used to draw his ideas and scan them in, but now he frequently creates basic drawings in a drawing program and then imports them into the image before treating it in Painter.

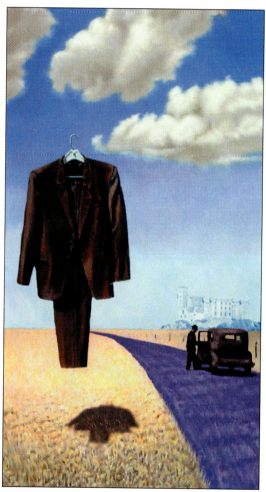

9.3

To get the atmospheric perspective in the sky, Pat selected the sky using the Magic Wand tool and then filled the area with a gradient. He said that the sky is never as intensely blue as we think it is, so he always uses colors a bit flatter than what he sees in the palette swatches. After he colored the sky correctly, he used the Just Add Water and the Liquid Smeary Mover variants and the Airbrush to create the cloud edges. Pat really likes the way the Liquid Smeary Mover variants break up the image while they are moving it. Using them, he can obtain effects he can't get even with oil paints. (Pat says, "But oil paints are still very cool.")

USING CLONING AND CLONING BRUSHES TO COMPOSITE IMAGES

Painter's cloning commands and its cloning brushes enable you to paint a clone (or copy) of one image into another image. As you paint, you can create unusual effects by changing opacity and by choosing different Cloners brushes. For example, the Driving Rain Cloner recreates an image as though it were seen through driving rain. The Van Gogh Cloner clones as if the image were painted by Van Gogh.

To use an image as a clone source, open it and load your final image onscreen. To designate the clone source, choose File ➤ Clone Source. Switch to a Cloners brush and start painting. In this section you see how cloning truly can add dimension and power to a painting.

THE BLESSING

Pat Watson created *The Blessing* (9.4) by using an image as a clone and another as a clone source. Pat started by taking photographs of hands and mountains specifically for this image. Although he wasn't quite sure where the image idea was going, the original concept for it rather intrigued him, so he kept shooting pictures.

In *The Blessing*, Pat created the wall separately, added texture from the Effects menu, and then greatly enlarged it. The calligraphic/symbol elements were created in Adobe Illustrator, imported into Painter, and blended with the background. To place

Chapter 9 Composite Techniques

the arms into the wall, Pat made the wall a clone and the arms/hands the clone source. Then he used the Straight Clone brush variant to paint in the clone source.

Pat Watson said the title of this image "refers to the notion that most people would not understand if they had been blessed, and so their inability to decipher the symbols or understand the language of gifts and blessedness leads them to worship icons they don't understand and invent incomprehensible rituals."

MEMORY PORTRAIT

Andrew Faulkner created *Memory Portrait* (9.5) for a series of illustrations for M&Co's *Copylight* project, in which artists were asked to submit work to be

> **HOW THE CLONERS BRUSH VARIANTS PAINT**
>
> As you use Cloners, you must understand that they all don't clone the same way. The secret to understanding how Cloners brushes paint is to analyze the Cloners brush's Stroke Type setting in the Brush Controls: Spacing palette. If the Stroke Type is set to Single (Pencil Sketch Cloner, Felt Pen Cloner, Chalk Cloner, Met Cloner, Driving Rain Cloner, Soft Cloner, Straight Cloner), the color changes to match the clone as you paint a single stroke. However, if the spacing is set to Multi (Hairy Cloner, Oil Brush Cloner, Hard Oil Cloner, Van Gogh Cloner), the color does not vary. Thus, when using these brushes you probably want to paint in short strokes. As you paint in short strokes, you see the clone emerge. If you don't, you may wonder whether cloning is working at all.

9.5

9.4

made into back-lit transparency lampshades. The following steps outline the process Andrew followed to create *Memory Portrait*:

1. Andrew scanned a rough pencil sketch of the image.
2. With the scanned sketch in Painter, Andrew created a clone of the image (File ➢ Clone). He then deleted the image onscreen and turned on Painter's Tracing Paper mode. This allowed Andrew to see his original image as if it were behind tracing paper.
3. Andrew painted the background with different-sized Cloners brushes at different opacities. As Andrew worked, a landscape image evolved.
4. Andrew scanned old newspapers and pasted them as floaters over the painted background with difference composite methods. He did this to form a cohesive layered background.
5. He selected background areas and applied the Image Luminance option (in the Using pop-up menu) of the Applied Surface Texture command. The Image Luminance option applies the clone's brightness values as a texture to the image onscreen.
6. After Andrew scanned the photograph of the head, he colorized it as a sepia in Adobe Photoshop. Then he opened the sepia head in Painter, selected with a feather (Select ➢ Feather), and copied and pasted over the background.
7. He photographed the light bulbs and scanned, pasted, and rotated them as backdrops for the letters in the word *Memory*, which he typed in Painter and placed over the light bulbs.
8. After the bulbs were in place, he painted the red oval with connections on the head and pasted the spark plug over the oval.
9. The edge of this piece was framed by a stick placed on the scanner and scanned as final art. Then it was roughly cut and pasted. Andrew composited the image with the Hard Light composite method and duplicated and rotated it three times.
10. Finally, Andrew painted with the Cloners brush again over the edge of the photos. Andrew also used the Pencil and Charcoal brushes to trace the edges of the photos to create a natural look.

SONG OF PEACE

Cloning and floaters both played a major role in Jeremy Sutton's powerful image, *Song of Peace* (9.6). Jeremy's goal was to create an emotional portrait of Yitzhak Rabin, the former Israeli Prime Minister assassinated in 1995. Jeremy wanted to create a portrait that "expressed the horror of the murder; the shock that Israeli society had become so polarized; the miracle that a peace process had been initiated, and the hope that it would continue after Rabin's death." Here are the steps Jeremy followed to create *Song of Peace*:

1. Jeremy began by gathering material for the background of the image. As he worked, he was struck by the powerful image of the blood-soaked song sheet in Rabin's pocket that the fatal bullet had passed through. The song sheet served as the anchor image for the portrait, around which Jeremy planned to arrange all other images.
2. Jeremy started the production process by scanning all the images he collected at 300 dpi.

9.6

3. He selected each image and copied and pasted them into a working file, where they appeared as floaters. He rotated, resized, and repositioned the floaters and experimented with different compositional ideas (9.7). As he worked, Jeremy adjusted floater opacity and the relative order the floaters were in above the canvas.

4. He edited each floater mask to determine what part of the floater was visible. (To find out more about editing floater masks, see Chapter 5). When he was satisfied with the arrangement, he dropped all the floaters onto the canvas.

5. Jeremy then used one image (of the Western Wall) to generate an embossed effect in selected areas of the image. To produce this effect, he pasted the wall into a canvas the same size as the background image, and then used this image as a clone source. To create the embossed effect in the background image, he set up the wall image as a clone source (File ➢ Clone Source). He then chose Effects ➢ Surface Control ➢ Apply Surface Texture.

In the Apply Surface Texture dialog box, Jeremy choose the Original Luminance option in the Using pop-up menu. This caused Painter to apply the luminance values of the clone source into the background image. The result: The texture of the wall appeared in Jeremy's image (9.8). Jeremy saved this file under a new name, and then he used the Soft Cloner Cloners brush variant to clone parts of the image back into an earlier version of the background image.

6. Jeremy painted the actual portrait of Rabin in a previously saved version of the background file (9.9). He used a photograph as a visual reference but did not scan or trace the image. Jeremy generally starts his painting with rough strokes using Chalk, Loaded Oils, Broad Water Brush, and Distorto brush variants. He accomplishes the finer detail with Airbrush variants and the Just Add Water variant. As Jeremy works, he constantly saves different versions of the file. For the Rabin portrait, Jeremy saved 21 different versions!

7. He then selectively cloned the painted portrait back into the last version of the background file to produce the final composition. To do this, he set up the portrait as the clone source (File ➢ Clone Source) and cloned the portrait into the background using the Soft Cloner brush variant. As he worked, he kept both images visible onscreen until he found the appropriate mix of image elements.

9.8

9.7

9.9

THE OWL AND THE PUSSY CAT

In *The Owl and the Pussy Cat* (9.10), Doug Lockyer makes extensive use of Painter's cloning features in his affectionate rendition of Edward Lear's poem of the same name. Doug painted the image to celebrate his marriage in 1997 to Katarina (Kitty-Kat). As you can see, the image was a highly complex piece to put together; it was created over three very full days and nights.

Doug executed the image in the following five phases:

1. He created a character drawing.
2. He inserted background texture and created the borders.
3. He created the boat illustration.
4. He cloned the image and composited the image from several sources.
5. He used Painter's Make Mosaic command to tile and blend the final image.

Character drawing

Doug started *The Owl and the Pussy Cat* by creating a rough sketch of the figure in pencil (9.11). He then scanned the sketch. Next he cloned his original scan, deleted it, and turned on Painter's Tracing Paper mode. Doug selected a handmade paper texture (large scale) and sketched a red chalk/silverpoint style onto a plain white background (9.12). As he worked, he used the 2B Pencil and Single Pixel Scribbler variants at a low opacity, allowing plenty of grain to show through, and then switched from Build-up to Cover method.

Background and border

After loading a scanned piece of parchment from Artbeats Wood and Paper collection, Doug applied

9.10

9.11

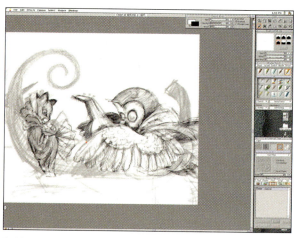

9.12

texture and lighting effects to roughen up the image a little, and then colorized it with soft, low opacity and grainy overlays of the Artist Pastel Chalk variant (9.13). He cloned the border from a drawing he created earlier with a fine hard pencil effect, primarily using the Single Pixel Scribbler variant using imported Adobe Illustrator paths for the repeated floral embellishments.

Next Doug cloned again from his drawing using the Artist Pastel Chalk variant, which he set to a low opacity Buildup so that the white wouldn't show. (He cloned with this brush by setting the Method Category to Cloning.) The raised, straight-border edges are the result of adding a bevel texture. The background image was also softly re-cloned to soften the effect.

Boat modeling and illustration

Doug opened a 3D boat image he modeled in MetaCreation's Raydream Designer (with texture maps made in Painter) (9.14). To create ripples in the reflections, he used the Liquid Brush and Coarse Distorto variants. He then selected the boat with a luminance mask (in Painter 5, Select ➢ Auto Select: Image Luminance), inverted it (Select ➢ Invert), and copied it. Next he opened the parchment texture background, cloned it (File ➢ Clone), and pasted the boat as a floater so that he could scale and position it accurately and move and scale it later.

Cloning and compositing

Doug then cloned in the sketch of the owl and pussycat underneath the boat floater (9.15). With the floater selected, he re-cloned the parts that appeared over the boat, using varying degrees of opacity with the Artist Pastel Chalk and 2B Pencil variants. To do this, he selected the brushes and set the Method Category to Cloning. He also cloned parchment over the bow of the boat to soften it.

When all was in place, Doug dropped the floater and re-cloned the owl and pussycat over it with low opacity Chalk and Pencil brushes. (Again, Doug set the Method category to Cloning.) He cloned more parchment back over parts of the boat to get the faded-into-the-page look, and then sketched in

9.14

9.13

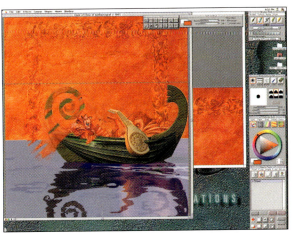

9.15

refined details with the Single Pencil Scribbler and Pastel variants. Doug tried to loosely define some areas with scribbly sketched pencil point, while adding form and density to others (the cat's face and owl's wing) with heavier pastel highlights. The mandolin and parts of the boat he left solid.

To create the moon, Doug made an oval selection and then a smaller oval. He positioned them so that he could cut the smaller from the larger, which produced a rim selection. This he filled in with a Large Chalk variant. Next he added Spatter Water brush (a Water Color variant) effects, retouching with the Wet Eraser.

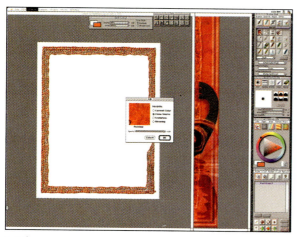

9.16

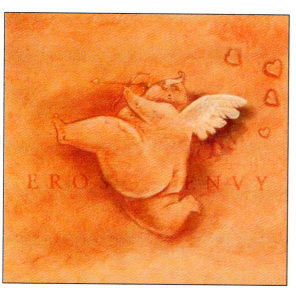

9.17

Tiling and final touch-ups

To create the border, Doug used Painter's Make Mosaic command, which can create a mosaic from a clone color (9.16). Doug selected the Clone Color option in the Painter Art Materials: Color palette and made another clone of his image. He created the mosaic using white grout. Using the tracing paper option, he created bulky outer rows, following the straight edge of his beveled outer border, and then fine inner rows, following the irregular contours of the inner border. The tiles pick up the color of the background clone image, making them more subtle and complimentary in hue.

Doug then used Painter's Apply Surface Texture command to apply texture to the 3D tiles to give them a soft look with a low shine. Doug advises, "The trick to getting the chalky look with the background image superimposed is to make a color selection of the white grout, allowing a little feathering and diffuse color selection from the tile highlights." He then filled this selection with the clone source (the parchment background with boat). "Voila! Instant weathered Mediterranean terracotta." Finally, Doug added a few chalky lines and soft, cloned parchment effects to either highlight or mute, and then he dropped in a gemstone on the stern post of the boat.

USING FLOATERS

Painter's floaters are like rectangular sheets of acetate that you can paint on and freely move around onscreen. Painter also provides numerous commands for compositing floaters and the masks within floaters. (For more information about using floaters and masks in floaters, see Chapter 5.) Many artists use floaters to blend together objects in their images and apply striking special effects to their images. This section provides you with an idea of how floaters can be used in painting.

DOUG LOCKYER'S FLOATER MAGIC

Doug Lockyer makes extensive use of floaters in most of his paintings. To create *Cupid* (9.17), Doug painted in Chalk over watercolor paper, with a superimposed 50% floating layer of parchment texture. He created the texture by using a scanned image and Painter's

Capture Pattern command (found in the Art Materials: Pattern palette).

Doug Lockyer's *Mancala* (9.18) is a packaging project for Pressman Toys (makers of Mastermind and Othello). Doug created the image for a game called Mancala for Kids. It is an example of the power of floaters, utilizing a unique feature of the overlay mode of composition along with some rich paper textures.

To create *Mancala*, Doug started by blocking the carved border shapes in neutral gray and then used Alien Skin's Black Box Inner Bevel filter to dimensionalize the shapes. This produced a gray-clay look against a pure-white background.

Doug created a solid floating panel of wood-grain texture, which he cloned from pieces of Artbeats redwood texture. By compositing the panel in Overlay mode (in the Controls palette), he was able to pick up the tones of the beveled surfaces through the wood. The white background rendered the wood transparent (as does 100% black), "so the effect is one of cutting out and dimensionalizing the shapes from the wood. Instant wood carving!" according to Doug.

Doug later added separate layers of a custom burlap texture he previously created, and then added the product as a floater. The *Rhino* (9.19) and *Turtle* (9.20) images were created separately and also dropped in as floaters. To create the characters, Doug drew the animals using some simple selections. He varied the texture of the paper—he used eggshell, basketball, and handmade paper—and then inverted the textures to stress the shadows. Doug used Artist Pastel Chalk, the Airbrush, and the 2B Pencil. Finally, Doug created the type and mechanical dielines in Adobe Illustrator and QuarkXPress.

9.19

9.18

9.20

Touchstone Energy (9.21) is a section of a storyboard sample from a Bozell advertising spot Doug Lockyer created for Touchstone Energy. Here are the steps Doug followed to create these images:

1. Doug began with a pencil drawing of the images, using Painter's 2B Pencil variant on a pure white background.

2. He floated the entire page (use Select ➢ All and then click the selection with the Floater Adjuster tool).

3. He chose Multiply as the floater composite mode in the Controls palette. Multiply makes the dark lines darken whatever is painted underneath, and knocks out the white. (In Multiply mode, painting white over a color equals that color.)

4. Being careful to first deselect the floater by clicking below it within the Floater List palette, Doug filled the page with a neutral, dark-gray/brown hue.

5. To finish the image, Doug loosely colored the image with a Flat Grainy Artists Pastel variant of the Chalk brush, working from dark to highlights, as in a traditional pastel drawing.

9.21

9.22

Richard Noble created *Lamp* (9.22) and *Deck Chair* (9.23) by combining traditional drawing techniques with photographic images. Richard completes the main image using a variety of drawing and painting tools. For example, he primarily used the Water Color brush to create *Lamp*. Next he scans images (or in the case of *Lamp* and *Deck Chair*, he takes digital photos) that he wants to use as textures for the background of the image. After the textures have been created, Richard creates floaters of these textures and applies the Overlay Composite Method. Using this technique, the image shows the pasted item only where the main image appears. It is very flexible and can also be subtle.

SWORD AND BUTTERFLY

John Ennis's *Sword and Butterfly* (9.24) provides a simple use of a floater. To create the image, John painted with the Chalk brush over a photograph he had taken. When painting, he used the Grainy Soft Cover Method Category and applied a texture he created himself. He then added the butterfly as a floater by pasting the butterfly into the image. (When you paste an image into a file, the pasted image becomes a floater.) Next he applied a drop shadow to the butterfly (Effects ➢ Objects ➢ Create Drop Shadow).

FEAST OF FOOLS AND THE CRACK

Dan Crowe created *Feast of Fools* (9.25) with several floaters. He created the image for COD Tuxedo Records, the Swiss record company of the band The Wild Bouquet. The image appears in the band's CD booklet.

To create *Feast of Fools*, Dan Crowe scanned different black and white images from a number of clip art books (9.26). Dan cleaned up the images and then pasted them into the cityscape as a floater. He also

9.23

9.24

9.25

9.26

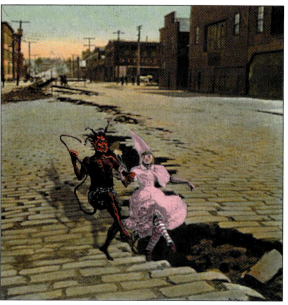

9.27

added the images to a new floater portfolio. All the figures ended up in one portfolio, which enabled him to change individual scale and rotation. Later, this portfolio was used to create another portfolio of shadows for each figure. Cloning was used to bring back the background and redo figures when the painting began. Each figure was painted and colored using Airbrush and Chalk variants. Dan usually uses the Water Brushes Just Add Water variant to blend.

Dan Crowe created *The Crack* (9.27) by scanning separate black and white images from different sources. He scaled and placed each scanned image as a separate floater, and created the shadows as separate floaters. He then painted in the image using Cloners brushes, along with the Airbrush and Chalk brushes. He also added glass distortion effects by choosing Painter's Effects ➤ Focus ➤ Glass Distortion command.

SKY DREAM

Margaret Sweeney's *Sky Dream* (9.28) illustrates how floaters can be used to create a collage from other paintings. Margaret created this complicated image over a long period of time. She started by painting the figure, and then she began applying backgrounds and skies from other images she had painted previously.

She used many different textures, patterns, and lighting effects over and over. She just copied an image, flopped it under the original figure, and added different lighting and effects to each half. She created the circle using the Oval tool and used the Airbrush on the edges to make it stand out. She also kept

9.28

Chapter 9 Composite Techniques

adding images and other sections from other paintings, which were added as floaters. To create the floaters, she selected an area in one painting and then copied and pasted it into another. She changed opacity and composite methods in the Controls palette.

ANGUISH AND COFFEEHOUSE/LAST RITES

Steve Campbell began *Anguish* (9.29) and *Coffeehouse/ Last Rites* (9.30) with a finished, scanned pencil sketch. He made selections in the sketch to section off areas of prospective color, background, and so on—whatever seemed to work. To apply color, Steve initially used Painter's Effects ➢ Fill command. This technique resulted in color that was too flat, so he eventually softened it up with brush and pencil work. He then applied lighting to create depth and roundness, and used selections once again to apply textures.

COSMOLOGICAL CONSTANT

George Krauter created *Cosmological Constant* (9.31) for an article in *Astronomy* magazine. After airbrushing the outerspace background, George imported images rendered in a 3D program into Painter and turned them into floaters. He then used Painter to assemble the floaters in the image.

9.30

9.29

9.31

SHUBAT TULIPS

To create the etching style and slight Oriental feel of *Shubat Tulips* (9.32), Dorothy "Pat" Erickson used floaters. Here's how:

1. With a new canvas onscreen, Pat painted using a deep brown color with her own version of the Very Small Artist's Pastel Chalk variant to sketch the tulips, leaves, grass, and mulch.

2. When Pat was satisfied with the drawing, she duplicated and floated the canvas by selecting the entire canvas (Edit ➢ Select All). With the entire canvas selected, Pat then selected the Floater Adjuster tool and pressed and held the Option/Alt key while she clicked the canvas.

3. Next Pat filled the floater with white using the Effects ➢ Fill command (without affecting the underlying sketch) and set the floater's Composite Method in the Controls palette to Gel.

4. Working in different floater layers, Pat used the Airbrush Fat Stroke variant to add color to the sketch. With the Eraser tools, Pat cleaned up areas and removed unwanted color when necessary. When a layer satisfied Pat, she would use the Drop command in the Objects: Floater List palette to drop the floater. She would then create another floater and execute the previous steps, each time dropping the completed floater onto the completed painting.

5. After the last floater was dropped into place, Pat used the Airbrush Thin Stroke and Feather Tip variant, the Chalk Very Small Artist Pastel variant, the Water Color Simple Water variant, and the Eraser Ultrafine Darkener for linear accents.

9.32

CATS, DOGS, COWBOYS, AND NOCTURNE

Chet Phillips created *Cat's Pajamas* (9.33) and *Dog Flight* (9.34) using brushes and a floater. The following steps outline how:

1. Chet created the black and white line work with the Pens Scratchboard variant by filling an area with black and scratching out with white.

2. Next he selected the entire image, floated it (Select ➢ Float), and changed the floater Composite Method to Gel.

3. Chet then deselected the floater and used masks, the Paint Bucket tool, and the Airbrush to add color.

Chapter 9 Composite Techniques

Chet created *Literate Cowboy* (9.35) by using the Pens Scratchboard variant to create the black and white line work. Chet worked by filling areas with black and scratching out with white.

After creating the cowboy and cactus, Chet tried something different for the background area. There are four levels of floaters behind the cowboy. Three of the floater levels are mountains; the fourth is the sky. For these levels, Chet created the detail in black and white with the Scratchboard brush variant, and converted them to color using the Apply Screen command (Effects ➢ Surface Control ➢ Apply Screen). He chose two colors and a paper texture for each.

9.34

9.33

9.35

Chet used this technique to a lesser extent in *Nocturne* (9.36). In this image Chet used the Apply Screen command with a paper texture on the two back levels of jungle growth.

SEA, MAID, AND LANDSCAPE

Jay Paul Bell creates both natural-looking landscape paintings (as seen in Chapter 8) and more surrealistic and sometimes semi-abstracted images, including *Sea . . .* (9.37), *Sea . . . (detail)* (9.38), *Maid . . .* (9.39), and *Landscape Fragment No. 3* (9.40).

9.36

9.37

9.38

Jay feels that "The total freedom of manipulation and experimentation the computer offers has made the creative process more spontaneous than with many traditional disciplines." Jay's secret in creating *Landscape Fragment No. 3* was to use KPT's Seamless Welder and to overlay floaters and vary the Composite Method for each floater. Here's how Jay created *Landscape Fragment No. 3*:

1. Jay scanned a contour drawing of a landscape.
2. He added color to the scanned drawing by using the Airbrush Feather Tip variant and the Airbrush Thin Stroke variant. As he worked with these brushes, he created and used different-size brushes.
3. Next Jay created the sky by filling it with a gradation he created and then adding clouds using the Image Hose Cumulus Clouds nozzle. He manipulated the clouds with the Airbrush variants at various sizes.

4. After Jay finished coloring the landscape (9.41), he saved the file and then applied KPT's Seamless Welder until he was satisfied with the fragmented/geometric appearance. This fragmented/geometrical image (9.42) became the background. Jay selected this background, copied it, and then pasted it, creating a floater above the fragmented/geometrical background.

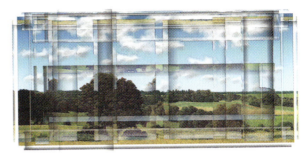

9.40

9.41

9.42

9.39

5. Next Jay applied KPT's Find Edges & Invert to the floater and adjusted the value with the Effects ➢ Tonal Control ➢ Equalize command (9.43).

6. He pasted a second floater and set the Composite Method to Hard Light and the Opacity to 65%. Jay pasted a third floater and this time set the Composite Method to Multiply and left the Opacity at 65%.

7. Jay pasted a fourth and final floater, set the Composite Method to Normal, and reduced the opacity to 35%. This floater added resolution and clarity to the land area of the image but overdid the sky. Jay deleted the sky by painting with the Airbrush Feather Tip, the Thin Stroke, and the Fat Stroke variants, with the Brushes palette Method Category set to Mask and the Method Subcategory set to Soft Mask Cover. He chose white in the Art Materials: Color palette and painted in the sky to remove it.

ARGON ZARK!

The art in Charley Parker's online "virtual comic book," *Argon Zark!* (`http://www.zark.com`), is an entertaining example of floaters and many other Painter techniques in action (9.44). In it, our heroes

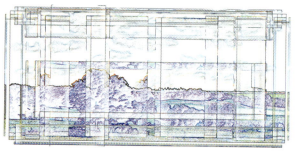

9.43

9.44

are *crashing* a virtual meeting of "The Nine or Ten Guys who Secretly Run Everything," who are represented in cyberspace by bizarre avatars. The story calls for Argon, Zeta, and Cybert to emerge into the scene right through the avatar of the group's CEO. Got it? Here's an overview of how Charley created the images in *Argon Zark!*:

1. Charley created a rough sketch with a 6% opacity variant of the 2B pencil that he calls a *2H pencil* (9.45). He knew that he would be repeating the bottom-middle image across the bottom three panels. To get a picture of the final composition, he copied the drawing in the bottom-middle panel by selecting it and Option/Alt+clicking in the selection with the Floater Adjuster tool to float a copy. He then dragged the selection into place and repeated the process for the last panel. He then dropped all the floaters.

2. Charley created the background of the first panel in KPT Bryce. To correctly position the figures in the panel in relation to the background, Charley pasted a copy of the Bryce PICT image into a floater, chose Effects ➤ Orientation ➤ Free Transform, and used the Floater Adjuster tool to size and position it to the panel. He then reduced the floater's opacity to 20% in the Controls palette so that he could see through it easily while revising the drawing underneath.

3. After refining the pencil drawing, Charley turned off the visibility icon for the Bryce image in the Floater List and deselected it by clicking outside the image in the Floater List. He then created a new full-size floater for the final *ink* drawing. To do this, he selected the entire image and Option/Alt+clicked with the Floater Adjuster tool to float a copy. (He was careful to float a copy so that he didn't lose the original sketch.) Charley then filled the floater with white. By reducing the opacity of this floater to about 80% in the Controls palette, the floater served as what Charley calls *adjustable tracing paper*. (Charley prefers this technique to Painter's Tracing Paper feature, which requires a clone image and is restricted to 50% opacity.)

4. To create his cartoon inks, Charley used a variant of the Pens Scratchboard variant. His settings in the Brush Controls: Size palette were Size: 1.5, ±Size: 2.0, and Size Step: 1%. He then saved the variant and again reduced the opacity of the white-filled floater to 80%. This enabled him to draw over his pencil drawing with carefully controlled ink lines for the finished drawing. When satisfied, Charley returned the opacity of the floater to 100% and dropped it. ("This is every ink artist's dream: a one-click pencil eraser!")

5. At this point, Charley created a mask of the finished ink lines using the Auto Mask command (In Painter 5 the Auto Mask command is found in the Objects: Mask palette). This line art mask would later enable Charley to paint freely in areas without damaging the black lines.

6. With the Magic Wand, Charley created a mask of the Panel 1 background. To create the mask, Charley had to create a complex selection comprised of six non-contiguous areas of the same color. He made his initial selection and then chose Select ➤ Save Selection to save it as a mask. To view the mask, he clicked the mask's eye icon in the Mask List palette. With both the new mask and the canvas mask visible, he was able to see his masked area in red. Charley then added to it by selecting another area with the Magic Wand and choosing Select ➤ Save Selection. In the Save Selection dialog box, he chose Save to: New Mask 1

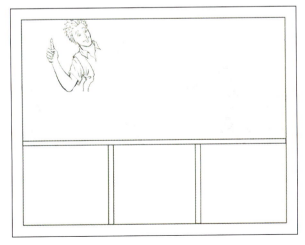

9.45

and selected the Add to Selection option. When Charley finished selecting his mask, he turned off the mask visibility and loaded the selection by choosing Load Selection in the Mask List palette.

7. Charley chose Select ➢ Invert to select everything onscreen except the Panel 1 background. He then used the Adjuster tool to float this above the Bryce image floater. He turned on the floater's visibility icon and chose Effects ➢ Orientation ➢ Commit Transform to turn the selection from a Reference Floater to an Image Floater. He then dropped the floater, which composited the background behind the Panel 1 figures (9.46).

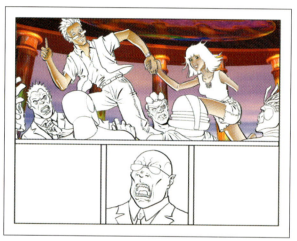

9.46

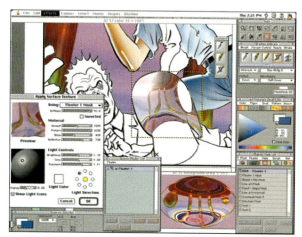

9.47

8. Charley began coloring in the figure by making selections with the Magic Wand tool. In the Controls palette he set Tolerance to 16, unchecked Anti-alias, and chose Selection as the Destination in the Controls palette.

9. He often revised the selections with the Lasso tool by holding down the Command/Control key to subtract from the selection, or by holding down the Shift key to add to it. He filled the selections with gradations using the Paint Bucket tool set to What to fill: Image and Fill with: Grad in the Controls palette.

10. To make the chrome avatar character appear to reflect the meeting room, Charley created a reflection map. Opening the PICT file of the KPT Bryce background image he created earlier, he chose Effects ➢ Surface Control ➢ Quick Warp. In the dialog box that appeared, he chose Sphere and adjusted the sliders to obtain what looked like an ovoid reflection of the image. He saved this file as *Background warp*, returned to the main image, and used File ➢ Clone Source to make *Background warp* the clone source. He then selected an area of the figure with the Magic Wand and turned the selection into a floater.

With the floater active, Charley chose Effects ➢ Surface Control ➢ Apply Surface Texture. In the dialog box that appeared, he selected the floater's mask in the Using pop-up menu and adjusted the sliders for Softness (50%), Amount (100%), and Reflection (100%) to get the look he wanted (9.47). He repeated this process for each area of the figure. Because the floater's mask is the same shape as the selection it's made from, the *reflected* image conforms to the shape of the area, adding to the illusion that the shape is reflecting the image.

11. To create the distortion of Zeta's hand coming through the CEO's face, he saved the floater that was floating over the center image into a new document, dropped it there, and applied the Effects ➢ Surface Control ➢ Quick Warp command. He created a new document because the Quick Warp effect only applies to the entire image, not to a selection or floater. He made the new document the same size as the floater by clicking the floater name and noting its size in the Controls palette.

In the Quick Warp dialog box, Charley chose Ripple and adjusted the sliders to achieve the look he desired. He then refloated the image, copied it back into the main document, and aligned it with the original floater using the Effects ➢ Objects ➢ Align command (9.48).

12. Charley reduced the opacity of the rippled floater to blend it with the underlying image, but he still wanted the face in the middle to be less distorted than the surrounding background. To achieve this effect, he edited the floater's Visibility Mask. With the floater active in the Floater List, he clicked the floater's mask in the Mask List but left the floater mask's Visibility eye off and the RGB mask Visibility eye on. Selecting the Airbrush and white as his current color, he was able to gradually paint out an area of the floater's Visibility Mask, revealing more of the image beneath the floater (9.49). He could also switch to painting with black to restore areas if necessary. By occasionally turning on the mask's visibility icon, he was able to see the mask itself and clean it up a bit.

13. Charley wanted a trail of semi-transparent images behind Argon and Zeta as they emerged into the room. To create this effect, he loaded the selection from the mask of the Panel 1 background, inverted it, and edited it with the Lasso tool—using the Shift and Option/Alt keys to add and subtract from the selection, respectively, until he had isolated just those two figures.

He floated a copy of the image and edited the edges of the floater's visibility mask to soften the areas where they fade into the background. He made several copies of the floater and arranged them behind the floater of "everything but the background" in successive stages of lowered opacity ("thanking myself at this point for buying extra RAM"). He then dropped all the floaters of Argon and Zeta as well as the large floater of "everything else."

14. The images of Zeta's hand pulling Cybert through in the bottom three panels were created essentially the same as the *motion trails* (Step 13) were completed for Panel 1: reduced-opacity floaters with their edges softened in the visibility mask.

15. For the image of Cybert (the robot) emerging in the last panel, Charley used Painter Shapes to get a more mechanical and precise line. He took advantage of Shapes when coloring by creating and painting on two transparent layers; one under all the Shapes, and one under the eye shapes but above the others (9.50). (Shapes, like Floaters, float above the background canvas.) This enabled him to paint freely onto the transparent layers behind the shape lines without having to be exact about where he met the edge. The second layer behind the eyes enabled him to paint behind those shapes but over the others.

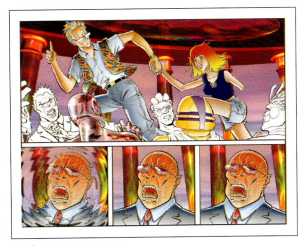

9.48

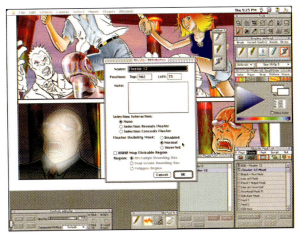

9.49

To see what he was doing more clearly, he temporarily put a small, white-filled floater at 70% opacity between the background and the layers he was working on. When he finished, he deleted the white floater and grouped and collapsed the other Shapes and Layers into one floater. He used the new Bulge brush to distort the CEO's face under the area of the robot's bubble. He also used the Bulge brush along with the Distorto brush to touch up areas of distortion in all the panels where figures and arms were emerging from the background.

16. After saving the final image, Charley also saved a version in JPEG format and reduced the image to 72 dpi. (Charley used JPEG Encoding Quality: Good.) Finally, he placed the final image in an HTML document with a white background for display on the Web.

MERLIN

James Dowlen created *Merlin* (9.51) for Hewlett Packard. The image was reproduced as a poster with a technical chart and other items at the bottom of the image.

This 17" × 22" poster is a collage of scanned photos, painted images, and some 3D modeling that James brought into the image as floaters. James airbrushed in the hat, hand, and sleeve in Painter using both Airbrush and Chalk brushes using Soft, Cover, and Grainy Method Categories. The lettering was created with the Pens Calligraphy variant, and the Celtic *M* was drawn with the Pens Scratchboard variant. Areas were filled with color and grads. James drew the curved electric cable with the Pen tool (stroke with no fill), allowing for an adjustable and perfectly shaped line that was then shaded with the Airbrush.

Journey of the Navigator (9.52) is especially meaningful to James Dowlen, who chose this image for the cover on his wife's memorial invitations. James was working on this image well before his wife, Eva, was gravely ill, and he finished it after she had died.

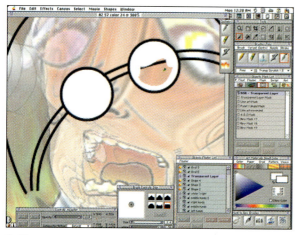

9.50

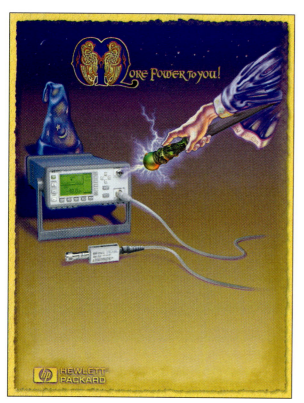

9.51

Chapter 9 Composite Techniques

James started with a black-and-white photograph of Eva with a winged headdress he had taken years earlier. In the original photo she was holding a lily. He changed it to the bird of paradise flower because it was not only her favorite flower but also the last words she spoke while looking at an arrangement of flowers before she died. He created the boat as a 3D model in Crystal Topas, and rendered and assembled it in Painter. The moon was hand-painted into the background.

Finally, James ran an Adobe Gallery Effects chrome filter over the entire image. He then reverted back partially with the fade command to diminish the effect 50 percent. Next he selectively cloned back most of the image, leaving some of the halo and interference lines around the boat and figure to add to the dream quality.

WORKING WITH SHAPES, FLOATERS, AND SELECTIONS

Shapes are a recent addition in Painter's repertoire. When Painter's programmers introduced Shapes in Painter 4, artists who liked to combine their drawing skills with painting skills had a new outlet to express their creativity. Painter's Shapes provide not only features primarily found in high-end drawing programs such as Adobe Illustrator, CorelDraw, and Macromedia Freehand, but also a powerful means of creating intricate floaters and selections. After you create a shape, you can easily turn it into a floater (Shapes ➢ Convert to Floater). If you do transform a shape into a floater, Painter automatically turns the shape into a floater mask that can be edited with a brush. Conversely, if you create a selection (or a mask that you convert to a selection), you can easily turn it into a shape (Select ➢ Convert to Shape).

VIVO

Adam Sadigursky created *Vivo* (9.53) by using a combination of shapes and floaters. As Adam works, he tries to provide dimension to his shapes with the Pen tool. To add depth, he often converts the shapes to floaters and overlays each of the floaters with different Composite Methods. After the floaters have been created, Adam applies textures using Painter's Effects ➢ Surface Control ➢ Apply Surface Texture.

9.52

9.53

KEN'S MURAL

Kenneth Gore's *Van Gogh Mural* (9.54) is a 6½-by-26½-foot mural created extensively with shapes and floaters. The mural appears in the Marriot hotel in Somerset, New Jersey. Here are the steps Kenneth used to create the mural:

1. Kenneth scanned a pencil sketch (9.55) in grayscale. He resized the sketch in Photoshop, and then divided the image into three sections and converted it to Photoshop's RGB Color mode.

2. In Painter Kenneth used the Pen tool to outline the shapes in the sketch.

3. Kenneth then converted the Pen shapes to selections to be used as masks. As he worked, he named each selection.

4. Kenneth filled the selections with color from a color set he created called the *Van Gogh Set*. To fill a color from a color set, he clicked the color in the Color Set palette and then executed the Effects ➤ Fill command. In the Fill dialog box, he chose Current Color.

5. After all the panels were blocked in, he used the Artists Van Gogh 2 brush variant for the finishing touches. While working, he adjusted the variability sliders in the Art Materials: Color palette, and he adjusted the brush size in the Brush Controls: Size palette.

6. Kenneth enlarged files using Macromedia's Xres batch convert mode. Before outputting the files, he converted them to CMYK in Photoshop.

THE TRANSCENDENTALIST

Sheriann Ki-Sun Burnham originally created *The Transcendentalist* (9.56) as a pen and ink drawing in the mid 1980s. She used the original drawing as the basis for creating a vector line-drawing of it, using Shapes in Painter. She then converted these Shapes into individual floaters. She worked on each floater individually, either adjusting contrast, focus, value, or with additional painting.

Sheriann built the composition by mirroring and altering areas (blocks) as she went along. She then copied and pasted each block, which created a floater. She then flipped the blocks and matched them up to the original block. Next she dropped the floater and continued painting. She did this over and over again until the image was complete.

9.54

9.55

Chapter 9 Composite Techniques

USING SELECTIONS AND FLOATERS

Painter's Lasso and other selection tools can often be used as painting aids. When you create a selection onscreen with the Lasso tool, or create a path with the Pen tool and convert it into a selection, you can use the selection as a mask. With the selection/mask onscreen, Painter protects the area within or outside of the mask as you paint—depending on how you set the mask icons in the lower-left corner of the Painter window.

The following examples describe how selections, as well as selections and floaters, can be used to enhanced the painting process.

FLOWERS AND CATS

Dorothy "Pat" Erickson created *Dampiera Diversafolia* (9.57) using the Lasso tool to create selections and then painting the selections with brushes. Here are the steps she followed to create the image:

1. Pat started *Dampiera Diversafolia* by creating a drawing with the 2B Pencil.
2. Pat cloned the drawing and turned on Painter's Tracing Paper mode.
3. Viewing the image through tracing paper, Pat isolated each segment of the flower, stem, and plastic container with the Lasso tool.
4. Pat colored the selections in the image using the Artist Pastel Chalk brush variant and the Water Color Pure Water brush variant. Pat created three variants from Artist Pastel Chalk: small, very small, and softer.
5. As Pat isolated each segment of the flower, she named it (numbered for the many stem/leaf segments) to keep the sections somewhat "under control." Pat often used the Magnifier tool to check the segments for color and shading. She also erased, bleached, and darkened to add definition. (Pat prefers the Eraser Method Category to the Burn and Dodge tool because she feels she can have more control for small images.)

9.56

©1996 Sheriann Ki-Sun Burnham

9.57

Dorothy "Pat" Erickson also created *Life is Good* (9.58) by using the Lasso tool and Brushes. This image is a favorite of Pat's, who frequently uses cats as the subject of her artwork. Because her earlier career was printmaking, she has tried to produce a print in a serigraphic manner, as seen here. Pat used the following steps to create *Life is Good*:

1. Pat first created a drawing using the Pencil.
2. She cloned the drawing, deleted the image in the clone document, and turned on Painter's Tracing Paper mode.
3. Pat used the Lasso tool to create a cat shape.
4. She used the Airbrush and her version of the Small Artist Pastel Chalk variant to produce the essence of a cat print in the drawing.

9.58

9.59

AUGUST FLOWERS

Stacy A. Hopkins created *August Flowers* (9.59) on a pink background. He created clouds with the Chalk brush and the leaves and flowers using the Lasso tool. Stacy colored the flowers and leaves with the Chalk brush using paper textures. He then applied Effects ➢ Tonal Control ➢ Posterize to the image.

To create the frame, he used the Rectangular Shape tool to create a rectangle about the size of the flower painting. Next Stacy converted the rectangle shape to a selection. Then he inverted the selection and applied paper grain, color, and lighting.

MORE POSTERS

Kenneth Gore created *Peacock Alley # 2 Poster* (9.60) using the Image Hose brush to create the outer space sky. He used gradations for the blue part of the sky and the Airbrush to create the gas clouds. Kenneth also used the Airbrush to make the glow around the objects in the image. Before he painted with the Airbrush, Kenneth created and loaded a feathered mask for each object. Kenneth also used Effects ➢ Surface Control ➢ Apply Lighting on the table and lamp.

9.60

PATRICK'S COMPUTERS

Patrick Lichty created *St. Joan of the Cross* (9.61) with many floaters. Patrick created the surrounding frame as a black-and-white mask in CorelDraw and used Painter to cut out through selection masks and the Magic Wand. By using Apply Surface Texture with the Image Luminance option selected, and MetraCreations Convolver's Relief features, he built up the texturing. Using the KPT Gradient Designer 2' Gradients on Path, he built up the gold lining around the outer frames.

To create the gridded inner area, Patrick used three layers. The background is a landscape he painted long ago, to which he applied a rainbow KPT Gradation Designer II effect. He then used KPT 3 Twirl.

The Grid was merely a grid pattern to which he applied a couple of iterations of KPT II Gradients on Paths, Vortex tiling, and then more gradients on paths. The central figure is a rendering from 3D Studio, and he enhanced the detail using the Airbrush and 2B Pencil. The floater was set as a 60% transparency.

9.61

THE IMAGE **AXIS** GROUP

CHAPTER 10
TYPE EFFECTS

Many digital artists love creating type effects because it enables them to produce attractive and startling art—and convey a message. Unfortunately, mastering type effects in most painting and image-editing programs can be a long affair, often involving numerous steps that require loading and reloading selections and masks.

In Painter, however, striking type effects can be achieved with only a few simple clicks of the mouse. Why so simple? Most painting programs and image editing programs create only bitmap type—the type is locked down to the background pixels. If you enlarge it, you often sacrifice quality. In contrast, Painter creates type as shapes—vector graphics that can easily be resized, moved, and converted to selections or floaters.

Painter's text-editing tools are the tools of choice for all Web headline art and any non-vector type. Painter's great texture application options allow very easy special effects as well.

DOUGLASS LOCKYER

CREATING VECTOR TYPE EFFECTS

Much of Painter's type power lies in its ability to create text as vector shapes, rather than as a bitmap that immediately dries onto the background canvas. The vector properties of Painter's type mean that the type not only can be easily stroked and filled, but also restroked and refilled. Furthermore, text in Painter can be quickly and easily resized, expanded, and contracted simply by clicking and dragging the mouse. Because the type is based on paths, it can also be easily altered by clicking and dragging the path's anchor points. (For more information on working with vector shapes, turn to Chapter 4.)

EDITING VECTOR TEXT

Vector type is extremely versatile in Painter. To create the first row of type in this figure (10.1), we typed the text in Frutiger Bold and then changed the stroke and fill using Shapes ➢ Set Shape Attributes. We didn't use the Effects ➢ Fill command because we didn't want the type to be converted into a floater. (As discussed in Chapter 4, you can change stroke and fill attributes by choosing Edit ➢ Preferences ➢ Shapes. This sets the stroke and fill as you create the text. If you use Shapes ➢ Set Shape Attributes, you must select the individual letters first.)

AXIS PITCH COVER
Douglass Lockyer

To create the second row of type, we duplicated the first row by pressing and holding down Option/Alt while selecting the text with the Floater Adjuster tool and dragging down. Next we changed the stroke and fill (again using Shapes ➢ Set Shape Attributes) and used the Floater Adjuster tool to move, scale, and rotate the type. To rotate the type with the Floater Adjuster, we pressed Command/Ctrl and dragged a corner.

To create the last row of type, we again duplicated the type from the previous line and then changed the stroke and fill (using Shapes ➢ Set Shape Attributes). Next we distorted the actual shape of the text. To alter the text, we selected the edge of a letter with the Shape Selection tool to display the anchor points. We clicked the anchor points and dragged them with the mouse. You can use the arrow keys on your keyboard to move selected type or anchor points one pixel at a time.

To add the extra leg to the second *M*, we added anchor points with the Add Point tool, converted the points to curve points with the Convert Point tool, and then dragged the anchor points with the mouse. The background of the figure is a Painter pattern, which we applied to the background using the Effects ➢ Fill command. We then made adjustments to the pattern using the Effects ➢ Focus ➢ Glass Distortion and Effects ➢ Tonal Control ➢ Correct Colors and Effects ➢ Surface Control ➢ Apply Surface Texture commands.

In this next figure (10.2), we typed the word **Winter** and then used the Floater Adjuster tool to resize, move, and rotate the type. We used the Shape Selection tool to select the outline of the text to display the anchor points. Next we selected individual anchor points and moved them with the mouse to alter the text. We then selected individual letters with the Floater Selection tool and filled, stroked, and changed the fills opacity of each letter separately using the Shapes ➢ Set Shape Attributes command.

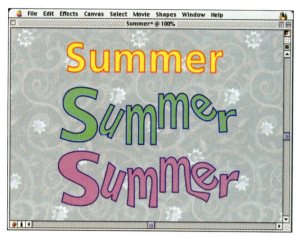

10.1

> **NOTE**
>
> Be aware that if you click and drag over a letter with the Shape Selection tool, you select the entire path, including all of its anchor points. If all anchor points are selected, you won't be able to click and drag to alter the path. Clicking and dragging a path that has all of its anchor points selected moves the entire path.

10.2

We added even more alterations to the next figure (10.3). To do so, we converted the text from shapes to floaters by first selecting all the letters with the Floater Adjuster tool and then selecting Shapes ➢ Convert to Floater. Next we applied a drop shadow to some of the letters with the Effects ➢ Objects ➢ Create Drop Shadow command. In the Drop Shadow dialog box, we made sure the Collapse to one layer option was not selected. When the check box is not selected, Painter creates another floater layer for the drop shadow. This enables you to change the opacity, position, and even the color of the drop shadow.

For the drop shadow of the *W*, we used the Dropper tool to change the shadow's color to the color of the *W*, and then we selected the *W* drop shadow floater and filled it with that color. Next we applied the Effects ➢ Surface Control ➢ Image Warp command to *W* to warp the letter. Then we deselected the text and filled the background with different gradation, patterns, and weaves.

We weren't satisfied with the look of any background, so we saved the file in Photoshop 3 format and imported the file into Photoshop. In Photoshop we applied the Filter ➢ Render ➢ Clouds command, using cyan and white foreground and background colors. To apply the Clouds command to only the background, we deselected all layers (Painter's floaters).

In the next figure (10.4), we imported the file from Photoshop back into Painter. Then we applied the Effects ➢ Esoterica ➢ Blobs command to the letters and the background. Before applying the Blobs command to an area, we used the Dropper tool to select the color in the area that we were filling. Then we dragged the Color Variability sliders in the Art Materials: Color palette so that the blobs varied in hue, saturation, and value.

10.3

USING AVERAGE POINTS TO EDIT VECTOR TEXT

If you don't want to spend your time clicking and dragging anchor points, you can let Painter automatically adjust the text with the Shapes ➢ Average Points command. The Average Points command averages the distance between anchor points.

The next figure (10.5) shows some type before and after it was altered with the Average Points command (using the Horizontal option). To edit vector text with the Average Points command, follow these steps:

1. Select the Type tool and type text into a new file.
2. Set the fill attributes by choosing Shapes ➢ Set Shape Attributes. In the Set Shape Attributes dialog box, make sure the Fill option is selected. Change colors by double-clicking the fill color swatch and choosing a color.
3. In the Tools palette, select the Shape Selection tool. If the Shape Selection tool isn't visible, click the Floater Adjuster or Selection Adjuster tool and hold the mouse button and drag until you can select the Shape Selection tool.

10.4

10.5

4. With the Shape Selection tool activated, click and drag over your text to select all the anchor points. This shows the actual path points of the text.

5. To distort the text, choose Average from the Shapes menu. In the Average dialog box, click Horizontal. After you close the dialog box, the text endpoints will be averaged together, creating an unusual text distortion.

6. If you want to change the size of the type or further distort it, click and drag any of the anchor points with the Shape Selection tool.

In Figure 10.5 we enhanced the effect by filling the text with a weave (Effects ➢ Fill). Using a weave, we turned our text into a floater, which we then beveled using the Bevel World plug-in found in the Objects: Plugin floaters palette.

> **TIP**
>
> You can also apply the Average Points command to text selected with the Floater Adjuster tool.

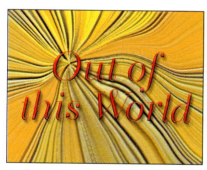

10.6

USING APPLY SURFACE TEXTURE TO RAISE TYPE

In the next figure (10.6), we used Painter's Apply Surface Texture to raise the type and give the background some depth. Here's how we did it:

1. Use the Type tool to create text onscreen.

2. To move or resize the text, click the text with the Floater Adjuster tool. To move the text, click in the middle of any letter and drag. To resize the text, click and drag a corner point.

3. You can fill or stroke the text by choosing Shapes ➢ Set Attributes.

   To use the Apply Surface Texture command with text (that is still a shape), you need to convert it from a shape into a floater. You can do this by selecting the text, choosing Group in the Objects Floater List palette, and then choosing Shapes ➢ Convert to Floater. If text is filled with the Effects ➢ Fill command, the shape is converted into an image floater.

4. In the Apply Surface Texture dialog box, click the Using pop-up menu. In the list of choices, you see the name of the mask created from the text. Click the mask choice and then move the Softness slider to the right until you create the desired effect. You can invert the 3D effect by clicking the Inverted check box. Click OK to apply the effect.

5. To change the background, make sure you deselect the text and drop shadow before you fill the area. We filled the background with a custom gradation and then used the Effects ➢ Surface Control ➢ Image Warp command.

> **TIP**
>
> You can apply a drop shadow to text by using the Effects ➢ Objects ➢ Create Drop Shadow command.

USING APPLY SURFACE TEXTURE TO CREATE CHROME TEXT

You can create startling chrome-like text effects by combining Painter's Liquid Metal plug-in filter and the Apply Surface Texture command. We used both commands to create the chrome text shown in this figure (10.7).

For this effect, an image created with Liquid Metal is used as a reflection map by the Apply Surface Texture command. The reflection map is a clone source that Apply Surface Texture uses to wrap around the text. The mapping is controlled by the Reflection slider in the Apply Surface Texture dialog box. Here are the steps we used to create this effect:

1. In a new file, create a metal-like image using Painter's Liquid Metal plug-in. To access the plug-in, chose Liquid Metal from the P.Float palette's pop-up menu.

2. In the Liquid Metal dialog box, choose Standard Metal from the Map pop-up menu. Select the Paintbrush icon and paint some liquid metal onscreen (10.8). The liquid metal serves as your reflection map. Leave Refraction set to 0 and Amount to 1.

3. Create a new file onscreen and enter some text. Convert the text to a floater by choosing Shapes ➤ Convert to Floater.

4. Set the metallic file as your clone source by choosing File ➤ Clone Source. Choose the metallic file in the pop-up menu that appears.

5. Choose Effects ➤ Surface Control ➤ Apply Surface Texture. In the apply surface texture dialog box, choose the type's mask in the Using pop-up menu. To create the Chrome effect, adjust the Reflection slider and the Softness slider. Drag both sliders to the right to enhance the effect.

> **TIP**
>
> To enhance the final effect, you may want to warp your metallic file using Effects ➤ Surface Control ➤ Quick Warp. Try the Cubic option.

10.8

10.7

RAISING TEXT OUT OF A DIGITAL IMAGE

By turning text into a selection, you can easily create unusual effects that rise right out of a digital image (10.9). Follow these steps to create the effect:

1. Open a digital image. (This image can be a scanned image or an image that you created in Painter.)
2. Use the Type tool to create text onscreen.
3. Convert the type to a selection by choosing Shapes ➢ Convert to Selection.
4. Use the Bevel World Plug-in floater to create the raised text effect.

10.9

> **TIP**
>
> If you want to make a pattern out of 3D text, create a Paper texture out of black text on a white background. To turn the text into a pattern, drop it (choose Drop all in the Floaters menu in the Object Floaters Palette). Select the text and then execute the Capture Texture command in the Art Materials: Paper palette.
>
> After you create the Paper texture, it will be the selected texture in the palette. Next load an image and apply the texture to your image by executing Effects ➢ Surface Control ➢ Apply Surface Texture. In the Apply Surface Texture dialog box, choose Paper Texture in the Using menu.

To load the Bevel World plug-in, open the Objects palette by choosing Window ➢ Show Objects. In the Objects Palette, choose P. Floater. Open the palette drawer and choose Bevel World. Then click the Apply button. In the Bevel World dialog box, adjust the settings to achieve the effect you desire—visible in the Preview area. (Note that previews of high-resolution images can take quite a long time to appear onscreen.)

5. Copy and paste the floater into another image if you want to use the text in another file.

CREATING BEVEL WORLD TYPE EFFECTS

The previous section illustrated a simple example of how Painter's Bevel World can be used to create a raised text effect. If you start experimenting with text and Bevel World, you'll quickly discover that the type effects possibilities are endless.

For example, the next figure (10.10) displays an image created by painting onscreen with an Image Hose nozzle composed of text. To create the 3D text effect in the Nozzle file, we used the Bevel World plug-in. After creating the beveled letters, we chose the Commit command in the P. Floater menu (in the Objects palette) to commit the image into a floater. We then created a drop shadow for each letter by choosing Effects ➢ Objects ➢ Create Drop Shadow

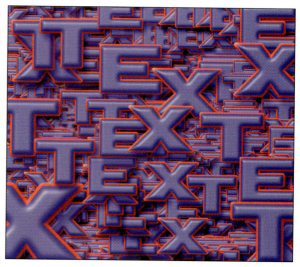

10.10

Chapter 10 Type Effects

(with Collapse to one layer selected). Next we assembled the letters onscreen and created the Nozzle file by choosing the Nozzle from Group command in the Brush palette's Nozzle menu. (See Chapter 6 for more information about creating Nozzle files from floaters).

The next nine figures illustrate more effects and settings for creating text using Bevel World. To create these examples, we typed a letter onscreen, filled it with color, and then selected it with the Floater Adjuster tool. Then we applied the Bevel World plug-in. As you look at the examples, notice that Bevel World's Outside Portion slider enables you to create a colored edge around the border of the text (10.11–10.19).

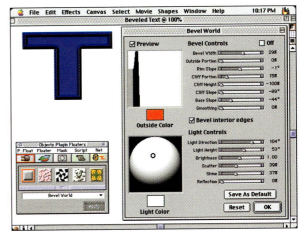
10.13

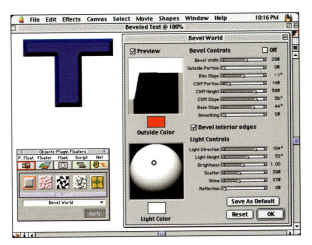
10.11

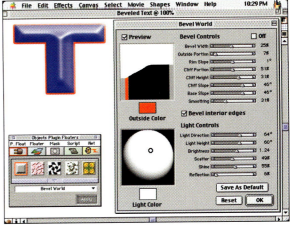
10.14

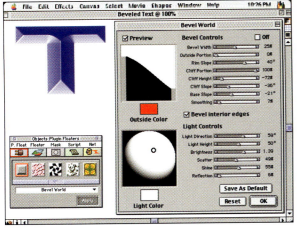
10.12

10.15

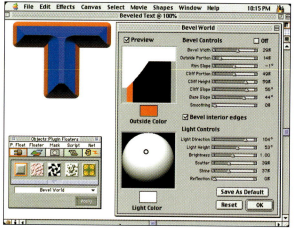

10.16

USING TYPE AND PAINTING TOOLS

Painter enables you to create endless effects by combining painting tools and text. To create *Studio Gecko* (10.20), Doug Lockyer beveled type with Alien Skin's Black Box plug-in, and then used Painter's Water Color Spatter and Simple Water brush variants to create the final effect. He created masks and colored the image with the Water Color brush, using both the Cover and Buildup Method Categories to create the "mess of hair."

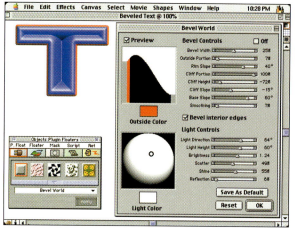

10.17

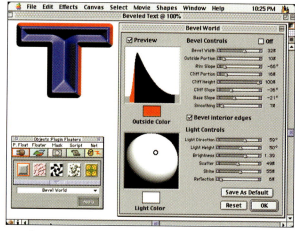

10.18

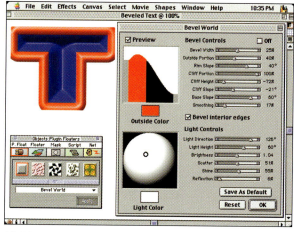

10.19

To create the Russian Glasnost coin (10.21), Doug Lockyer produced the 3D effect with the Airbrush brush and added highlights with Painter's Chalk and Airbrush brushes. In the I-Com logo (10.22), Doug Lockyer combined cut-out text with deep paper textures and lighting effects.

Doug Lockyer used a variety of techniques to create the Axis pitch cover (10.23). This image is a proposal and presentation cover for Image Axis, one of New York's leading graphics services studios. Following are the steps Doug took to create the image:

1. Doug started by generating the Axis Group Logo as paths in Adobe Illustrator. He then turned them into floaters in Painter and airbrushed them in with the Airbrush brush.

2. Next Doug scanned a page of parchment and imported it into Painter, along with a grayscale TIFF texture library document. Then Doug applied the texture to the scan (Effects ➣ Surface Control ➣ Apply Surface Texture) to give it its richly shaded depth.

3. By copying and pasting the layered the logo in a combination of Overlay, Multiply, and Normal composite modes, Doug was able to create a reasonable facsimile of a deeply de-bossed and, in places, cut-out image. This image made the logo integral with the paper-textured page.

10.21

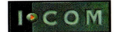

10.22

10.20

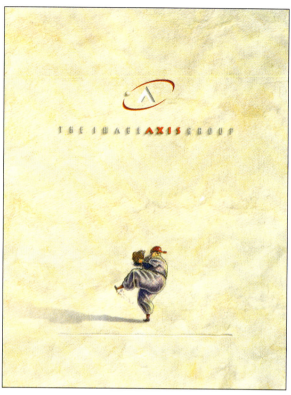

10.23

4. Doug created a separate illustration against a white background for the pitcher image by tracing a scanned outline with the 2B Pencil brush variant in a sepia color and then floating the whole Pencil layer.

5. He composited this floating layer in Multiply mode (found in the Controls palette when the Floater Adjuster tool is selected) and painted with the Simple Water brush. Doug calls this "one of Painter's most subtly sophisticated and exquisite brushes."

6. As Doug worked, he regularly "dried the canvas" (Canvas ➤ Dry) to allow overlapped brush-strokes to sit atop one another without bleeding wet-on-wet, thereby enhancing the watercolor look.

7. To complete the pitcher and suggest motion, Doug threw some spattered brush-strokes around the leg area.

8. Next Doug added highlights and shadows over a dry canvas with the Airbrush brush, in Cover and low-opacity Buildup modes, respectively. The image was then copied and pasted layer by layer over the parchment background.

9. Doug added type in Painter, except for the logo font, which was a set of Adobe Illustrator paths. Doug says that Painter handles anti-aliased type "far better than Photoshop," so he was able to create quite nice, soft, tracked-out text on a floating layer with a two-pixel feather to soften the edges.

10. He added the text with the Text tool and then converted it to a selection. To create the beveled look, Doug used the Apply Surface Texture command (Effects ➤ Surface Control ➤ Apply Surface Texture) and adjusted the effect with the softness slider.

11. Finally Doug added the drop shadows along with an Alien Skin Black Box Motion Trail plug-in, to simulate cast shadows.

CREATING A MOSAIC OUT OF TEXT

Painter's digital mosaic maker is one of Painter's more fascinating effects. Not only can you use the Canvas ➢ Make Mosaic command to transform a digital image into a mosaic, but you can also turn type into a mosaic (10.24). Here are the steps we took to create the mosaic effect:

1. We started by creating a rectangle with the Rectangular Selection tool for the background mosaic.

2. We converted the rectangle to a selection by choosing Shapes ➢ Convert to Selection. (Before we filled the selection with mosaic tiles, we selected a yellow color in the Art Materials: Color palette and dragged the Color Variability Value slider to the right.)

3. We applied the mosaic by choosing Canvas ➢ Make Mosaic. In the Make Mosaic dialog box, we clicked the arrow pop-up menu and chose Fill Selection. We manually filled in the areas not filled in by Painter by clicking and dragging the mouse. (We first selected the arrow icon in the bottom left of the dialog box.)

4. After we created the mosaic in a rectangle, we selected the Pens Calligraphy variant and chose Select ➢ Stroke Selection to stroke the mosaic rectangle. Then we saved the file.

5. We created a new file where we created the mosaic type.

6. After typing the letters onscreen, we converted the type to a selection by choosing Shapes ➢ Convert to Selection. Before we filled each letter with a mosaic, we dragged the Art Materials: Color palette Color Variability Hue, Saturation, and Value sliders to the right.

7. To create the mosaic inside each letter, we chose Canvas ➢ Make Mosaic. In the Make Mosaic dialog box, we clicked the arrow pop-up menu and chose Fill Selection. We manually filled in the areas that were not filled in by Painter.

8. To stroke the letters, we selected the Pens Calligraphy variant and chose Select ➢ Stroke Selection.

9. We needed to paste the text into the background file (the rectangular mosaic file). To do so, we selected the letters with the Floater Adjuster tool and copied them. Then we activated the rectangular mosaic file and pasted the letters into the file. We then moved the letters into position and saved the file again.

10.24

CHAPTER 11
ENHANCING DIGITAL AND PAINTED IMAGES

In traditional painting, artists use many tricks to turn the realistic world into a painting. Some artists use photographs to help them get started with their work; others use slides or an overhead projector to help them start. When it comes to helping an artist begin a digital painting, Painter is very obliging. For example, Painter can automatically transform a digitized image into a digital version of a Van Gogh painting. Of course, Painter's Auto Van Gogh command is unlikely to fool anyone into thinking the digital version was actually created by Van Gogh. Nevertheless, you can use Auto Van Gogh to create painter-like effects and backgrounds. Later, you can use your creative skills to turn the digital image into a work of art.

In this chapter you'll see how artists transform scanned images into paintings using Auto Van Gogh, as well as Painter's Auto Clone and Tracing Paper commands. You'll also see how paintings can be enhanced by adjusting colors and textures with Painter's Effects ➢ Tonal Control and Effects ➢ Surface Control commands.

CONVERTING PHOTOGRAPHS INTO PAINTINGS

This section provides a look at how artists use Painter's cloning tools such as Auto Van Gogh and Auto Clone to turn photographs into paintings. In many respects Auto Van Gogh and Auto Clone are like plug-in filters. After you run the effect, your realistic digital image is automatically transformed into a painting. There's no need to pick a brush and manu-

Margaret Sweeney starts most of her images as rough sketches onscreen, occasionally from sketches made while traveling.

ally paint. The longer you let the effect run, the more painter-like effects are added to your image. After you run Auto Van Gogh or Auto Clone, you may want to touch up the image by painting over it, or you may want to use the automatically generated painting as a background in another painting.

PAINTING WITH AUTO VAN GOGH

Dutch Flowers (11.1) is an example of a painting created using Auto Van Gogh. You can judge for yourself how close our example simulates a true Van Gogh. We started the image by scanning a photograph of flowers (11.2). Then we loaded the scanned image into Painter and created a clone by choosing File ➢ Clone. Next we selected the Artist Auto Van Gogh brush variant in the Brushes palette. To run the Auto Van Gogh effect, we selected Effects ➢ Esoterica ➢

NIGHT GARDEN
Margaret Sweeney

Auto Van Gogh. In a few moments Painter began turning our digital image into a painting with Van Gogh brush strokes. We stopped the effect by clicking the mouse.

PAINTING WITH AUTO CLONE

If you don't like the Auto Van Gogh effect, you can use Painter's Auto Clone command to automatically create a diverse range of painterly effects. To use Auto Clone, first clone your image (File ➢ Clone). Next, pick the brush you want Painter to use when it automatically paints your file (such as the Artists Impressionist brush variant). Then choose Effects ➢ Esoterica ➢ Auto Clone. The effects of using Auto Clone with the Artists Impressionist brush variant (11.3) and the effects of using Auto Clone with the Artists Piano Keys brush variant (11.4) is shown. We used the Artists Flemish Rub brush variant with Auto Clone to create this final figure (11.5).

11.1

11.2

11.3

11.4

11.5

PAINTING WITH THE VAN GOGH 2 BRUSH

If you don't want to give Painter carte blanche with your works of art, you can use the Van Gogh 2 brush variant to manually create a Van Gogh effect. You can see the Van Gogh 2 brush at work in Kenneth Gore's *Peacock Alley poster #1* (11.6). This image was output as an Iris poster and can be viewed in the Peacock Alley restaurant at the Waldorf Astoria hotel in New York City.

Kenneth started this image by scanning a sketch and then using the Pen tool to create selections in broad areas. When Kenneth had all the selections he needed, he began to paint the image.

To create the sky, Kenneth first painted a rough sky with the Pastel Artist Pastel brush variant, and then applied the Apply Surface Texture command with the Image Luminance option selected (Effects ➢ Surface Control ➢ Apply Surface Texture). Kenneth finished creating the sky using the Van Gogh 2 brush variant. He also used the Van Gogh 2 brush to paint the inside area of the cup. The cup was created using the Oval Selection tool and the Pen tool. Kenneth painted the cup using the Artist Pastel Chalk variant. In the shadow areas he applied a pattern using the Soft Cloner brush variant. He also used the Apply Surface Texture command in these areas to bring out the fabric detail. Kenneth also used the Van Gogh 2 variant to create the bottle.

To create the patterns inside the pear, Kenneth filled the pear with a red marble pattern and a black marble pattern. He had created these patterns by putting pieces of red and black marble on the scanner and scanning both of them. Then he selected a section of each marble image with the Rectangular Selection tool and chose Capture Pattern from the Pattern pop-up menu in the Art Materials: Pattern palette. To create the glow around the pear (the pear was a floater), Kenneth applied the Effects ➢ Objects ➢ Create Drop Shadow command. Ken intensified the shadow using the Effects ➢ Tonal Control ➢ Correct Colors command using the Brightness and Contrast option. He created the drop shadow of the plate in the same way. (The plate was photographed and scanned.) Kenneth also used the Liquid Distorto variant to soften the plate edges.

To create the wood at the bottom-right side of the image, Kenneth first loaded a library of textures from the MetaCreations *Sensational Surfaces* CD-ROM. He then selected one of the CD's wood textures in the

> **TIP**
>
> You can use the Canvas ➢ Grid command to align and make a more precise pattern.

> **TIP**
>
> To convert a shape to a selection, use the Shapes ➢ Convert to Selection command.

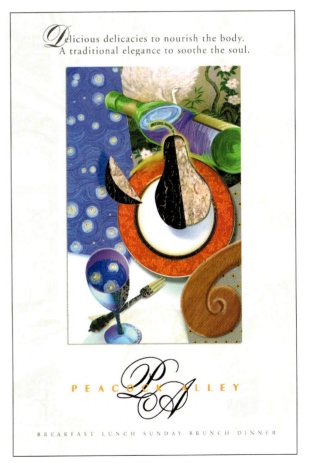

11.6

Art Materials: Paper Palette. Kenneth applied the wood grain texture with the Apply Surface Texture command. To create the napkin, Ken used three or four textures and the Apply Surface Texture command to apply some texture. Ken also used the Large Chalk brush variant, starting with a dark color and working toward a light color. The peacock and flowers behind the bottle were originally a piece of wallpaper that was added to this image with a Cloners brush variant.

TRACING OVER DIGITAL IMAGES

Painter's Tracing Paper mode provides another means of transforming a digital image into a painting. However, unlike Auto Van Gogh and Auto Clone, you manually create the final image using a digital image or sketch as a guide—and your creativity and skill when choosing and painting with brushes.

11.7

11.8

To use Tracing Paper, start by cloning your original image with File ➢ Clone. Select the entire image (Select ➢ All) and delete the image in the clone document by pressing the delete/backspace key. After the clone is deleted, your next step is to turn on Tracing Paper so that your original image appears in the clone, as though tracing paper was placed on top of it. To activate Tracing Paper, click the Tracing Paper icon in the upper-right corner of your document window, or choose Canvas ➢ Tracing Paper. This allows the original image to show through, enabling you to paint over it. *Pears* (11.7) by Adele Droblas Greenberg is a realistic painting created with the underlying help of Tracing Paper.

To create *Pears*, Adele scanned a photograph of a plate of pears (11.8). Next she cloned the scan by choosing File ➢ Clone. She then selected the entire clone image, deleted it, and clicked the Tracing Paper icon in the top-right corner of the document. On the screen, a dimmed version of the pear file appeared, which Adele used as a guide for painting. Next Adele used the Pens Calligraphy brush variant to create the outline of the pears with black ink. She then used the Water Brush Stroke variant (Water Color brush) to fill in the pears. As she worked, she painted with the Clone color. If she accidentally painted outside the black dry stroke, she could easily remove the wet stroke by painting with the Wet Remove Density Subcategory. Because she was painting with Water Color brushes, the Wet Remove Density subcategory removed only the watercolor paint and not the black *dry* stroke created with the Calligraphy brush variant.

TIP

When using Tracing Paper, you can toggle back and forth between the ghosted tracing paper view and a full color view of your image simply by clicking the Tracing Paper icon.

USING THE CLONERS BRUSHES

Another technique for turning digital images into paintings is to use Painter's Cloners brushes. (See Chapter 8 for more information on Cloners brushes.) When you paint with Cloners, you can paint into the image you're currently working in onscreen with the actual image or color information from a cloned source. *Baseball* (11.9) and *Hockey* (11.10), by David Obar, are excellent examples of images created with Cloners brushes.

David started both images by opening a Photo CD scan of a photograph and cropped it to the height and width he desired. (David normally uses no larger than the Photo CD base resolution for images up to 11 in. × 17 in. "It's easier to see brush strokes if the resolution of an image is not too large," David advises.)

David then determined the color palette he wanted for the images and made the initial color changes in Adobe Photoshop.

In Painter, David cloned the image, selected it, and deleted it. (David approaches cloning as if he is painting on a blank canvas.) David painted in the clone using the Chalk cloner with the Clone Color check box selected in the Art Materials: Color palette. As he painted, a chalk-like version of the original scan appeared onscreen. Basically, he followed the lines and planes when cloning. As he worked, David traced over lines, varying the brush size according to the width of the original image.

David created the remainder of the images by varying brush sizes, depending on how much detail he wanted to keep. His biggest concern was not to end up with an image that appeared to be a photograph manipulated with a filter.

11.9

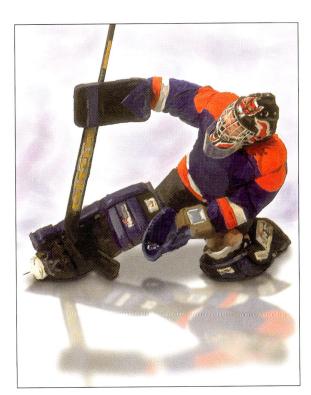

11.10

CONVERTING BLACK-AND-WHITE IMAGES TO COLOR

John Stephens converted an old black-and-white photograph (11.11) into three different color images using Cloners brushes.

11.11

11.12

In the first color image (11.12), John's goal was to create the semblance of an actual oil painting. First John created a mask of the white areas of the black-and-white image using the Auto Mask command (found in the Objects: Mask palette's Mask menu). John then filled the white areas with colors using the Paint Bucket tool. Next he painted the basic picture primarily with the Big Wet Oils brush variant using the Pencil brush for detail.

John created several versions of the oil painting of the ship. He applied surface texture (canvas 2) in the library More Paper Textures on one of the versions. On another version he used the Van Gogh Cloner and then Auto Van Gogh. John then sharpened parts—he even used the Aldus Gallery Effects emboss filter from Classic Effects #1 (these filters are now incorporated into Adobe Photoshop). John says that the Liquid Distorto variant worked well for the ocean and parts of the clouds. John says that "It really seemed to emulate gooey oil paint."

John then used Cloners brushes to piece each version together, taking pieces from part of the different versions to create the final image. Some parts of some of the images worked well. Using the Straight Cloner variant, he was able to pick and choose which parts he liked for his final painting. For example, John cloned only the paper texture to the canvas area and no place else. John played around with this technique, cloning back and forth, until he obtained his desired effect.

To create the next color images, John started by filling the white areas of the ship with color. He primarily used the Water Color brush to paint the ship, and he used the Pencil brush to add detail. John created a marbleized version of the image using Painter's marbleize feature (Effects ➤ Esoterica ➤ Apply Marbling) and cloned the Water Color version into it (11.13). To create the next figure (11.14), John blurred the Water Color version of the ship, and then used the Image Hose brush to create the realistic looking drops on the porthole. To make the porthole, John used the Oval Selection tool to create a mask, and then he painted it.

Pat Watson is another artist who often starts with black-and-white images to create his color paintings. Pat usually starts with an image and "sort of plays around with it in his mind until an intriguing idea comes."

When working on *Galaxie Drive-In* (11.15), Pat wanted to create an image of a drive-in. He had in mind a western desert suburban drive-in. With camera in hand, he went to the outskirts of Reno and shot pictures of mountains that had the "correct look." Pat never uses colored scans, because the color from the scan distorts his visualization of the image. Working from black and white and adding his own color enable Pat to exercise principles from color theory. Working this way also gives him a chance to reclaim black-and-white detail from a clone source without having the scanned color intrude on the color ideas he's working on in the clone. Pat feels that a scanned black-and-white image has a much different look than a scanned color image that is subsequently converted to grayscale.

To create the sky, Pat used some old cloud photos and scaled them dramatically to exaggerate the horizontal aspect, and drew the sagebrush by hand. The highlights on the tops of the sagebrush were created using the Chalk brush. To make the more geometric structures look accurate, Pat built the ticket booth, marquee, and screen/fence in Adobe Illustrator. He then created the striations in the fence using the Liquid Smeary Mover. He used the Straight Cloner to reclaim areas from the original black-and-white image. To add the touch of anomaly that Pat finds intriguing, he added the car in the sky. The car came from another image.

11.14

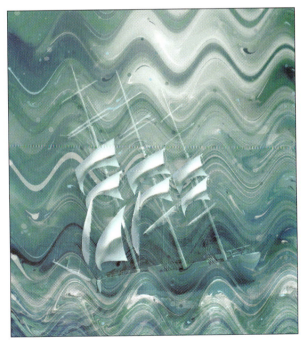

11.13

11.15

Pat Watson also created *Guardzilla* (11.16) from a black-and-white image. To create the image, Pat used the Pens Scratchboard tool brush variant against a black background. Pat painted the image freehand, going for a deliberately distorted image. Then, using the black-and-white image as the Clone source, he built a blurred color image that had an appropriate-looking light source. He then blended the two together.

ADJUSTING PAINTINGS AND DIGITAL IMAGES

At times you may find that you need to make adjustments to an image (sketch, painting, or photograph) or enhance it. You can do this many different ways in Painter. You can use the commands in the Effects ➢ Tonal Control submenu to alter the color in an image, or use the Effects ➢ Surface Control ➢ Apply Lighting command to add or change the lighting in an image. You can also use the Cloners brushes to restore images.

Margaret Sweeney started both *Night Street* (11.17) and *Night Garden* (11.18) as daylight sketches and converted them into nighttime images using the Apply Lighting command to obtain the overall nighttime tone. The light areas (mostly yellow) were selected, masked, and added separately. Margaret added the trees in *Night Garden* as a pattern and then painted over the pattern.

> **TIP**
>
> You can use the Effects ➢ Tonal Control ➢ Adjust Color command to convert a color image to grayscale. In the Adjust Color dialog box, drag the Saturation slider all the way to the left. By removing all the color saturation, you change it into a grayscale image.

11.16

11.17

Chapter 11 *Enhancing Digital and Painted Images*

Here are the steps Margaret took to create *Night Street*:

1. Margaret scanned a day scene drawing that she had sketched (11.19).
2. She added some canvas area to the left, right, and bottom (Canvas ➢ Canvas Size) of the scanned image.
3. Margaret drew in part of another house on each side with Colored Pens (11.20).
4. Margaret painted over the drawing with the Loaded Oils variant before using the Apply Lighting command.
5. Margaret created a selection of the background and areas of the houses that are in shadow with the Lasso tool (11.21). Margaret said that if she needs to, she corrects her selections by selecting the areas with the Shift key to add to the selection, and with the ⌘/Ctrl key to subtract. Margaret applied a fill (Effects ➢ Fill) at 90% so that she could still see the lines underneath (11.22).

11.19

11.20

11.18

11.21

6. Margaret inverted the selection (Select ➢ Invert) and used the Effects ➢ Surface Control ➢ Apply Lighting command. In the Apply Lighting dialog box, Margaret chose golden yellow and blue colors with side lighting, and changed the position of the "flashlight" (11.23).

7. Margaret completed the image by painting with the Loaded Oils brush variant and Airbrush brushes.

Margaret created *Old Fence* (11.24) from a drawing she sketched of a porch. The rest of the house was added around the porch. Margaret originally created the image in large blocks of flat color, to which she added the texture of the house, fence, and foreground with the Loaded Oils, Sargent, and Palette Knife and dry brushes. She selected the house changes using Effects ➢ Tonal Control ➢ Correct colors with the advanced colors selected. She added blue and decreased reds to give the area a cooler color tone. The area was then inverted, and the opposite color corrections were made to give the area a warmer color tone.

Chelsea Sammel's *Black Lillies* (11.25) is another example of how Painter's tonal controls can be used to alter an image. When creating this image, Chelsea

11.22

11.24

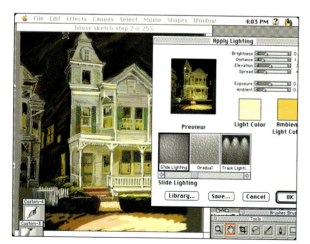

11.23

11.25

Chapter 11   Enhancing Digital and Painted Images   163

used the new Painter 5 Hue Add plug-in brush. To load the Hue Add brush variant, click the Photo icon in the Short Cut to New Brushes palette. (Window ➤ Custom Palette ➤ Shortcut to New Brushes, or choose the Load Library command in the Brushes pop-up menu and choose Load Library.) After selecting Load Library, open the New Brushes folder and choose Photo. Then choose Hue Add in the brush variant pop-up menu.

Black Lilies was based on a photograph Chelsea took of a single lily. She scanned in the photograph and used floaters to Free Transform (Effects ➤ Orientation ➤ Free Transform) and copy the lilies. She also painted in a few that she wanted in specific positions.

Next Chelsea cloned in a photo of some buildings, but they did not show up. To solve this problem, she floated the buildings and used the Dissolve Composite Method and Tonal Controls to make a negative (Effects ➤ Tonal Control ➤ Negative) to add background *noise*. She also found Confusion Brush, the new Painter plug-in, to be helpful in certain areas. She then painted over the image with the Chalk brush and canvas paper grain. Next she painted over everything with the Painter 5 Photo plug-in brushes. She added paint with the Sargeant brush, and then dragged through it all with the Palette Knife. She also used the Hue Add brush, which leaves the range of values intact while changing the hue.

Dan Crowe's *Rabbi* (11.26) is an example of how a real painting can be restored digitally in Painter. Dan started by first scanning an original acrylic painting he created in his youth (11.27) that had lost a lot of color and had some smoke damage. Due to the large size of the original work, Dan had to scan the painting in quarters before it would resemble a whole picture. He then restored the original acrylic by cloning the original image and using the Airbrush and Chalk brushes, as well as Painter's Glass Distortion command (Effects ➤ Focus ➤ Glass Distortion).

11.26

11.27

Dan also created *The Age Of Reason* (11.28) by retouching and combining Kodak Photo CD images (11.29, 11.30).

11.28

11.29

11.30

To create *Tour Poster* (11.31), Dan Crowe took a video grab of the Chinese woman. The earth was a Planet Art CD European poster, which Dan cleaned and retouched with Painter's Airbrush and Chalk brushes and Eyedropper tool. Dan posterized the entire image (Effects ➢ Tonal Control ➢ Posterize) and changed the color using the Effects ➢ Tonal Control commands. He added the type as the finishing touch.

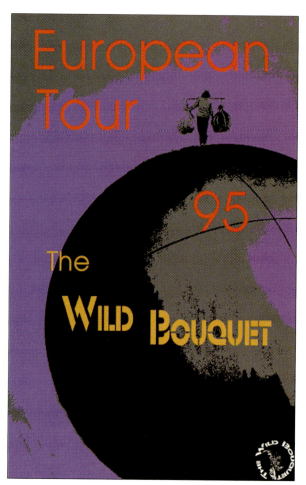

11.31

Chapter 11 Enhancing Digital and Painted Images

In *Deus ex Machina* (11.32), Pat Watson reworked scanned images to achieve the painterly effect he sought. The idea for the image came from a photo montage he created for a show at The Center For Photographic Arts (formerly The Friends of Photography) in Carmel, California. The montage, which used the same concepts as this image, was difficult to produce and contained too much contrast to suit his original visualization. Scanning the original image proved insufficient, so Pat reprinted the original negatives and worked from them.

Reworking scans to get a certain look and feel is an interesting process to Pat. He holds specific expectations for a photographic image, and a different set of expectations for a painterly image. In his experience he found that he can't just color a photograph to get the effect he wants. To get the slightly abstracted effect he's after, Pat frequently requires extensive simplification of the photographic image. For example, in the image the actual dried lake bed was much more detailed than it appears in the final image. Furthermore, the sense of perspective was directly linked to the complicated interlace of the cracks in the mud. After he simplified the cracked patterns, Pat wanted to flatten and dramatize the foreground perspective, in keeping with traditional teachings on compositional devices for drawing and painting. Although he considers these *representative* images, real life doesn't look this way. Pat feels that not only are the symbolic references not possible, but the lake bed, the mountains, and the clouds are not the way they really would be.

11.32

11.33

Pat created *Therapist* (11.33) using the techniques described previously. When Pat works, he either scans photographs he's taken or uses images from old books and magazines—and he means old. Pat goes to old bookstores and finds publications that are at least 40 years old. One reason Pat searches for old materials is that he doesn't ever want his work to look like someone else's montage. Another reason he uses old images is to avoid copyright complications; not because the copyright has expired, but the older images were printed so poorly that he has to redraw them extensively before the resulting image is useful. This solves the copyright problem, because when he's finished, the original isn't discernible from the form he has created in the image. In the end, Pat doesn't mind if it looks like he's drawing from the original (literally and metaphorically). Pat doesn't want his images to look like he's drawing somebody else's image.

John Ennis created *Tall Chief* (11.34) as part of the cover of a romance novel about a native American artist. He created the work in much the same way he used to work in oil. He began by using colored pencils to create a line drawing of the tall chief figure. To help create the image, John imported a photograph and used the tracing paper overlay.

John then applied watercolor washes to establish tonal value and to approximate final color. He used watercolor because it also enabled him to preserve the line drawing at this stage. During this process he used the Small Canvas texture from the More Paper Textures library.

Next he applied the oil paint layer, but he used the Large Chalk brush variant set to Soft Cover to simulate oil. Here he turned off the canvas texture because "real oil paint tends to obscure real canvas as it builds up." Finally, John applied the Adobe Gallery Effects Texturizer (canvas) filter to create the final image.

Chapter 11 Enhancing Digital and Painted Images

11.34

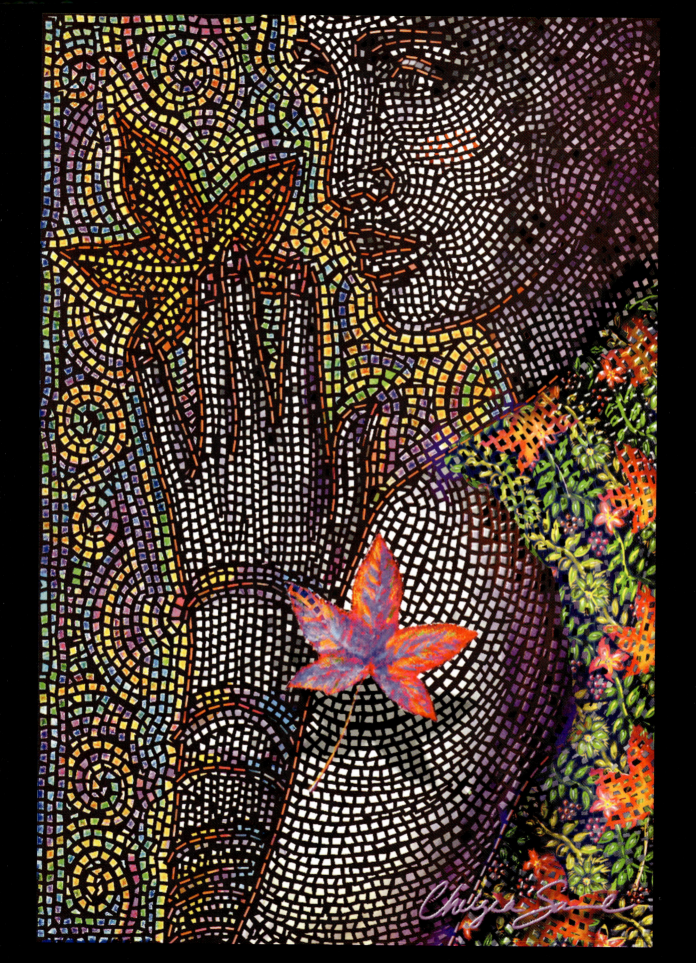

CHAPTER 12
CREATING SPECIAL EFFECTS

Although Painter is billed as a painting program, it could also be sold strictly on its merits as a digital special effects generator. Where else can you turn if you want to transform your image into blobs or pop art, or paint with a brush that sprays out digital images?

As you've seen throughout this book, Painter enables you to distort images, turn them into mosaics, and add depth using the Apply Surface Texture command. You can also easily alter an image to make it look as if it were seen through driving rain or a pane of glass. This chapter takes you on a tour of how artists use special effects to create Painter art. You will see not only how effects such as mosaics and glass distortion can add interest to an image, but also how artists use Painter's new Plugin floaters to enhance their work.

Chelsea Sammel said she has never created a mosaic in the natural medium, and that this is an interesting cause-and-effect situation wherein the computer version has actually inspired her to try creating a mosaic the old-fashioned way.

WORKING WITH GLASS DISTORTION

Chelsea Sammel used Painter's Glass Distortion effect to create most of the unusual textured effects in *Eye* (12.1). To Chelsea, "This image was an experiment with Glass Distortion, based upon suggestions from artist Mark Snoswell." Chelsea had always used the default settings of Glass Distortions, but she found that Mark had been getting completely different results by changing these settings. Chelsea sums up the experience this way: "It was as if we were using two completely different functions—or perhaps the effect was simply inverted because we were on opposite sides of the equator."

12.1

HER MOTHER'S DRESS
Chelsea Sammel

12.2

12.3

12.4 ©1997 Sheriann Ki-Sun Burnham

To create *Eye*, Chelsea started with a photograph of an eye. Based on Mark's instructions, Chelsea added some noise to the image. She did this by using the Effects ➤ Apply Surface Texture command and choosing the Paper Grain option in the Using pop-up menu. Next Chelsea used the Effects ➤ Focus ➤ Glass Distortion command. In the Glass Distortion dialog box, Chelsea changed the Map option to Vector Displacement and increased the Amount and Variance sliders. She also changed Direction but didn't add any Softness. Chelsea discovered that by tweaking all these parameters, Glass Distortion added an almost brush-like quality to the photograph. She is not often attracted to the use of filters over an image, but she found this effect interesting.

Chelsea emphasized the effect by increasing the saturation of the colors with Tonal Controls ➤ Adjust Colors. She then floated the eye over a background of applied paper grains. To create the torn edge effect (she created the image before Painter's Torn Paper plug-in was available), she cut the edges of the floaters with an oval shape and then converted this shape to a selection. She softened the edges and applied a drop shadow. As a finishing touch she slightly emphasized the colors and directions of the Glass Distortion effect by using the small Airbrush and painting in the lines a bit stronger.

Dan Crowe's *Eastside#1* (12.2) is another example of how Glass Distortion can enhance an image. To create *Eastside#1*, Dan scanned a photograph (12.3) and cloned out the cars. He completed the image by applying the Effects ➤ Focus ➤ Glass Distortion command. In the Glass Distortion dialog box, Dan changed the settings as desired to achieve the effect he wanted.

Lagoon (12.4), by Sheriann Ki-Sun Burnham, is another example of Glass Distortion in action. In this image Sheriann used Glass Distortion with the Paper Grain texture throughout this image. Other textures in the image include scanned rice paper and photographs. To create the thin, branch-like shapes, Sheriann scanned a photograph of leaves that she applied to the image with the Apply Surface Texture command.

WORKING WITH APPLY SURFACE TEXTURE

Painter's Apply Surface Texture is one of Painter's most popular effects. Many artists turn to this command to give their images depth or to emboss them. You can use Apply Surface Texture to apply texture to an entire image, or you can use the command to apply surface texture to a floater.

When you use the Apply Surface Texture command, the Using pop-up menu in the Apply Surface Texture dialog box enables you to apply texture to your images based on the current paper texture selected in the Art Materials: Paper palette. If you choose Image Luminance, Surface Texture is applied based upon the brightness values of your image. If you choose Original Luminance, Surface Texture is applied based upon a clone source or the currently selected pattern in the Art Materials: Pattern palette. Choose 3D in the Using pop-up menu, and 3D brush strokes are applied based on the difference between the onscreen image and a clone source.

The images in this section illustrate the many ways the Apply Surface Texture command can be utilized.

Steve Campbell's *Face* (12.5) provides an example of how Apply Surface Texture can be used to create an impasto effect. Steve started by scanning a pencil sketch of the image. He touched up the sketch with brushstrokes within selections. He finished off the image by running the Apply Surface Texture command with the Image Luminance option selected to create the impasto effect. Finally Steve added some lighting within a selection to create depth.

Patrick Lichty created *Texas* (12.6) for the *FringeWare Review* (a magazine devoted to the examination of fringe culture and information age society). The background was originally taken from a texture gallery CD-ROM. Patrick then created a

12.5

12.6

> **TIP**
>
> Painter creates a mask out of text when you turn a shape into a floater. This means you can create texture in an image based on text you've typed onscreen. See Chapter 9 for more details.

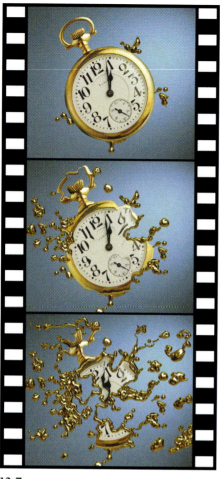

12.7

grayscale paper texture of 1s and 0s by using the Capture Texture command in the Art Materials Paper menu. Next he used the Apply Surface Texture command with the Using pop-up menu set to Paper Texture. The gears are all Kinetics 3D Studio MAX renderings (but they could have been done in MetaCreations RayDream as well). The Glowing and Drop Shadow effects were created with Alien Skin's Black Box filters.

WORKING WITH PLUG-IN FLOATERS

Painter's plug-in floaters enable you to create a variety of special effects. With plug-in floaters you can automatically bevel selections, text, and floaters; you can paint chrome and metal onscreen with Liquid Metal; you can simulate impasto; and you can even turn your images into kaleidoscopic patterns. The

> **NOTE**
>
> Chapter 5 covers the fundamentals of using plug-in floaters in more detail. Turn to Chapter 9 to see how plug-in filters can be used to create text effects.

THE BEGINNINGS

Interview with Mark Zimmer, Chief Technical Officer at MetaCreations, and John Derry, Director Natural Media Research

Q: How did all the special effects in the Effects menu come about, such as mosaics and the plug-ins?

MZ: Each one of these effects came from "idea sessions." Some from Chicago in July 1992; some were even earlier. Marbling was something we thought up in Chicago after visiting the bookstore of the Art Institute of Chicago. The mosaic feature came about in the summer of 1995 while Mark was traveling in Denmark. Most of the code for Mosaic was written in Skagen, at the tip of Jutland.

When an effect was coded, it became the "miracle du jour," and we experimented with it until we felt the effect was honed enough to be usable. Usually the first version of the effect was so byzantine as to be completely impossible to understand.

Q: What happened in Chicago in July 1992 that helped you come up with some of the Effects commands? And what do you mean when you say that some of them came about even earlier? How was Marbling thought up in a visit

Chapter 12 Creating Special Effects

following images illustrate how some professional artists have used plug-in floaters.

Melting Watch (12.7), by the Mark Jenkins/Rucker Design Group, dramatically illustrates the effects the Liquid Metal plug-in floater provides.

Melting Watch began as a watch in a separate floater above the blue background. First Mark created a new layer and applied Liquid Metal from the Objects: Plugin Floaters palette. In the Liquid Metal dialog box, Mark set the reflection map to Standard Metal and painted a few metallic drops around the watch with the brush tool.

For the second frame, Mark copied the art onto a new layer and painted into this layer with the Liquid Distorto brush from the standard Brushes palette. This allowed him to erase and distort the watch floater. Then he applied the Liquid Metal plug-in again and added more metallic drops.

He used the same process once more for the last frame, but this time he completely distorted the watch and painted in generous amounts of Liquid Metal.

Beate Fritsch/Rucker Design Group created *Burning Heart* (12.8) using several plug-in floaters. Beate created the image using three floating layers: one for the inner detail of the heart design, one for the flame edges around the heart, and one for the background. Beate started by painting in the base color of the heart, and then added painterly detail using various natural media brushes. She created the yellow texture with the Impasto plug-in floater. Beate painted into the inner design floater with lighter colors to bring it forward.

To create the background layer, Beate started by filling it with a radial gradation of red to darker red. Then she used the new Painter 5 Fire FX brush, which allows you to "paint with fire." When you paint with this brush, it adds flame-colored yellow shapes to an object. Finally, Beate created the speckled edge by applying the Tear plug-in floater from the Objects: Plugin Floaters palette.

12.8

---

to the bookstore of the Art Institute of Chicago?

MZ: The books *How To Marbleize Paper*, by Gabriele Grunebaum, and *Marbling Paper and Fabric*, by Carol Taylor, were both purchased in that bookstore. These books introduced us to the variety of approaches taken in a very traditional field, and led me to analyze just what happens physically when a dowel or a stylus is dragged through the liquid paint and ink in a tray.

This analysis was not by any means trivial. We also found that the volumes of books that exist that contain techniques for multiple passes in marbling could be encoded into processes and steps inside the computer. We also invented a tremendous number of the steps and processes ourselves.

JD: SIGGRAPH '92 in Chicago was probably the first time Mark and I got to spend some time together after having gotten to know each other (we started working together in April of '92). And, of course, SIGGRAPH is a great place to get inspired about computer graphics.

We had talked about several of the concepts for some of the Effects/tools, but in Chicago we actually formalized the ideas in a notebook.

We happened to see some books on marbling in the bookstore at the Art Institute of Chicago, and that got us to thinking how cool it would be to apply marbling techniques to something like a photograph.

Q: Mark, in regards to the Mosaic feature in Painter, were you inspired by anything in particular in Denmark?

Mark Jenkins/Rucker Design Group created *Wooden Home Button* (12.9) by starting with a button shape and filling it with a wood texture. Applying the Bevel World option in the Plugin Floaters palette, Mark adjusted the bevel and lighting controls until he obtained the effect he was seeking. Afterwards, he added the embossed type to create the final figure.

Mark Jenkins/Rucker Design Group also created *Groovy Back Button* (12.10). Mark first created the psychedelic pattern using the KPT Vortex Tiling filter. He made the button shape into a floater and then applied the Bevel World plug-in. To provide the button with a soft, pillow-like texture, he set the smoothness slider in the Bevel World palette to 100. He later added the embedded type as a separate floating layer.

12.9

12.10

12.11

What was it about Skagen, at the tip of Jutland, that inspired you to write most of the code for Mosaics?

MZ: The fine brickwork and cobblestone work in the streets led me to think about how to simulate that hard work on the computer. The interlaced-arch cobblestone street formation is still unduplicated on the computer. But I also came across some Dutch books on the Byzantine Mosaic work in churches and basilicas in the Mediterranean, which impressed me and led me to do the basic work. These obscure bookstores were in Copenhagen. I didn't actually study it until I had some "quality time" with the computer in Skagen.

The light in Skagen is unusual since it is at the northern tip of Jutland. That also was inspiring.

To create *Skipping Stones* (12.11), Margaret Sweeney turned to the Impasto plug-in floater. She started the image as a quick sketch using oil brush variants and then painted over it with the Impasto plug-in floater. She found that using the Impasto plug-in to create an entire painting was too slow and RAM-intensive. She soon discovered that the best way to work with the plug-in was to create a selection, apply the plug-in, and then paint over the selection. When painting, she used the Extra Art Materials brushes in the folder on the Painter 5 CD-ROM, which she loaded using the Load Library command in the Brush pop-up menu in the Brushes palette. She set the shine and depth low because she didn't want a plastic look. Margaret suggests: "It's interesting to use these brushes with different settings of the regular brushes and with different paper textures selected—it changes the character of the strokes in dramatic ways."

Jeremy Sutton created *Joe Williams* (12.12) with the Impasto plug-in floater. He started by painting the image with Painter's Brush (12.13, 12.14) and then used the Impasto plug-in floater to add texture to the image. Some of his favorite Brush variants include the Cover Brush variant, Coarse Hair variant, Big Dry Ink variant, Digital Sumi variant, and the Camel Hair variant. Jeremy also likes to create different versions of his impasto image and then add a transparent layer set to Difference composite method. (Jeremy recommends a visit to Joe's PixArt Web site at www.ruku.com, as well as a visit to his own Web site at www.portrayals.com).

Chelsea Sammel painted the entire image of *Abstract Background* (12.15) with the New Paint tools. Chelsea said that she finds the New Paint tools to be so expressive that she has found a whole new

12.13

12.14

12.12

series of abstracts that seem to have just flown out of her. "They tend to suggest landscapes, mental or referential, by their very nature."

Chelsea started *Abstract Background* with a warm-up exercise (12.16). She tried all the tools and brushes in Painter until something began to suggest itself to her (12.17). Then Chelsea defined the landscape that was beginning to emerge with the New Paint Tools—specifically the Big Wet Luscious and the Palette Knife.

Next Chelsea selected the entire document by using the Select ➤ All command and created an Impasto plug-in floater from the canvas. Using various Impasto brushes, she added depth while painting with colors in the image (Paint with Depth enabled only). She also added new colors by closing the Impasto options windows, which enabled her to select colors from the image. She finished the image by enabling the Negative Depth Box and disabling Paint with Color options in the Impasto Options dialog box. By closing the Options dialog box, she could then paint with any brush. She used several brush variants to carve out paint from existing brushstrokes and depth.

WORKING WITH MOSAICS

Ever wonder why you're seeing more and more mosaics in commercial art and digital paintings? The simple reason is that everyone seems to be using Painter's amazing Canvas ➤ Make Mosaic command. With Make Mosaic you can fill and stroke a selection with mosaic tiles. You can also fill in mosaic tiles with a clone source. This is quite an effective way of creating a mosaic out of an image.

To create a mosaic out of a clone source, first load the image from which you want to create a mosaic. Choose File ➤ Clone to clone it. Next choose Canvas ➤ Make Mosaic. In the Make Mosaic dialog box, click the Use Tracing Paper option. Before you start to brush in mosaics, click the Clone Color option in the Art Materials: Color palette to select paint with the color of the image.

The following images provide a varied look at how artists are using Painter's Make Mosaic command.

Her Mother's Dress (12.18), by Chelsea Sammel, is one of a series of images Chelsea created after her mother's death. It is also one of her first digital mosaic images and an exploratory one. Chelsea said she has never created a mosaic in the natural medium, and that this is an interesting cause-and-effect situation wherein the computer version has actually inspired her to try creating a mosaic the old-fashioned way.

Chelsea's interest in mosaics started after looking at a book about ancient Pompeii and then looking at some mosaics her grandmother had created. Chelsea found that in many cases the artists started with a sketch of the mosaic, which was done by laying down long, thin tiles to define the compositional areas.

12.15

12.16

12.17

Chelsea did the same. She started outlining her digital mosaics using very thin tiles.

Next Chelsea used black grout and painted with white—she wanted to add color effects afterwards. Later, when she needed to return to work on the image, Chelsea used Painter's Keystroke Settings: Command Option to click a tile and return to the same color and dimensions of the tile previously used.

As she worked, Chelsea used the Darken tiles icon to add shading to the face and body of *Her Mother's Dress*. With the Lighten tiles icon selected, she highlighted areas of the tiles, especially areas of the face and arm where she wanted more dimension. After completing the tiling, she chose the Render Tiles into Mask Layer command.

After closing the Make Mosaic dialog box, she converted the mask into a selection. "Because all of the tiles were individual selections, I was able to do all kinds of interesting functions that work within selections," said Chelsea. For example, she used Cloning to clone a pattern from the patterns library into the tiles on the dress without touching the grout. She also painted with watercolors into the tiles. She used the Simple Water brush and increased the Diffusion (Brush ➢ Controls ➢ Water). She also decreased the Wet Fringe so that it wouldn't interfere visually with the edges of the tiles. Then Chelsea painted with bright colors, alternating between Building up and Abrasive methods for the Simple Water brush. As a final touch, she painted a leaf against another background. She selected it with the Magic Wand, floated it, and then added a drop shadow in an attempt to add more depth to the mosaic.

Gary Clark's *Carver* (12.19) provides another look at integrating Painter's mosaic feature into a painting. Gary used a floater to create the colors in *Carver*, which he created for a literary magazine cover. Gary started by using a digital camera to take a picture of a building. Then he imported the picture into Photoshop and removed the color by converting it to grayscale so that he could apply color to it himself.

In Painter Gary used the Make Mosaic command to apply the mosaic to the image. Next he pasted an image of rust (which he had photographed and scanned) over the mosaic. After the image was pasted, Painter automatically converted it to a floater. Gary used the Pseudocolor Composite Method to blend the mosaic image and the rust floater together.

To produce the duotone version of *Carver* (12.20), Gary imported a grayscale version of the mosaic image into Photoshop. To create the textures in this image, Gary used a grayscale version of clouds that he had photographed.

Stacy A. Hopkins used Painter's mosaic feature to create *Trees* (12.21). Stacy began by importing a digital photograph that he took with a digital camera. He then applied a mosaic to a few branches. To apply a mosaic to the branches, Stacy created a clone of the file and then chose Canvas ➢ Make Mosaic. In the Make Mosaic dialog box, Stacy selected the Tracing Paper option so that he could see the branches as he painted the mosaic into the areas he wanted.

Stacy selected the black background with the Magic Wand and filled it with a gradient. On the back-

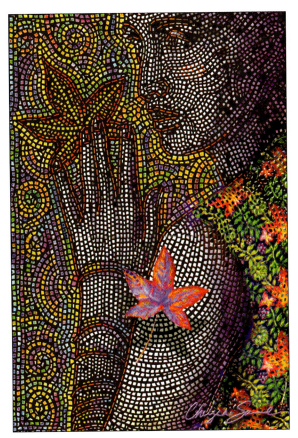

12.18

12.19

12.20

ground he also used the Apply Surface Texture command with the Original Luminance option selected. At the bottom of the image he used the Driving Rain and Chalk Cloners brush variants. Finally, he selected the entire image and stroked it with the Chalk bush. He also applied the Alien Skin Eye Candy (Black Box) filter for the round-edge look.

John Ennis also used Painter's Make Mosaic command to create *Highland Secrets* (12.22), a commissioned book cover, published by Zebra Books.

Kenneth Gore created *Mosaic Tile* (12.23) by scanning a pencil drawing. He then used the Pen tool to create selections, which he filled with mosaics. His last step was to use the Apply Lighting command to create the 3D look.

12.21

Chapter 12   *Creating Special Effects*

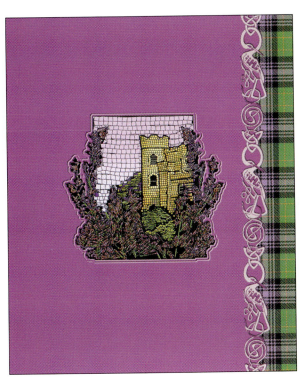

12.22

12.23

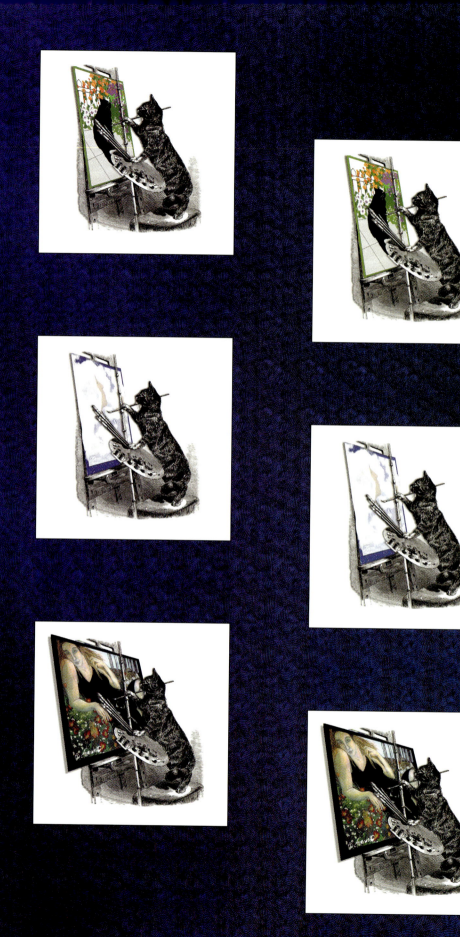

CHAPTER 13
PAINTER, MULTIMEDIA, AND WEB ANIMATION

Painter is one of the few painting programs that not only enables you to create images that can be used on the Web and in multimedia productions, but also allows you to liven up your artwork by turning it into a movie.

Fortunately, you don't need to set up row after row of seats in front of your computer screen. Audiences can view your movies in a multimedia production or on the World Wide Web. Follow along as we take a look at how several professional artists use Painter to enhance their multimedia productions and Web sites. As you read through this chapter, you'll see examples of how Painter can be used to create movies for interactive multimedia productions and how floaters can be used to streamline movie production. If you haven't begun using Painter as a multimedia tool, you'll undoubtedly find this chapter not only instructive but also inspiring.

BANGLES, BUTTONS, AND BACKGROUNDS

What's the most important part of a Web page or multimedia production? To many Painter artists, it's the backgrounds and buttons. Painter's bevy of tools and commands for creating colorful background textures and beveled buttons is seemingly endless. In fact, if you start using Painter for multimedia productions, you'll soon view it as your Home Depot for digital handiwork. Painter's Patterns and Gradations provide a quick start for any background. When you want to add texture, the Apply Surface Texture com-

An artist's Web site isn't some magical path to fame, fortune, and recognition; it is a digital portfolio available worldwide 24 hours a day.

DEBI LEE MANDEL

mand is invaluable. After your backgrounds are completed, beautiful 3D buttons are a few mouse clicks away with Apply Drop Shadow and the Objects: Plug-In Floaters palette's Bevel World.

BUTTONS FROM BEVEL WORLD

We created two buttons for a multimedia production for a New York City slide library company. We created the 3D background area of the buttons by filling a floater with a gradation and then applying Painter's Bevel World plug-in (found in the Objects: Plug-In Floaters palette). After we created the button, we dropped it onto the background canvas by choosing Drop in the Objects: Floater List palette. Then we added the text by typing it in using the Type tool and converting it into a selection by choosing Shapes ➢ Convert to Selection. We dragged the selection over the button and created the 3D effect by applying the Bevel World plug-in. We created two different versions of the text: an outer bevel for the off state of the button (13.1), and the inner bevel for the on state (13.2) of the button. We later saved the images as PICT files so they could be imported into Macromedia Director (Windows users can save in BMP format before importing their files into the Windows version of Director).

13.1

13.2

13.3

CREATING AN INTERFACE

Another example of multimedia work created in Painter is this interactive opener (13.3) from our CD-ROM, *The Ultimate Interactive Guide to Painter 5*. We created the background by painting it with the Brush tool and then applying different Effects commands, particularly Apply Surface Texture. The buttons were created using Adobe Illustrator and Painter Shapes. To give the buttons and text a 3D look, we used Painter's Apply Surface Texture command and the Bevel filter of Alien Skin's Black Box (note that the screen was created before the Bevel World plug-in was available). We then turned to Photoshop for our final production needs. We imported the background, buttons, and text into a Photoshop file—each element was placed into a separate layer so that we could move it or edit it as necessary. Then we converted the Photoshop file to Indexed Color mode so that the image would only contain 256 colors. By reducing the number of colors in the image, we kept the file size of the production small. Additionally, reducing the number of colors helps ensure that virtually any computer user with a color system can view our CD-ROM.

Chet Phillips used Painter to create this elaborate opening screen (13.4), which introduces his portfolio on an interactive CD-ROM. Chet says that "every baby boomer has some memory of the various dashboard play stations that were advertised during Saturday morning cartoons. They let you drive or fly a souped-up car, plane, or rocket and, in some cases, came with a view screen that let you watch a primitive animation while listening to the sound of plastic gears painfully grinding away. My interactive illustration portfolio pays homage to them with a main screen to play, I mean, work with."

After scanning an initial sketch and setting up transparency areas, Chet started blocking in large areas of color by creating masks. He created the gray plastic grill panels by applying various Painter textures with Apply Surface Texture. This helped achieve the raised 3D look. Next he used Painter's Effects ➢ Surface Control ➢ Color Overlay command with textures to fill in the lights; for the two side lights he added a slight glass distortion.

Chet started the steering wheel and side blue panels by creating a mask and then painting with the Airbrush, which was set to the Soft Cover method category. He converted the type to floaters, which enabled him to label buttons. He then used Apply Surface Texture (with the Mask option selected in the Using menu) to bevel the edges. Chet created the inset rocket image separately in Painter as a simple animation and later placed the elements into Macromedia Director. All the buttons either link to another area in the portfolio or play sound clips when pressed.

Doug Lockyer's Invisible Dog Films Web page (13.5) is another example of how Painter can be used to create a multimedia interface. Doug created this highly textured Web page by applying textures in Painter and creating floating, metallic-airbrushed buttons with beveled type over the top. To produce the type and metal panels, Doug created paths in Illustrator and imported them into Painter.

CREATING AND EDITING MOVIES

Painter is one of the few painting programs that enables you to create movies out of digital images. What do you do with a movie you create in Painter? Save it as a QuickTime (Mac) or AVI (Video for Windows) movie. After you create a QuickTime or AVI movie, you can integrate it into a multimedia production. Most multimedia programs, such as Adobe After Affects, Adobe Premiere, and Macromedia Director, allow you to import QuickTime or AVI files. Painter 5 even allows you to output your animation as animated GIF files for the Web.

Making movies in Painter is a simple process: Just create a new file by choosing File ➣ New. In the Picture Type section, choose Movie instead of Image. After you specify how many frames (how many individual images) you want to create in your movie, click OK. After you name your movie, Painter opens up a window that enables you to decide how many colors you want to have in your movie. If you want to turn your movie into an animated GIF file for the Web, be sure to choose the 8-bit color (256 colors) or 8-bit black and white (256 shades of gray) options. (You can reduce the colors even more when you out-

put the movie to animated GIF format). At this point you can also activate Painter's Onion Skin feature. Using this feature enables you to see dimmed previous frames superimposed in the frame in which you're painting. Using the previous frames as a guide can be especially helpful when you need to create fluid, smooth motion in your movies. After you've specified your color and onion skinning choices, Painter opens up a window in which you can paint your movie frame by frame. This makes creating a movie in Painter much like creating a flipbook, which displays animation when you flip through the pages.

In this scene from a Painter movie that appears in our CD-ROM production, "The Ultimate Interactive

13.4

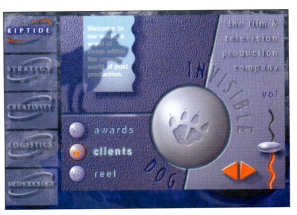

13.5

Guide to Painter 5" (13.6), the movie starts as soon as the user enters the frame. By clicking the knobs on the TV, the user can start and stop the movie. The movie on the TV screen is actually a combination of several QuickTime movies created in Painter. We created the shapes and colors using effects such as Blobs and Marbling. We combined the movies in Adobe Premiere, which we used to edit them together and add transitions and sound. When the editing was complete, we exported the final QuickTime movie into our multimedia production, which was produced in Macromedia Director.

Here's a little known fact: File ➤ Open opens QuickTime or AVI movies directly into Painter. Using this command, you can use Painter to edit QuickTime or AVI movies that have been created in other programs. When you open a QuickTime movie in Painter, each frame of the original QuickTime movie appears as one frame in a Painter frame stack movie. After the movie opens, you can paint and apply Painter effects to the pre-recorded movie.

As an example, we captured some video and edited it into a QuickTime movie using Adobe Premiere. Then we opened the QuickTime movie in Painter. In one of the frames, we created a path with the Pen tool, turned it into a selection, and painted the selection mask using the Image Hose brush. This frame was taken from the QuickTime movie before it was altered in Painter (13.7). The next figure shows the same frame after it was masked and painted over (13.8).

13.6

CREATING WEB ANIMATION

One of the simplest and most entertaining ways to jazz up a Web site is to add a bit of animation. The easiest technique for adding animation is to create an animated GIF movie. Animated GIFs are basically a series of individual GIF files played sequentially to create animation. Many artists began creating animated GIF movies by using GifBuilder, a simple shareware program that enables you to assemble your animation as well as control transparency and speed. Painter not only includes all the features of GIF animation programs, but also allows you to paint and create special effects.

13.7

13.8

TIP

If you want to keep an image onscreen through multiple movie frames, turn it into a floater. As you click from frame to frame, Painter automatically copies the floater into the next frame.

THE ANIMATED CD-ROM

We used Painter's GIF animation feature to produce a glowing CD-ROM graphic for our Web page at `www2/infohouse.com/~addesign` (13.9). We began this simple animation project by creating the CD image in Adobe Illustrator, which we chose because it allowed us to easily create text on a curve. We saved the file in EPS format and then imported the image into Painter. Then we pasted the image into a Painter Frame stack movie and created the animated glow effect by simply running the Effects ➤ Esoterica ➤ Highpass command on each of the frames. To save the image as an animated GIF file, we chose File ➤ Save As. In the Save Movie dialog box we chose the Animated GIF option. In the animated GIF dialog box we specified that we wanted the image to display only 16 colors. We also set the animation to be interlaced, meaning it would gradually appear onscreen as pages downloaded. In the Loop field we specified how many times we wanted the movie to repeat. In the Frame Delay field we entered **25** to have each frame delay a quarter of a second before appearing. (The Frame Delay field pauses your frames in 100ths of a second.)

MAKING CATS PAINT…

Figure 13.10 shows three frames from another animated GIF movie. The images, which appear on Debi Lee Mandel's Web page (`www.catsprite.com`), were created in Painter (13.10). As you might guess from viewing these stills from the animation, when you arrive at Debi's page, you see the cat paint! As Debi created the images, her goal was to showcase several different styles of her work to serve as the front door to her site, a sort of sneak preview. Debi says that the hardest part was making the three varying sizes of the work she selected fit the easel.

Debi started by separating the cat and the bamboo and creating a floater with the easel in the background. Next she imported the three color graphics, slipping them in between the cat and bamboo (each as their own floater). She then sized and distorted the graphics to the proper perspective, and saved each graphic with floaters so that she could import the file into Photoshop and have the floaters appear as layers.

(Debi often relies on Photoshop for quick production, "saving Painter for what it does best—painting!")

In Photoshop Debi created a flattened layer of each of the three paintings, with their own "corresponding" cat and easel, and saved them as separate PICT files. She then opened all three paintings into the same document to create a single, dithered super palette. "This cuts the number of total colors and the size of the final file tremendously!" says Debi. She then used Photoshop's Indexed Color command to convert the color palette of each image to match her dithered super palette. Her final steps were to save the images in GIF file format. To create the animation, she opened the images in GifBuilder (as mentioned earlier, Painter now includes all the features of GifBuilder).

> **TIP**
>
> Because most Web users access the Internet via modems, downloading a large GIF movie with lots of colors could prove interminable to some users. If you want to create animation on the Web, here are a few suggestions: Keep the dimensions small, the length short, and the number of colors to a minimum.

> **TIP**
>
> To have your animated GIF continually repeat, enter **0** in the Loop field.

13.9

13.10A

13.10B

13.10C

...AND MICE JUMP THROUGH HOOPS

Where else but on the Web can you see a mouse jumping through a hoop? Ben Barbante, the technical editor for this book, created this humorous animated GIF (13.11) for his own Web site (http://classroom.cea.edu/benb). This animation appears as the splash screen for his Painter Tips and Tricks session. He created the monotone image to match the overall color scheme of the Web site and also to reduce the file size for quicker downloading.

Ben created the base image by sketching with real paper and pencil. He darkened the lines with a black felt-tip marker and scanned the image. He opened and cropped the picture in Painter and cleaned up the drawing using the Pen brush's Pen & Ink variant. Next he chose Effects ➢ Surface Control ➢ Color Overlay, filled the image with a flat color, and saved the image as a TIFF file named 01.tif.

Ben duplicated the file at the Macintosh finder level by selecting the document's icon and pressing ⌘/Ctrl+d until he had created ten separate files. Then he renamed the documents so they were numbered 01.tif to 10.tif. He numbered the files in this fashion so that he could have Painter load them sequentially as a movie.

In Painter Ben chose File ➢ Open and clicked the Open Numbered Files box. He opened 01.tif when prompted to open the first numbered file. The dialog box then asked him to open the last numbered file, so he opened 10.tif. In the Open As Movie dialog box, he chose three onion skin layers and the 8-bit color system palette as the storage type. The movie opened with 10 identical frames, which he used as the base.

Ben created a floater out of the mouse's body and left out the legs. He pasted the floater into frame 1 and clicked the Frame Foreward button. This dropped a copy of the floater in the frame he was in but kept the floater floating in the same spot when he got to the next frame. To add movement, Ben pressed the arrow keys to nudge the floater one pixel at a time. After repositioning the floater, he clicked the Frame Forward button and then repeated this procedure until he positioned the mouse's body in each of the frames in the animation.

Next Ben added a few special effects to the animation. He returned to frame 1 and edited the floater with the Eraser brush to make the mouse appear to be behind the curtain. With the Pen brush's Pen & Ink variant, he drew in the legs separately in each frame so that the mouse appeared to be running. He painted tiger colors in the frames after the mouse had jumped through the hoop.

Although Painter 5 has the capability to save directly to animated GIFs, Ben wanted to optimize the files so that the overall download size was smaller. He saved the movie as numbered, RGB TIFF files. He used Equilibrium DeBabelizer to change the bit depth to 4-bit (16 colors).

In Painter Ben chose the Rectangular Marquee tool, went into each frame, and selected only the portion of the frame that showed change in the animation. He then noted the exact T (Top) and L (Left) coordinates from the Controls palette. He chose Edit ➢ Copy and then Edit ➢ Paste into new image. He saved each cropped image as a GIF file.

Ben used GifBuilder to build the animated GIF. Then he opened all the GIF files in numerical sequence. He went into each subsequent frame and changed the coordinates of where the top-left corner would appear within each frame by entering the T and L numbers he had noted earlier. In GifBuilder he set the animation to loop six times. Ben says that executing the extra steps in DeBabelizer and GifBuilder was a big savings in file size—45K as compared to 105K, which would have been the file size if he had created the animated GIF from within Painter. Ben notes that 55K is significant when you consider that a 14.4 bps modem can download roughly 1K per second.

13.11A

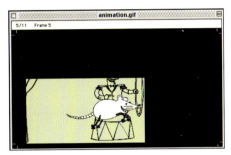

13.11B

13.11C

13.11D

CHAPTER 14
USING PAINTER WITH OTHER PROGRAMS

There's no question that Painter is one of the most powerful and versatile painting and digital imaging programs on the market. But Painter can't do everything.

Often times, artists need to use more than one program to achieve the look they want in their artwork. For example, Painter artists frequently use 3D programs to create perspective and lighting effects instead of spending hours painting them. Some artists use 3D programs such as MetaCreations Ray Dream Designer, Strata StudioPro, and 3D Studio Max to create 3D models, and then use textures created in Painter to apply bumps, cracks, and shadows to the surfaces of their models.

Many artists use Adobe Illustrator with Painter to create their artwork. Artists use Illustrator to create 2D, flat art, and then import the art into Painter using the File ➤ Acquire ➤ Import Illustrator file command. In Painter the artists can use any of Painter's brushes or Effects commands. (Shapes can also be exported to Illustrator.)

A large number of Painter artists also go back and forth between Photoshop and Painter. Painter enables you to save in Photoshop format and can load a Photoshop file. Layers and paths from Photoshop appear as floaters and masks in Painter. Painter floaters and paths also appear in Photoshop. Photoshop is also widely used by Painter artists as a production tool for retouching, color correction, and converting RGB files to CMYK format for printing.

Painter can do a lot of fancy footwork on its own, but as you'll see from the artwork in this chapter, it

I am absolutely fascinated with the Distorto (the Liquid brush). I have found it so helpful for things like ocean and clouds.

JOHN STEPHENS

can also tango, waltz, rumba, and jitterbug with a host of other software partners.

USING PAINTER WITH 3D MODELING PROGRAMS

Painter artists use 3D modeling programs to create intricate 3D images, rendering them with sophisticated lighting effects and textures. Many Painter artists who use 3D programs turn to Painter to create textures that they wrap around their 3D objects; others use programs such as MetaCreations Bryce to create surrealistic terrains and backgrounds. In this section you'll see examples of how Painter artists use a variety of 3D programs, including MetaCreations Poser, which allows you to quickly create three-dimensional human figures.

NOVARIS IV
George Krauter

CREATING DAY DREAM CHARLIE

Artist Doug Lockyer used 3D programs such as Strata StudioPro, Bryce, and MetaCreations RayDream Designer, as well as Live Picture, to help create *Day Dream Charlie* (14.1), which won the Fractal Design Painter competition in 1996. Creating this elaborate and humorous image took Doug over one month of steady work. Here are the basic steps he took to create the image:

1. Doug started by creating a highly detailed composite drawing, which he later scanned in as several different pieces.

2. Doug separated each character and created the leaves and background components using Painter's Airbrush, different Chalk and Water Color brush variants, and Pencil brush variants.

3. Doug created a repeat pattern for the fern leaves from one frond, which he duplicated and stretched, duplicated and stretched, and so on.

4. Using a combination of Strata StudioPro, MetaCreations Bryce, and RayDream Designer, Doug created the marble pillars and curving fern fronds and generated a fractal landscape for the background mountain range. Some of the faces of the characters with spherical faces were also generated in these 3D programs.

5. While working on the image, Doug created a hairline fine-felt tip brush variant. Doug calls this particular variant "most useful and unique." Doug says the variant "tapered beautifully." Using this variant, he drew onscreen quickly in Soft and Hard Cover mode. He used this custom brush to paint the hair, butterfly wings, and feathers. Doug painstakingly painted every animal hair by hair. He painted the hair with a dark neutral blocked-in base layer and built up dark to light, with extra depth and shading supplied by low opacity Airbrush strokes in Buildup and Cover mode. To add texture to the clothing, Doug scanned real fabric and used it as a clone source.

6. Doug created the snake, a fifty-layer piece of composited 3D modeling. Doug created the scale pattern in Painter using the tiling function. The patches of snake skin were wrapped around donuts, cylinders, and spheres, and then cloned together in Live Picture.

7. Doug created the shadows as separately drawn elements. He created them by cloning the characters in Painter and erasing them. He then used Tracing Paper to view a 50 percent transparent image that he used as a template. By blocking in a shadow region, selecting it with the Magic Wand,

14.1

Chapter 14 Using Painter with Other Programs

and then shading and fading it from dark umber to white, he created a shadow layer for each character. He then saved these shadows as separate files to paste into the Live Picture composite with varying degrees of opacity.

8. When compositing all the characters, leaves, twigs, and background elements, Doug *simply* brought the characters and their shadows in separately, scaled them, and retouched the fine hair areas by brushing and cloning in Live Picture. (This is what Doug means by *simply*: "The process involved over a gigabyte of separate files, and three Live Picture 'Fits' documents of 50 odd layers each, composited together for a final 800 dpi TIFF file that measured 19 in. × 12¼ in. and took up 568MB!")

9. Next Doug chopped the TIFF file into equal manageable rectangles. He then retouched them in Painter so that the overlapping hairs blended perfectly with the background.

10. Finally, Doug "laboriously pieced the file together again, waiting up to 40 minutes for screen redraws. I read several books and studied two computer program manuals during the pasting process!"

BLOCKS OF PRODUCTS

James Dowlen created *BLOCKSA* (14.2) using Painter and Crystal Topaz, a 3D program. The image was created for Hewlett Packard.

James says that a large part of the project was brainstorming with the project directors at Hewlett Packard before generating many thumbnail sketches and agreeing on an effective concept for the illustration. The idea here was to express the expandability, versatility, and upgradability of their test instrument. James created models of the instrument and building blocks in Crystal Topaz. When creating the models, James placed them exactly, with the precise perspective to match the lines of the instrument photo. Then on separate square canvasses in Painter, he created the letters and symbols for the blocks, and then added drop shadows to give a little dimension. By copying the image to the clipboard, James could then paste it into the final image canvas. Next he chose

Effects ➢ Orientation ➢ Distort so he could pull the square-shaped floater into position and add the proper perspective to make it become part of the blocks. James painted the hand with the Airbrush using his own hand as a model.

GLOWING BUDDHAS

Patrick Lichty created *Glowing Buddhas* (14.3) in 3D Studio MAX from a Viewpoint Datalabs mesh (a wireframe model) using a texture map he created in Painter.

To create the texture map, Patrick successively built up Pastel and Large Chalks using metallic colors. He intensified the metallic effect by using Painter's Apply Surface Texture command with the Image Luminance option chosen in the Using pop-up menu.

Patrick rendered the Buddha in 3D Studio Max and imported it into Painter. He masked out the surrounding black using the Lasso tool. Then he used Alien Skin's Black Box filters to create the

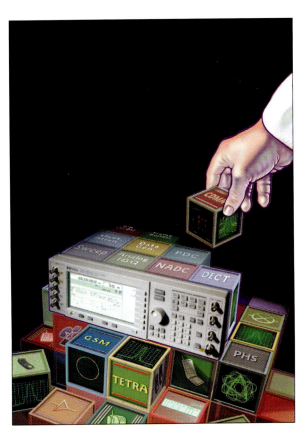

14.2

glow, "but this could be as easily done through the new Glow Brush." He created the background using MetaCreations Bryce.

Patrick applied a glow and a bevel to the hand, which was taken from the MetaCreations Synergy Quilt. He then assigned it as its own floater. Patrick feels that the radiating burst from the hand is one of the most interesting parts of the image. He created a floater that filled the entire screen and colored it white. He then used successive applications of KPT Gradient Designer 3 to create rays, and applied the same gradient in Darken Only Mode to create the interference pattern. Next he applied a slight Lens Flare in Photoshop.

ROBOT + PICASSO = ROBOCASSO

Stacy A. Hopkins created *Robocasso* (14.4) using both Painter and Strata StudioPro, a 3D modeling, rendering, and animation program.

Stacy painted the model using the Sharp Chalk brush variant. As he worked, he used the selection tools and filled selections with color. The paintings leaning against the wall are just something that Stacy had "hanging around" on his hard disk. Stacy built the elements and rendered them in Strata StudioPro. He then loaded the image into Painter, where he created the word *Robocasso* at the bottom using the Type tool. Stacy turned the type into a selection and filled it with a gradient. He then used Painter's Apply Surface Texture command with the Image Luminance option selected. He enhanced the 3D effect by dragging the Apply Surface Texture's Softness slider to the right.

THE BIKER

Stacy A. Hopkins created *The Biker* (14.5) using the 3 P's: Painter, Photoshop, and Poser.

Stacy started by creating the human figure in Poser and then imported it into Painter. Using Painter's Selection tool, he selected an area and filled it with a gradient using Effects ➤ Fill. He then used the Airbrush and Pencil brushes and the Water brush's Just Add Water brush variant to *work in* that selection. Next Stacy selected another area next to the previously selected one and worked on it. Stacy followed the shape of the face or body to make the selections. A selection may have been one eye or half of the nose down to the corner of the mouth over to the cheek bone. He then used Apply Surface Texture with the Paper Texture option to add texture to the skin. He created the leather

14.3

14.4

14.5

vest in much the same way, except he used Effects ➤ Tonal Control ➤ Brightness/Contrast to obtain the shine of the black leather. The design on the vest is a paper grain. To obtain the desired effect on the vest, Stacy applied Painter's Edit ➤ Fade command. Stacy finished the image in Photoshop, where he created the background and pieced the image together.

FLOWER SELLER

Margaret Sweeney used Poser to help create *Flower Seller* (14.6), which she created after a trip to Savannah, Georgia. She created the woman in Poser and imported the image into Painter. She created the stone from paper textures and different brushes.

SPIRIT OF 'INDE'PENDENCE

Chet Phillips created the *Spirit of 'Inde'pendence* (14.7) for the *Dallas Morning News* for its annual Oscars spread.

To create the image, Chet used Painter and Poser. He arranged figures and added drums in Poser 2. He imported these figures into Painter and reworked the details with Painter's Airbrush and Water brushes. In general, Chet created masks from the base, film sections, and figures in the background, and he painted with the Airbrush tool.

USING PAINTER WITH ILLUSTRATOR AND FREEHAND

Long before MetaCreations added its Shapes feature to Painter, many artists created their digital drawings in Adobe Illustrator and Macromedia FreeHand. Both programs are so packed with features that many Painter artists who use Shapes still keep Illustrator or FreeHand handy.

A NEW LOOK AT LAKE TAHOE

Pat Watson's *Philosopher* (14.8) is an example of an image created using both Adobe Illustrator and Painter.

Pat wanted to do something different, with Lake Tahoe as his subject matter. He began considering how he could combine Lake Tahoe with an unusual rocking stone in Truckee, California, that somebody put a shrine over. Pat originally considered putting the shrine/rock in the water. But after looking through different images in his collection, Pat found a scaffold

14.6

14.7

image he had created in Adobe Illustrator for a previous project. The board scaffold holding up this giant boulder with a shrine on top seemed like a good idea.

Pat believes that scans of photos rarely translate into good-looking painterly images. Therefore, he reworked a scan of water to obtain a convincing look, which entailed darkening up some areas to produce a more convincing shadow in the troughs of the wavelets, and then adding a soft highlight at the top. Pat used the Airbrush to add the color and Painter's Smeary Mover brush variant to push the color, which he feels usually makes a great wave effect. Next Pat used the Just Add Water variant to smooth out the image area. He didn't like the highlights, even though they made the water look more realistic, so he softened them up substantially using the Straight Cloner (cloned from the original image) variant. Because the boards were built in Illustrator, they didn't have any shadows, so Pat had to imagine the direction of the sun and add the shadows. After working on the image, he felt that the background didn't look the way he wanted, so he used hills from another photo and repainted them to match. The original shrine image had the shadow facing in the wrong direction. To obtain a convincing shadow, Pat drew straight lines a shade lighter on one side of the column and a shade darker on the backside. He then used Just Add Water to smear the lines and soften them up.

14.8

14.9 ©1997 Rodney A. Greenblat/Interlink/Sony Creative Products

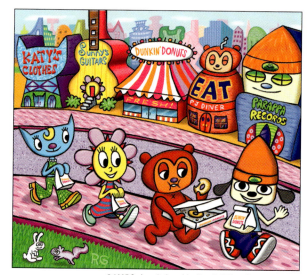

14.10 ©1997 Rodney A. Greenblat/Interlink/Sony Creative Products

Chapter 14 Using Painter with Other Programs

RODNEY'S JAPANESE PLAYMATES

In the United States, artist Rodney Alan Greenblat is primarily known for his children's books and "Dazzeloids," a whimsically entertaining interactive CD-ROM. In Japan Rodney is famous for a series of cartoon characters that appear in Sony's Playstation games.

Rodney's *The Secret Donut Protector* (14.9) and *Donut Town* (14.10) were featured on a tin lunchbox promotional premium given away at Dunkin' Donuts in Japan. It features characters from the Sony Playstation game "Parappa the Rapper."

Rodney created *InfoDog with Email* (14.11) and *InfoDog Underwater* (14.12) as covers for a quarterly brochure for InfoWeb, Fujitsu's online service.

To create these images, Rodney first sketched them out on paper and scanned them. Next he traced the images in Macromedia FreeHand. After the images were sketched, he saved them in EPS format and loaded them into Painter. Generally, Rodney works by filling the characters using the Paint Bucket. Afterwards he uses the Pencil and Charcoal brushes to fine tune the images and enhance details.

14.11   ©1997 Rodney A. Greenblat/Interlink

14.12   ©1997 Rodney A. Greenblat/Interlink

USING PAINTER WITH PHOTOSHOP

What computer program would you choose if you were stranded on a desert isle? Most of the artists featured in this book would choose Painter as their top choice. Undoubtedly, their second choice would be Adobe Photoshop. Even though Painter usually surpasses Photoshop when it comes to creating stunning painterly effects, Photoshop leaps ahead of Painter at many production tasks. For example, artists who need to convert RGB images to CMYK and edit and color correct their images frequently turn to Photoshop. Making a selection in a layer is a simple matter in Photoshop, but try making a selection in a floater and see what gets selected. The examples in this section provide only a small sampling of how artists combine Painter and Photoshop to create great art.

WOMAN, SHIP & PEARLS

John Stephens created *Woman, Ship & Pearls* (14.13) using Painter and Photoshop. He scanned a pearl into Photoshop and then duplicated it to create the string of pearls. To create the ocean and clouds, John used Painter's Liquid Distorto brush variant. To create the woman, he used both Painter and Photoshop. The woman's dress was painted using the Distorto brush variant. John created the ship using RayDream Designer. He then imported it into Photoshop, where he tweaked it to his liking.

A SOFTWARE PACKAGE COVER

Anton Atzenhofer created *Copy* (14.14) for a cover of a software package that copies computer files.

Anton began by scanning an original drawing that he created. In Painter he worked with the Felt Pens, Airbrush, and Pencil. His next step in Painter was to paint with the Hairy brush variant, Charcoal, and Airbrush.

In Photoshop Anton enhanced the color and brightness correction using the Levels command. He

14.13

14.14

14.15

also created a radial blur with a 50 percent mask over the complete picture. (Although this step was completed in Photoshop, Anton sometimes does this type of work in Painter.)

THE BUDDY SYSTEM

Steve Campbell created *Buddy System* (14.15) by scanning a pencil sketch he had created. In the scanned image, he made selections. He filled the selections with color and applied textures and lighting. To complete the image he applied several Photoshop filters.

USING PAINTER WITH MULTIPLE PROGRAMS

Digital art sometimes requires the artist to dip in and out of many different programs. For example, in a complicated project it may be necessary to create textures in Painter and two-dimensional images in Adobe Illustrator. Next, these images might be imported into a 3D program. The illustrations are extruded into 3D models, and the textures are mapped onto the final 3D image. The last step might be to combine all the images in Photoshop and apply the final color correction.

KIDSTUFF

Doug Lockyer created *Tilt 'n' Tumble* (14.16) and *Tri-Ominos for Kids* (14.17) using Painter, Photoshop, and MetaCreations RayDream Designer. Doug recalls that producing these images involved creating "masks, masks, and more masks." Using floaters and layers that he imported and exported between Painter and Photoshop, Doug created the three-dimensional look for the people and animals. He applied subtle texturing with squiggles, circles, and cross-hatches. He then produced the final images by rendering them in RayDream Designer.

14.16

14.17

14.18

14.19

BENEVOLENCE AND PROPHECY

Debi Lee Mandel used a combination of Adobe Illustrator, Adobe Photoshop, Painter, and occasionally even KidPix (to create roughs and textures) to create *benevolence* (14.18) and *prophecy* (14.19). She created *benevolence* for Dai Nippon (Japan) for its 1996 digital art calendar. (Dai Nippon is one of the world's largest printer and print supply companies. The calendar was published as a promotional piece for its products and services.)

When Debi works, she chooses an application based upon what she wants to create at the time. As a natural media painter, Debi always works in mixed media— water-based crayon, oil pastels, polymer paints, and graphite. When she paints digitally, she uses the best tool for different functions within the same piece. She relies heavily on Painter for paper texture and *after-the-fact* surface texture for gaining the effects of natural media, like a stroke that sits *on top* of a rough substrate. Debbie *builds her substrate* (she likens this to gessoing and sanding a canvas, and so on), paints, and draws in Painter. She also draws and manipulates (and sometimes paints) in Photoshop and creates text and graphical elements in Illustrator.

When creating *benevolence*, Debi primarily used Photoshop. However, for added elegance she painted the swan and its reflection on the water surface in Painter from scratch. She imported the image into Photoshop and skewed it to suggest the motion of the swan. To blend it in with underlying layers, she used the Photoshop Multiply blending mode at 55 percent opacity.

THE AGE OF AQUARIUS

Ben Barbante, art director at *InfoWorld* magazine, created *Aquarius* (14.20) using Painter, KPT Bryce, Adobe Illustrator, and Adobe Dimensions. Ben created the image as a self-promotion piece that he wanted to output on a 35mm digital film recorder. He called a service bureau to obtain the proper dimensions (always a good idea when outputting to a film recorder)— height: 2048 pixels; resolution: 1365 pixels, 72 pixels per inch.

Ben used KPT Bryce, a 3D terrain-building program, to create the sky, the plateau in the background, and the rippled water surface. He used

Adobe Illustrator to create the designs on the vase and to fine tune art created in Dimensions. Ben turned to Adobe Dimensions to create the vase. In Painter he painted the dolphins and added the finishing touches, such as the shading and highlights, to the vase. He also used Painter to manipulate the photo of the desert floor as well as to composite the water surface with the desert floor to achieve translucency. Ben also used Painter as his final compositing area, where he experimented with the sizes and positions of floaters for all the elements.

14.21

DOG DAYS

Anton Atzenhofer created *Dog* (14.21) using Adobe Photoshop, Adobe Streamline, Macromedia FreeHand, and Painter. He started by creating a black-and-white ink drawing (14.22), which he converted to a path object with Adobe Streamline (Anton wanted the clear lines of a vector illustration). Then he colored the drawing in Macromedia FreeHand. He used Painter's floaters (if you ever use the German version of Painter, Anton tells us that *Schwebebereich* is the German word for a floater) to create the background and add some brush effects to make the image a bit more friendly.

14.22

14.20

UNICORN GIRL

John Ennis created *Unicorn Girl* (14.23) using KPT Bryce, Photoshop, and Painter. The image was created for the cover of a book published by Harper Collins.

LOOKING FOR AMERICA

Gary Clark created *Gone off to Look for America* (14.24) with the help of Photoshop, KPT Bryce, and Painter. Gary started with a picture of a statue, which he had taken with a digital camera. He loaded this image into Photoshop, masked it, made an alpha channel out of the mask, and saved the image as a PICT file. Next he created the background with MetaCreations KPT Bryce. Even the reflection of the statue and the beam of light over the statue was created in Bryce. He imported the entire image into Painter, where he pasted in the telescope. To enhance the telescope, he used the Dodge and Burn brushes.

OTHER WORLDS

If you venture into the world of science fiction, you're likely to come across the fantastic artwork of San Francisco artist George Krauter. George created *Finder's Fee* (14.25) for the April cover of *Analog*

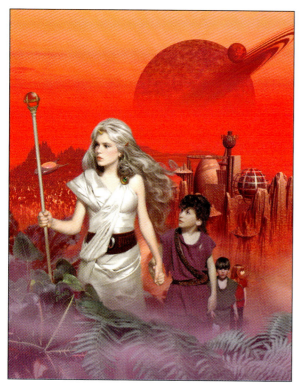

14.23

14.24

14.25

Science Fiction and Fact magazine. He created *Novaris IV* (14.26) for the September cover of *Science Fiction Age*.

To create both images, George used Painter, Macromedia Extreme 3D, Adobe Photoshop, and Adobe Illustrator. George likes to use Painter as his creation tool for texture maps for his 3D work. All the textures in these two images were created in Painter. Textures maps are applied to 3D models to create the texture wrapped around the 3D objects.

In *Finder's Fee*, George used Painter textures to create the bumps (the *rot*) that can be found on the cactus plants. The stone-looking bumpiness on the domed buildings was also created in Painter.

George also occasionally uses Painter to composite his images. The butterfly and flower in the foreground of *Finder's Fee* were traced from a scanned pencil drawing (14.27) in Adobe Illustrator. George turned the finished Illustrator EPS art into a floater in Painter and modified it with painting tools. George used the Camel Hair Brush, Sable, Dry, Coarse Hairs, and other brush variants to flesh out the butterfly and the flowers' petals. George also created the people in the image by painting over a hand drawing in Painter. The butterfly's wings were modeled in Extreme 3D, but their texture map was created in Painter. The rendered wings were also brought into Painter as a floater. George also used the Image Hose brush to make the pollen-bearing part of the flowers. When George was satisfied with the whole image, he opened it in Photoshop and added some noise to touch up the image.

14.27

14.26

CHAPTER 15
PAINTER GALLERY

T his chapter is composed of a variety of eye-catching Painter images selected specifically for your viewing pleasure. We hope you enjoy your gallery tour.

SUN MULE, Doug Lockyer
Doug Lockyer created this image for Sun Systems. The illustration is a rough charcoal and pastel sketch over purple paper.

FAMILY
Ayse Ulay

ÆGYPT, Steve Campbell
This illustration by Steve Campbell is an award-winning entry in Fractal Design's (now MetaCreations) annual Painter art contest. The image was collaged together from scans of several sketches.

THE BEGINNINGS

Interview with Mark Zimmer, Chief Technical Officer at MetaCreations

Q: Where does the inspiration for new features come from?

MZ: Where else? To be creative, you have to be open to new concepts. You have to become familiar with lots of new things. But actually going to see lots of traditional art helped, too.

Q: Any insights, tips, techniques, or undocumented information?

MZ: Check out the new masking in Painter 5. It seems different at first, but once you get the hang of it, it's pretty easy. In a lot of cases, it's much easier.

Q: What does the future hold for Painter?

MZ: The magic of dynamic plug-in floaters has me interested in creating more.

I've got some more projects, which will probably turn into new plug-ins. I'm sure more plug-in brushes are on the way as well.

Chapter 15 Painter Gallery

PARAPPA CD COVER, Rodney A. Greenblatt
Rodney A. Greenblat created this illustration for the Playstation game "Parappa the Rapper," published by Sony Computer Entertainment. The game features artwork and characters designed by Rodney. ©1997 Rodney A. Greenblat/Interlink/Sony Computer Entertainment.

SILICON GAMING FACE, Corinne Okada
Corinne Okada created this image for Silicon Gaming in Palo Alto, CA. The project entailed creating illustrations of face cards and card backs for a digital card game. Software is to be installed in Silicon Gaming machines, which will be played in Las Vegas casinos. The client wanted all the royals to look as if they were characters from 1920s traveling magician shows. To create the images, Corinne used Adobe Illustrator, Adobe Photoshop, and Painter. William Scott was the Art Director for this project.

BEATLES, Susan LeVan
Susan LeVan had fun creating this image for Spread Live! magazine. Susan used textured, Chalk Pastel variants to create the image.

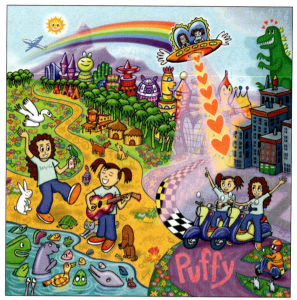

PUFFY SAVES THE WORLD, Rodney A. Greenblatt
This image of Rodney's was designed as cover art for two CD singles for the hit Japanese pop group "Puffy." The image was divided in half and used for two covers. When the cover is closed, the two images appear as one. ©1997 Rodney A. Greenblatt/Interlink/Sony Computer Entertainment.

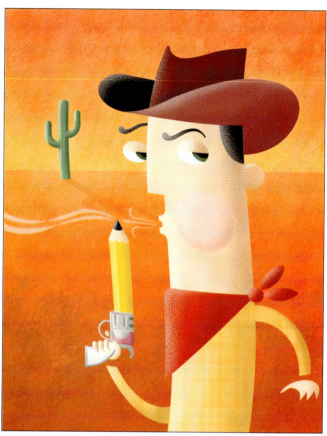

COWBOY, Ben Barbante
Ben Barbante created this image as a self-promotion. It appears on his Web site.

PARAPPA PLAYSTATION RIDE, Rodney A. Greenblatt
Rodney created this illustration as cover art for an inhouse corporate magazine called Sony Family, *distributed by Sony, Japan. ©1997 Rodney A. Greenblatt/Interlink/Sony Computer Entertainment.*

CYBERVICE, Ben Barbante
This is another image from Ben Barbante's Web site. Looks dangerous, huh?

Chapter 15 *Painter Gallery*

SUMMER SOLSTICE, Ayse Ulay
Ayse Ulay created this image as a poster and T-shirt illustration for Santa Barbara, CA, to celebrate events held in the city every year.

FAMILY, Ayse Ulay
Ayse Ulay created this piece as cover artwork for a water quality annual report for the city of Santa Monica's Environmental Programs Division.

SUSTAINABLE CITY, Ayse Ulay
Ayse Ulay created this illustration for the city of Santa Monica's Environmental Programs Division for an annual report on Sustainable City Programs.

FRENCH BOOKSTORE, Chelsea Sammel
The inspiration to create this image came to artist Chelsea Sammel at MacExpo Paris while working with what was then Fractal Design. Chelsea says she made sure to correct the mistakes she made on an earlier trip—she brought her sketchpad, and arranged time off at the end of the show. She walked all day through Paris and says, "It was the best day," as she made small sketches all the way. She had planned to do a series of Paris paintings when she returned to the United States, but due to a lack of time she compiled one image from several sketches. Chelsea says that by the time she began, she couldn't remember many of the colors, so she painted with exaggerated colors. Chelsea painted with the Colored Pencils brush variant and the Water Color brush. She added thin Chalk strokes over all, and a light surface texture to finish.

HEART AND HAND, Chelsea Sammel
Chelsea Sammel always paints one image for herself every year. **Heart and Hand** *was just such an image. She created it for a personal holiday card at the end of the year. She wanted to paint something showing a diversity of elements making up one human hand to portray a holiday message of togetherness and humanity. She created a selection for the hand first because she wanted to be able to recognize or ignore it at will. She did the same for the heart and then painted with the selections alternately active and dormant. She used the Pens Scratchboard tool, Chalk brush variants, and the Brush Big Wet Ink variant. Chelsea notes that "The computer changes your work style in so many subtle ways. For example, on a canvas I would have used a lighter hue of each paint color inside the hand. Here I painted the entire image, then used the selection to lighten the hand to visually separate it from the background."*

Chapter 15 Painter Gallery

LA, Patrick Lichty

This image is based on an image of Patrick's fiancee when she had posed with him on a holiday several years ago. In this image Patrick wanted to capture her firey spirit and dynamic nature. The photo itself was not used directly in any way; the image is a freehand painting.

The secret to this painting is the layering. First Patrick fleshed out the image using the Chalk tools, using mainly maroons and blacks. The gray shoulder was also sketched in. To create the swirling effects in the upper-right-hand corner, Patrick used a custom variant of the Liquid Distorto variant to manipulate the texture.

The facial curve, nose, and hair were created in a similar fashion, with only minor differences. Patrick masked out an area and then painted into it. In the facial curve, white chalks were applied, followed by an application of the Leaky Pen variant. The nose was created using the Chalks and Water Color brushes, and a faint texturing was applied using Kai's Power Tools version 2 Texture Explorer. The hair was slightly different. It consists of Oils and Chalk and was manipulated with the Distorto variant, and then was embellished with the Leaky Pen.

THE BLINDING LIGHT OF TRUTH, Patrick Lichty

The Blinding Light of Truth started with a light bulb Patrick had worked with in 3D Studio (but he says it could have just as easily been RayDream). The image had a lot of detail but lacked reflections on the glass as well as a background. To make the background, Patrick created a texture using Kai's Power Tools version 2 (which he still uses along with version 3). Next he used Effects ➢ Surface Control ➢ Apply Surface Texture with Painter's rag cotton and text paper textures.

Patrick used Kai's Power Tools version 2 to create the burnt and "brooding" look of the background. He used a series of radial Gradient Designer fills, using different modes such as Difference and Procedural, which give unexpected effects. Then Patrick used KPT's Gradient Designer in a radial mode, but mainly with Lighten Only effects to create the rays. At this time the image was brought in to Painter and resized by creating a reference floater and resizing it accordingly. The image was converted to a normal floater again, and the background was carefully removed using the Lasso tool. Now that Patrick had the background, he needed to make the bulb pop off the page. In this case he used the Airbrush variants along with a little Chalk for simple retouches. Reflections were sketched in and fleshed out, and Patrick used the Thin Airbrush variant to elongate the rays and add lens flares on the bulb.

Jay Paul Bell, a professor at the School of Art at Northern Illinois University, had his students use Painter to create their final projects. Here are a few of the images his students created.

BRADY BILL, Dennis Johnson

CYBORG, Fred R. Hopper

THE LOOK OF HER, Randy A. Halverson

Chapter 15 Painter Gallery

SLEDDING, Tina M. Kotlarz

IMAGINE, Karen M. Schuler

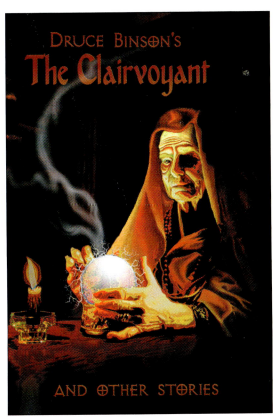

THE CLAIRVOYANT, Charles Rosenberg

UN MONDE UNIS, Debi Lee Mandel
Debi Lee Mandel created this image for Quarterdeck as a graphic for its original "Friendly Channel" banner.

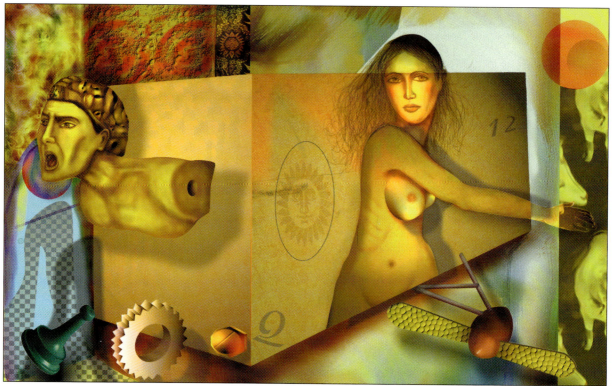

DESPERADO, Adam Sadigursky
To create this image, Adam Sadigursky used a combination of shapes, floaters, brushes, textures, and lighting.

EYE, Anton Atzenhofer

Anton says that he basically uses two techniques to create images in Painter. One technique is to draw with pen and ink and then create the basic colors with Aquarell brushes before he scans in the image. Otherwise (as he did in creating Eye), Anton first creates a pencil drawing with outlines (some are not completely overpainted and visible like those in the upper-right area). Then he scans the drawing and modifies it.

When modifying the image, Anton adjusts the contrast, making the gray pencil areas a little bit darker, and eliminating the light grays. Then he fills most parts of the picture (in this image, everything except the face) with big Water Color brushes for a basic background-coloring. The same technique is used for many of the other parts. Anton uses a basic color and then highlights it with a different color to obtain more color complexity in big areas. Anton says that this technique makes the color more lively.

Chapter 15 Painter Gallery

NORTH, Anton Atzenhofer

CLEARING, Dennis Orlando

ISLAND VIEW, Dennis Orlando
For information on Dennis Orlando's techniques, see Chapter 8.

LENGTHY CONSIDERATION, Pat Watson

TRANSITIONAL THOUGHT, Pat Watson
For information on Pat Watson's techniques, see Chapters 9, 11, and 14.

OYSTER BAY, Margaret Sweeney
Margaret Sweeney created "Burning Leaves," "Sketchers," and "Oyster Bay" using Painter 5. Margaret starts most of her images as rough sketches on screen, occasionally from sketches made while traveling. Margaret sometimes creates images using Illustrator and then imports them into Painter. In Painter she uses a variety of brushes and often paints using custom paper textures.

SKETCHERS, Margaret Sweeney

BURNING LEAVES, Margaret Sweeney

Chapter 15 Painter Gallery

AH, Hiroshi Yoshii
Hiroshi Yoshii is an award-winning Japanese artist whose Painter work is both colorful and whimsical. To create his images, Hiroshi sketches in Painter with the Pencil and Eraser. Hiroshi says that he rarely uses a real pencil and paper except for "idea" sketches. He primarily uses Painter's Chalk and Airbrush. Here are a few of Hiroshi's images; many have appeared in Japanese magazines. Blue Flower Face and Tree of Bird are original works of art that Hiroshi created for his own pleasure.

Ah appeared in Health & Life *magazine, Houken.*

BLACK NOSE, Hiroshi Yoshii
This illustration is a T-shirt design for a sales promotion for Macworld Japan, Macworld Communications Japan.

BLUE FLOWER FACE, Hiroshi Yoshii

CRAB, Hiroshi Yoshii
This image appeared in The Basic *magazine, Gijutuhyoron-sha.*

FLYING ROBOT, Hiroshi Yoshii
Hirsohi created this image as the cover illustration for an issue of NEXT Vision *magazine.*

SHELF, Hiroshi Yoshii
Shelf was used as the cover illustration for an issue of Internet Surfer *magazine.*

NEAR FUTURE OF AKIHABARA, Hiroshi Yoshii
This illustration appeared in Mac Fan Beginners *magazine, Mainichi Communications.*

Chapter 15   Painter Gallery 217

TWINS, Hiroshi Yoshii
Twins *appeared in* The Basic *magazine, Gijutuhyoron-sha.*

TREE OF BIRD, Hiroshi Yoshii

THE MOON & THE EARTH, Hiroshi Yoshii
The Moon & The Earth *was used as a magazine illustration in* HEART BEAT *magazine, Japan Telecom.*

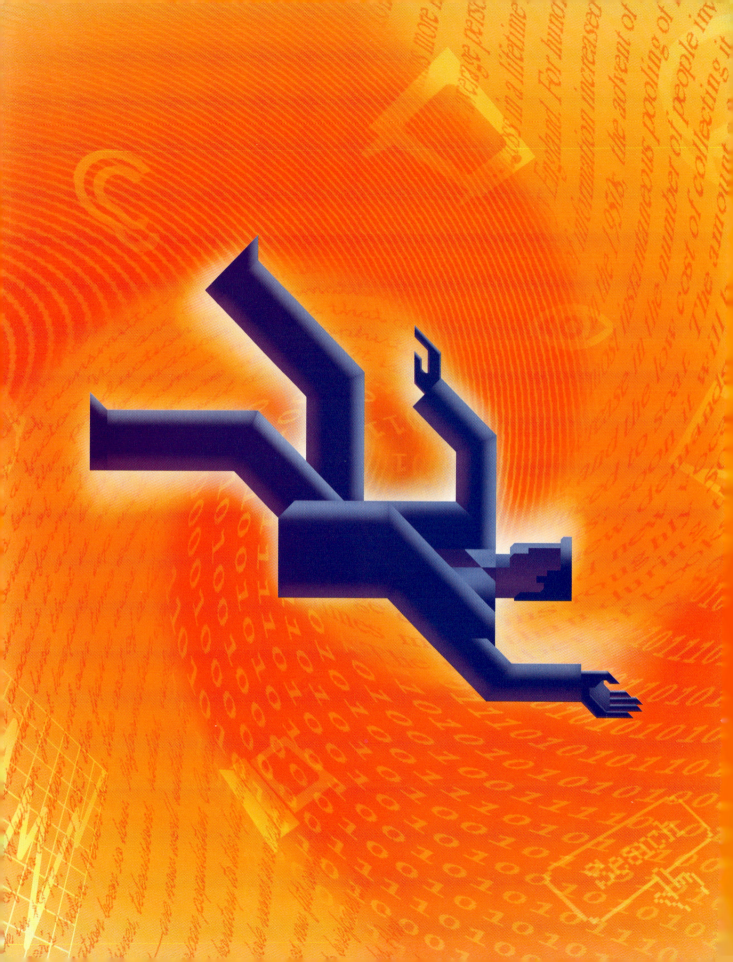

APPENDIX
USING THE CD-ROM

The CD-ROM included with this book is filled with goodies that will help you get more out of Painter 5. Many of the files on the CD-ROM supplement the chapters in the book by illustrating advanced Painter concepts, such as using floaters and masks.

CONTENTS

The CD-ROM includes the following:

- A demo version of MetaCreations' Painter 5. If you haven't purchased Painter yet, or haven't upgraded to Version 5, here's your chance to experiment with the best painting program available for both Macs and PCs. If you've never used Painter before, get ready for the ultimate art experience on your computer. The demo version of Painter 5 is located in the Painter 5 Demo folder (Mac), P5 Demo folder (PC). (For information on how to install the Painter 5 demo, consult the readme.txt file.)
- Several animated tutorials that teach you advanced concepts and some of the new features of Painter 5. Sit back, watch, and learn how to use Floaters and Masks, how to create an Image Hose out of floaters, and how to use Plug-in floaters to create text effects. Double-click the Tutorials file to load the tutorials (Mac), or double-click Tutor95 or Tutor31 (PC).
- Two sample chapters from our CD-ROM, *The Ultimate Interactive Guide to Painter 5*. One sample chapter shows you, step-by-step, how to use colors and how to create gradations, weaves, and patterns (A.1). The second chapter shows you step-by-step how to create movies with Painter (A.2). For more information about the CD-ROM, visit our Web page at `www2.infohouse.com/~addesign`.

A.1

A.2

- Tutorial images. Use the tutorial images to create your own Image Hose, and practice using floaters, shapes, and masks. We tried to include as many sample images from the book as possible. The tutorial images are located in the Images folder on the CD-ROM.
- Image Hose nozzles from Dennis Berkla's *The Garden Hose* CD-ROM. *The Garden Hose* CD-ROM is packed full of nozzle files of trees, bushes, grasses, and plants (A.3). Use the nozzle files to paint beautiful, natural looking scenes and backgrounds. Go to the Garden folder on the *Painter 5 Studio Secrets* CD-ROM for more information about ordering this amazing CD-ROM. The Garden Hose nozzles are in the Nozzles folder.
- Patterns, Textures, and Nozzles. We created several original patterns, textures, and nozzles for you to try in your Painter images.
- Artwork by Mark Zimmer, Chief Technical Officer of MetaCreations. Mark's artwork is found in the Zimmer folder on the CD-ROM.

A.3

MACINTOSH SYSTEM REQUIREMENTS

The Painter 5 demo for Macintosh only runs on Power Macs with System 7.5 or above (as does Painter). The minimum memory requirement for the Painter demo is 13,240KB, although 20MB is recommended. The minimum memory requirement for the tutorials is 12MB. In order to use the tutorials, QuickTime 2.0 or above must be loaded.

WINDOWS SYSTEM REQUIREMENTS

The Painter 5 demo for Windows only runs on Windows 95 or Windows NT (as does Painter). Minimum processor is a 486 DX chip with 16MB of RAM, and SVGA video. The tutorials included with the CD-ROM require that QuickTime be installed on your system.

INSTALLING QUICKTIME

To run the tutorials and *The Ultimate Interactive Guide to Painter 5*, you must have QuickTime installed on your machine. See the following installation instructions for Macintosh and Windows users.

MAC USERS

QuickTime is a system extension installed when the Mac OS is installed. If QuickTime has been turned off, you can turn it back on using the Extensions Manager found in the Control Panel folder.

WINDOWS USERS

If you do not have QuickTime installed, we included a Windows version in the QTIME folder on the CD-ROM. Double-click the installer and follow the screen prompts to complete the installation.

ARTIST INDEX

After looking at all the amazing artwork in *Painter 5 Studio Secrets*, you might have asked yourself, "Who are these talented folks and how can I contact them?" Here's a list of the artists in this book, along with his or her photo or self portrait, a brief biography, and contact information.

ANTON ATZENHOFER
E-mail: atzeat@aol.com or atze.atzenhofer@nuernberg.netsurf.de
Web site: http://members.aol.com/p1103/index.html

Anton says that he has been drawing and painting since he could hold a pencil. His profession as an illustrator and comic artist started at age 16, when he became a lithographer. During this time he also started creating his first illustrations for science fiction magazines. He then went to the Academy of Fine Arts in Nuernberg to study Graphic Design. In 1985 his artwork was seen in comic magazines including the German version of *Heavy Metal* magazine, *Schwermetall*. Anton has created a few "comic-albums," the first of which was a parody of horror and action movies called "Memoirs of a Chainsawer" (In German this translates to "Memoairen eines Kettensägers."); and the last, a Police detective-comedy called "Where the Fun Stops..." ("Wo der Spaß aufhört...").

Since 1990 Anton has been working as a freelance illustrator for several advertising agencies and publishers. His work ranges from storyboards to technical drawings, illustrations, and icons for multimedia CD-ROMs and CD labels.

Artwork found in Chapters 1, 4, 8, 14, and 15

BEN BARBANTE
Phone: 650-525-3414
E-mail: ben_barbante@ccgate.infoworld.com
Web site: http://classroom.cea.edu/benb

Ben Barbante has been the art director of *InfoWorld* since 1990. Ben teaches Painter at the Center For Electronic Art in San Francisco, and his electronically created artwork has been shown at Macworld, Seybold, and SIGGRAPH trade shows.

Artwork found in Chapters 4, 13, 14, and 15

JAY PAUL BELL
E-mail: jbell750@aol.com
Web site: http://members.aol.com/jbell750

Jay was born in 1945. He received a BA in Comprehensive Art (1967) and an MA in Painting (1968) from St. Cloud State University in St. Cloud, Minnesota. He received an MFA in Painting and Drawing (1975) from the University of Wisconsin-Madison. Jay has been on the faculty in the School of Art at Northern Illinois University since 1975. He has exhibited his paintings and drawings in numerous national and regional competitions and is represented in various public, corporate, and private collections.

Jay is represented by Neville-Sargent Gallery in Libertyville, Illinois; Broden Gallery in Madison, Wisconsin; Rule Modern and Contemporary Gallery in Denver, Colorado; and Silicon Gallery in Philadelphia, Pennsylvania.

Artwork found in Chapters 8 and 9

JAY PAUL BELL STUDENTS:

KAREN M. SCHULER
Phone: 847-437-8725

Artwork: *Imagine*, found in Chapter 15

TINA M. KOTLARZ
Phone: 773-252-2958

Artwork: *Sledding*, found in Chapter 15

FRED R. HOPPER
Phone: 630-681-1894

Artwork: *Cyborg*, found in Chapter 15

RANDY A. HALVERSON
Phone: 217-586-4791

Artwork: *The Look of Her*, found in Chapter 15

DENNIS JOHNSON
Phone: 847-473-4545

Artwork: *Brady Bill*, found in Chapter 15

CHARLES ROSENBERG
Phone: 847-438-7474 or 847-438-7475

Artwork: *The Clairvoyant*, found in Chapter 15

DENNIS BERKLA
E-mail: Dennis@DigArts or DigArts@gardenhose.com
Web site: http://www.dcsi.net/~digarts/

Learn about the Garden Hose, Dennis' CD ROM, at http://www.gardenhose.com
   DigArts (The Garden Hose)
   PO Box 4953; Chico, CA 95927-4953

Dennis was born in California. He studied art and filmmaking in college and graduate school. He worked in film, finance, and higher education before founding DigArts Software in 1994.

Artwork found in Chapter 6

SHERIANN KI-SUN BURNHAM
Phone: 562-433-5813
E-mail: kisun@earthlink.net

Sheri was born in Seoul, Korea, in 1959. She has a BA in Art from California State University, Long Beach, in 1982. Sheri has been a professional artist since 1980 and involved with computer graphics since 1981. She currently owns a freelance and design business, specializing in graphic and product/surface design. Though she does use the computer in much of her design work, her main interest with computers is in fine art. Her fine art has been presented in many exhibitions and publications in the US and abroad, including the 1988, 1989, and 1997 ACM SIGGRAGH art shows; the 1989-91 and 1997-98 ACM SIGGRAPH traveling art shows; the 1990 Artware—Art and Electronics in Germany, 1995; 1996 Fractal Design Art Expos; and 1989 and 1997 Connecticut College Niennial Symposiums for Arts and Technology.

Artwork found in Chapters 8, 9, and 12

STEVE CAMPBELL
Phone: 415-668-5826
E-mail: Campbell@sirius.com
Web site: http://www.sirius.com/~campbell/

Steve was born in Kansas City, Missouri, in 1947. A compulsive scribbler, one or two sketchbooks were necessary accessories wherever he went. For many years, as many of his daily hours as possible were spent filling sketchbooks with drawings. In 1972 he moved to San Francisco where his addiction to art finally began to feed him. He began a quarter of a century's involvement in graphics and publishing that continues to this day. In 1988 he got his first Mac (an SE with 4MB RAM) and Mac-based illustration quickly became a vital portion of his creative palette. Since then (currently running a PowerMac 8500 with 49MB RAM), the Macintosh computer has become his primary tool and instrument. Beginning with corporate pixel-pushing, he has recently been redefining and reinventing himself as a digital fine artist, having been three times selected to exhibit in Fractal Design's yearly Art Expo traveling gallery, and a finalist four times in the MicroPublishing/Iris Digital Art contest with awards ceremonies held yearly at the Seybold, San Francisco, trade show.

Artwork found in Chapters 8, 9, 12,14, and 15

GARY F. CLARK
Phone: 717-387-1689
E-mail: clark@planetxbloomu.edu

Gary is an award-winning artist who has exhibited his work in numerous exhibitions in the United States, Canada, and Europe. His work was also showcased in a solo exhibition at the United States Senate, Russel Rotunda, in Washington, DC, in 1994. Gary's work has also been published in a wide variety of magazines, including *Computer Artist*, *Macworld*, *MacUser*, *PC Today*, *Photo Electronic Imaging*, and *AV Video* magazines. His work has been in many books covering Painter, as well as in calendars published by Fractal Design (now MetaCreations) and Delta Informatics (located in Athens, Greece).

Gary is a Professor of Art at Bloomsburg University of Pennsylvania and has taught studio art since 1972. He presently teaches courses in Computer Fine Art, and Two-Dimensional Design and Drawing. Professor Clark holds a BFA degree in Graphic Design from Maryland Institute College of Art as well as an MA in sculpture from West Virginia University. He has also attended Penn State University, the Philadelphia College of Art, and Marywood College in Scanton, Pennsylvania.

Artwork found in Chapters 8, 12, and 14

DAN CROWE
Moving Image & Sound Works
Phone: 415-642-8250
Fax: 415-642-9660
E-mail: sparks1362@aol

Dan received a Bachelor of Arts degree in 1982 from Evergreen State College in Washington. He started to create computer artwork in 1992. In 1994, he was in a joint exhibition with artist Tom Brennan.

Dan has been a musician and touring sound engineer for the past 14 years. His work with performance art has included sound and systems engineering for Meredith Monk and Laurie Anderson.

Working from his San Francisco studio, Dan's main influences are the mythology and images of the Native American experience. Recycled, reused, and found images provide the initial foundation for much of his work. Fashioned in many stages, digital elements are built up, shaped, and layered with digital use of chalk, airbrush, pencil, pen, watercolor, oil, water emulations, and/or plug-in effects. Dan is currently working on CD covers and tour posters for several Bay Area bands and international record companies.

Artwork found in Chapters 8, 9, 11, and 12

JAMES DOWLEN
Dowlen Artworks
Phone: 707-579-1535
Fax: 707-573-9116
E-mail: artworks@sonic.net

James says that he has always been driven to draw and paint the universe he saw unfolding around him. Expressing and interpreting the experiences of his life with lines and colors from the time he was five or so was his natural pastime. Amazed by what he saw or thought he saw, he was most often puzzled by the unanswered questions surrounding the nature of things and people, and himself. He was never puzzled about what to do with his life: he wanted to draw and paint. This seemed the perfect way to attend the mysteries he loved to examine. His drawings and paintings have always been the key to his universe.

James grew up in Aurora, Colorado. He attended Colorado State University in the late 60s and early 70s, then various schools in California. James later became a commercial illustrator in San Francisco and now lives in Santa Rosa.

James was introduced to computer graphics in 1982 and was apparently not impressed and saw little or no use for it. Then late in 1983, he was again stuck in front of an early graphics machine at Time Arts, Inc., where he helped develop one of the very earliest paint programs, Lumena. Since then he has included computer graphics in his illustration career more and more as the technology became more useful. Painter has been one of those great breakthrough tools that helps him to accomplish nearly any look that he needs in the professional market place.

In June of 1995 James was sort of awakened or re-awakened when he held his wife as she died after a long and painful sickness. This event inspired a journey both in spirit and across the world. James says; "I guess it was a quest." James left for Tibet, a place where the people look at the immortal self with respect and where death is accepted as part of the nature of things. There he discovered for himself a place where the gentle Tibetan people keep alive centuries old traditions that he had read

Artist Index

about in old *National Geographic* magazines. Changed and inspired by the events in his life and the beautiful Tibetan culture mythologies and religious traditions, he has been at work painting from memories of his experiences.

Artwork found in Chapters 7, 8, 9, and 14

BEA DROBLAS
Phone: 248-737-1617 or 561-845-9211

Bea was born in Buenos Aires, Argentina. She studied at the National School of Fine Arts and the Fernando Fader Art School, both in Buenos Aires. Over the years she perfected her training in different work shops and museums in Europe.

Her main sources of inspiration are themes of every day life, which she expresses mainly through the enhancement of colors. Her works are an extension of her feelings. Like every artist, she has had to work hard before being able to find the right way to express herself. She has exhibited her work in Florida, Michigan, Europe, and Latin America.

Artwork found in Chapter 3

JOHN ENNIS
E-mail: ennis@voicenet.com
Web site: http://www.voicenet.com/~ennis

A book cover artist for over 15 years, John Ennis has illustrated for every major book publisher in New York City. Recognized internationally, his work is published in over two dozen foreign countries.

John trained at the Art Students League of New York as a traditional oil painter. Over the last few years he has made a remarkable and complete transition to digital art, which has led to the publication of his book *Going Digital-An Artist's Guide to Computer Illustration*, published by Madison Square Press. He is an active member of the Society of Illustrators of New York where he chaired the 1995 Paperback Show and sat as a juror in the more recent Digital Salon exhibition.

In August 1997, he appeared at the Macworld Expo in Boston as a speaker for the Advanced Imaging for Professionals seminar with Bert Monroy. In September 1997, he addressed the Artists Guild of Delaware Valley at the Art Institute in Philadelphia.

Artwork found in Chapters 2, 3, 9, 11, 12, and 14

DOROTHY PAT ERICKSON
Phone: 406-453-6103

Pat has been a working artist for 40 years. She was introduced to computers in 1991. Pat says that it took at least 15 minutes for her to realize that this was the medium she had been seeking most of her life. As a jeweler specializing in enamel Cloisonné and pen and ink drawings handled in what she dubs her Comic Book style, Pat discovered instant gratification in the unique tools of Fractal Design's Painter.

Pat designs clip art for a Montana-based Software Company, and her work has been included in competitions and local exhibitions. As co-owner of Gallery 16, Great Falls, Montana, she handles the graphics for advertising and in-house exhibitions.

Artwork found in Chapters 8 and 9

ANDREW FAULKNER
Phone: 415-332-3521
Fax: 415-331-4524
E-mail: afstudio@best.com
Web site: http://www.afstudio.com

Andrew Faulkner is an illustrator and designer working in Sausalito, California. His photo-collage technique relies heavily on the use of Painter's many realistic brushes and textures, particularly when used with the Wacom tablet. His work ranges from posters to book covers, and his clients include Apple Computer, Adobe Systems, Inc., and Harper Collins. Andrew's illustrations have appeared in *Macworld*, *MacUser*, *Worth*, and *Publish* magazines, as well as in the Los Angeles Times.

Artwork found in Chapters 3, 5, and 9

SIMON FELDMAN
Simon Feldman Studio, Inc.
Phone: 212-260-7890
Fax: 212-677-5206
E-mail: simager1@aol.com

Simon was born in 1960 and raised in Brooklyn. On his thirteenth birthday he received his first 35mm SLR camera and a black-and-white developing kit. As he unraveled his first roll of developed film, he knew he was hooked.

In 1982 he graduated from Antioch College in Yellow Springs, Ohio, with a BA in Psychology/Communications. Simon had taken painting as an elective and found deep satisfaction in pushing the paint around on the canvas. It occurred to him that it would be great if he could somehow combine the two mediums together, but he lacked the knowledge to do it. After graduating, Simon worked in NYC for a couple of TV broadcasting companies and tried to break into the video side, quite unsuccessfully. Simon turned back to photography and worked as a photo assistant for three years. In 1987, he opened his own studio. Soon after, he got his first Mac and began using Photoshop to compliment his photography. It wasn't long before he came across Painter and was able to finally realize one of his earlier dreams of combining photographic images with a paint medium. Simon says he had come full circle.

Artwork found in Chapter 1

BEATE FRITSCH
E-mail: beate@rucker.com

Beate is a senior designer and illustrator at Rucker Design Group in San Mateo, California. Having worked as an Art Director in a German advertising agency, her diverse skills include design, art direction, illustration, and conceptual thinking. After moving to the United States four years ago, she got hooked on the computer and digital design. She is still fascinated by the broad range of possibilities the computer offers, and loves exploring new technologies. An expert user of Photoshop, Illustrator, QuarkXPress, Painter, and Fractal Design Expression, she enjoys working on a variety of projects including artistic illustrations, complex packaging projects, and Web sites for clients like @Home, Hewlett Packard, and America Online.

Artwork found in Chapter 12

JACK GOLD
E-mail: marjak@gate.net

Jack grew up in the South Bronx of New York City and is retired after careers in journalism, broadcasting, and retail advertising.

Jack says the computer has reopened the door to painting not visited since his teens. He misses only the smells of turpentine and linseed. Unfortunately, he says, most of his time is spent trying to get the Macintosh away from his wife.

Artwork found in Chapter 1

KENNETH B. GORE
Phone: 212-966-5301
Fax: 212-334-1245
E-mail: ken40@ix.netcom
Web site: http://www.grandeillusionsart.com

Kenneth was born in Dallas, Texas. He studied 2D and 3D design at Oxford Polytech in Oxford, England. He received an MFA in 1985 at the University of California, Santa Barbara, and a BFA in 1983 from West Texas State University in Canyon.

Kenneth has also served in the military. His service includes six years in the US Air Force (1973-1979) at Cannon AFB in Clovis, New Mexico and in the Royal Air Force in Upper Heyford, England. Awards he has won include Emblem design for USAF 27th TAC Fighter Wing, Bicentennial art design/paintings for Cannon AFB, Early merit promotion to Non-Commissioned Officer, Mural commissioned for RAF, Upper Heyford.

In 1985, Kenneth and his wife Karina Cavat formed Grandes Illusions Studios in both Santa Barbara, California, and in New York City.

Artwork found in Chapters 7, 9, 11, and 12

RODNEY ALAN GREENBLAT
E-mail: rodney@whimsyload.com
Web site: http://www.whimsyload.com

Rodney Alan Greenblat is a creator of intriguing and whimsical art. His paintings and sculpture have been exhibited in galleries and museums around the world. He is the author and illustrator of children's books and the director of the Center For Advanced Whimsy, an independent company that creates artwork, design, and music for children and adults. Some of Rodney's commercial projects include character and graphic design for video games and consumer items distributed in Japan.

Artwork found in Chapters 14 and 15

ADELE DROBLAS GREENBERG
E-mail: addesign@infohouse.com
Web site: http://www2.infohouse.com/~addesign

Adele always enjoys extending her artistic knowledge, whether it involves using the computer or crayons. When Adele is not using Painter or Photoshop, she is having fun with her daughter and husband.

Artwork found in Chapters 2, 3, 4, 5, 6, 7, 10, 11, and 13

SETH GREENBERG
E-mail: addesign@infohouse.com
Web site: http://www2.infohouse.com/~addesign

Seth has been using a computer for more than 15 years. You can say that the computer is a major part of his life—for better or worse. Seth spends most of his time programming; occasionally he stops programming to create some artwork. When he's not using the computer, you can find him enjoying life with his family, reading, or swimming.

Artwork found in Chapters 2, 3, 4, 5, 6, 7, 10, 11, and 13

STACY A. HOPKINS
Phone: 302-737-3002
E-mail: Stacy162@magpage.com
Web site: http://magpage.com/~stacy162

Stacy is married, an ex-marine, rides a motorcycle, and is co-owner of High Energy (a gym in Newark, Delaware). Stacy started using Painter about four years ago. He doesn't have any training in art or computers; he just enjoys being creative and likes the challenge of learning art on a computer. Stacy says, "I guess I am proof that the average person can have some measure of success using a computer if the desire is there."

Artwork found in Chapters 1, 3, 8, 9, 12, and 14

MARK JENKINS
E-mail: mark_jenkins@rucker.com

Mark is a senior designer at Rucker Design Group in San Mateo, CA. His award-winning artwork has been exhibited internationally and has been featured in several books and magazines about digital art. Mark considers himself a jack-of-all-trades designer: his experience spans a broad range of areas, including illustration, corporate identity, packaging, and multimedia. Although he enjoys the experimental freedom of the Macintosh, Mark was trained traditionally and maintains high standards for typography and production. Mark is an expert user of Photoshop, Illustrator, Painter, and Fractal Design Studio, and has been a featured speaker at seminars on the subject of how to combine the most powerful features of those applications.

Artwork found in Chapter 12

DOROTHY SIMPSON KRAUSE
Phone: 781-837-1682
Fax: 781-834-1782
E-mail: dotkrause@aol.com
Web site: http://www.dotkrause.com

Dorothy is a Professor of Computer Graphics at the Massachusetts College of Art, Corporate Curator of IRIS Graphics, Inc., and a founding member of Unique Editions, a digital artists' collaborative. She is a frequent speaker at conferences and symposia and a consultant for manufacturers and distributors of products that are used by fine artists. Her work is exhibited regularly in galleries and museums and featured in more than three dozen periodicals and books. In July 1997, she organized "Digital Atelier: A printmaking studio for the 21st century" at the National Museum of American Art of the Smithsonian Institute and was an artist-in-residence there for 21 days.

Artwork found in Chapter 7

GEORGE H. KRAUTER
Phone: 415-753-5305
Fax: 415-665-7054
E-mail: kronos 1@aol.com

George Krauter is a San Francisco illustrator who specializes in science fiction and other related themes. His work can often be seen on the covers of such science fiction magazines as *Analog* and *Science Fiction Age*. George also works with science and technical magazines, including *PC Magazine* and *Astronomy*.

Most recently, his work was part of the 1995 Seybold, San Francisco, Digital Art Gallery and the annual show of the San Francisco Society of Illustrators. In 1996, he was nominated for a prestigious Hugo Award for Best Original Artwork. George also was awarded a Silver and Gold Award by the San Francisco Society of Illustrators (SFSI). The Silver Award was in the Science Fiction and Fantasy category for *Finder's Fee*. The Gold Award was in the Technical category for *3D Cubes*.

Artwork found in Chapters 6, 8, 9, and 14

SUSAN LEVAN
Phone: 617-536-6828
E-mail: slveb@world.std.com

Susan LeVan is a mixed media artist and illustrator who became interested in computer art when she discovered pressure sensitive graphics tablets and Painter. She is a principal with her husband Ernest Barbee of LeVan/Barbee, a digital studio in Boston whose work ranges from editorial illustration to large billboard advertising. She holds an MFA in Printmaking from the Cranbrook Academy of Art. LeVan's illustrations appear regularly in a variety of publications, and her work has been exhibited internationally in museums and galleries.

Artwork found in Chapters 8 and 15

Artist Index

PATRICK LICHTY
Creative Partner, Lichty Studio Design & Fine Arts
Phone: 330-494-5593
E-mail: voyd@raex.com
Web site: http://web.raex.com/~voyd

Patrick is an artist, writer, and partner of Lichty Studios, and has been exploring computer imaging since 1979. His media arts relate to the interaction humanity has with technology and mediated society. His writings address the impact of technology on American society as well as the emerging potentials in the electronic arts. He is part of the Haymarket RIOT performance project and Bruce Sterling's Dead Media research project. Recently, Patrick has been part of the New York Digital Salon and spoke before the 1997 International Symposium of the Electronic Arts (ISEA).

Artwork found in Chapters 6, 8, 9, 12, 14, and 15

DOUGLASS LOCKYER
Studio Gecko, Riptide Communications
Phone: 212-989-5000
Fax: 212-695-2823
E-mail: doug@ripsite.com
Web site: http://www.ripsite.com

Doug is a self-taught illustrator and designer from New Zealand. He exhibited impressionist landscapes in oils at the age of 13, and has won numerous fine art scholarships. Doug has also won numerous print and design awards from national art competitions in New Zealand, such as from BNZ Architectural Design in 1984, and National Print awards for design and illustration in Australia. He was recently the first-prize winner of the 1996 Fractal Design Painter Digital Art competition.

Doug is the creative director at Studio Designs, Inc., a leading digital art, illustration, and packaging design business in Manhattan, where he creates toy and game illustrations, advertising storyboards, and finished illustrations for some of the world's most prominent brands and advertisers. You will see his Painter images on toys and games from Pressman Toys, in magazines, and all over the World Wide Web.

Artwork found in Chapters 8, 9, 10, 13, 14, and 15

DEBI LEE MANDEL
Catsprite Studios
Phone: 916-389-8312
Fax: 916-389-9038
E-mail: dlm@catsprite.com
Web site: http://www.catsprite.com

Debi is a self-taught fine artist with 20 years experience in natural media. In October 1994, she bought a PowerMac 6100/60/CD, turned it on, and "started learning all over again." Within three months she had work accepted for inclusion in a book about painting with computers. Debi says that she is a figurative artist, and this has not changed with her new medium.

Artwork found in Chapters 13, 14, and 15

RICHARD NOBLE
Phone: 510-838-5524
Fax: 510-838-5561
E-mail: rnoble@nobledesign.com
Web site: http://www.nobledesign.com

Richard Noble attended the Ringling School of Art and is now the owner of a design and illustration business in San Francisco. He has worked in advertising for 25 years and has continued to paint as a sideline. His work has been featured in several fine arts shows, most recently at the Sausalito Art Fair, where he was featured with 12 other computer artists in the first computer arts exhibit.

Artwork found in Chapter 9

DAVID OBAR
David Obar Productions
Phone or Fax: 972-625-0794
E-mail: obarpro@aol.com

David graduated in 1990 with a BFA in photography from the University of North Texas in Denton. David freelances as a digital illustrator and a commercial photographer. He works with agencies, designers, and photographers, and has done work for corporations such as Texas Instruments, Nortel, Southwestern Bell Telephone, Bryan Foods, Nickelodeon, and Siemens.

He has worked with graphic programs since 1990 when he interned with J.W. Burkey Studios. He bought his first Macintosh in 1992, a Quadra 700 with a 200MB hard drive and 32MB of RAM. David works primarily with Macintosh computers but occasionally he gets a call for clients using PCs. He currently works on a PM8100/80 with 160MB RAM and 2GB hard drive space, as well as other removable drives. He uses a Calcomp Drawing Slate II tablet, which for him is invaluable when working in Painter.

Artwork found in Chapter 11

CORINNE OKADA
Phone: 415-325-3549
E-mail: cokada@ophi.com

Corinne Okada is a San Francisco Bay Area illustrator and graphic designer working in both digital and traditional media. Her creations have appeared in *PRINT*, *Communication Arts*, *Computer Pictures*, and *MacUser* magazines. Corinne's work experience ranges from museum graphics to animation, CD cover illustrations, and icon design. She enjoys illustrating for educational software and hopes some day to illustrate and write children's books.

Clients include Sony, Silicon Graphics, Silicon Gaming, Apple Computer, Wild Planet Toys, WebTV, PFMagic, Tenth Planet, Landor Associates, CKS Interactive, and West Office Exhibition Design.

Artwork found in Chapter 15

DENNIS ORLANDO
Phone: 215-355-5524
Fax: 215-355-6924
E-mail: dorlando@voicenet.com
Web site: http://www.voicenet.com/~dorlando (WWW Gallery) and
http://www.180079world.com (WWW Business)

Dennis Orlando is an award-winning artist with over 20 years of professional experience. He considers himself a "TraDigital" artist, creating traditional painterly images through the use of digital tools. Dennis has a diverse background as a fine artist, graphic designer, art director, creative director, adjunct professor, and a Web designer. He is co-founder and partner of SmallWorld Media Group (http://www.180079world.com). His paintings can be found on the Web at http://www.voicenet.com/~dorlando.

Artwork found in Chapters 1, 2, 8, and 15

CHARLEY PARKER
Phone: 610-872-2163
E-mail: cparker@zark.com
Web site: http://www.zark.com

Charley is a freelance cartoonist, illustrator, and Web designer living in the Philadelphia area. His online "virtual comic book," *Argon Zark!* (http://www.zark.com), has received numerous awards since its inception in 1995. The comic has also been featured in articles in the *Philadelphia Inquirer*, the *Houston Chronicle*, the *Richmond Times-Dispatch*, *Internet Underground* magazine, and Germany's *TV Movie* magazine, as well as a number of computer graphics books, including *Official Kai's Power Tools Studio Secrets* by Ted Alspach and Steven Frank from IDG Books Worldwide and *Designing Digital Media* by Nick Iuppa from Focal Press.

In what he jokingly refers to as his "spare time," Charley likes to draw with real pencil and paper just to remember what it's like.

Artwork found in Chapters 8 and 9

CHET PHILLIPS
Phone: 214-987-4344
E-mail: chet@airmail.net
Web site: http://web2.airmail.net/chet

Chet Phillips has worked as a freelance commercial illustrator for more than 12 years. He received his BFA degree in Painting and Drawing from North Texas State University in 1979. Since then, he has divided his time between working for advertising, design, publishing, and editorial clients, and selling and showing gallery work. In 1992, he traded in his pencils and brushes for a Macintosh and has since created digital work exclusively. Using Painter, the possibilities have been limitless. His work has been exhibited around the world in Fractal Design's annual traveling Art Expo since it began in 1994. Companies that he has worked for include American Airlines, MCI, Frito Lay, JCPenney, and GTE, and he is also a regular contributor to the *Dallas Morning News*.

"My artwork has influences in popular culture and surrealism with a large dose of humor thrown in," says Phillips. "Incongruities in life and stories that may have many meanings also intrigue me. Exploring these areas with my artwork is a constant source of inspiration. Most importantly, no electrons were killed in the creation of my artwork."

Artwork found in Chapters 8, 9, 13, and 14

CHELSEA SAMMEL
Chelsea Sammel Illustrations
Phone: 408-636-7443
E-mail: yochelsea@aol.com

Traditionally trained, award-winning artist Chelsea Sammel has been using the digital medium for the last 15 years. She has worked as a beta-tester, teacher, and demo artist for Fractal Design (now MetaCreations) since Painter's creation in 1991.

Chelsea's studio clients include IBM, Apple Computer, Microsoft, Sun Microsystems, Lodal, Gillette, and McKesson. Her artwork has appeared in more than 30 publications, including *Computer Artist*, *Computer Pictures*, *MacWeek*, *Discover*, *PC*, *Computer Graphics World*, *How*, *Confetti*, and *Art Product News* magazines, and in several books and on PBS Television's "Computer Chronicles." Chelsea recently developed the Painter 5 Curriculum book for Fractal Design, and currently teaches Painter at the University of California.

Artwork found in Chapters 8, 11, 12, and 15

EMILY STEDMAN
Phone: 212-941-0137
Fax: 212-941-0140
E-mail: estedman@tiac.net

Emily has been a traditional painter and illustrator for more than 20 years. She has had 7 one-woman shows of oil and watercolors in New York City, and numerous group shows, including shows at the Brooklyn Museum. Her paintings are also in corporate collections, including the collection of Schering-Plough Pharmaceuticals.

She received an MFA from the Pratt Institute and a BFA from Illinois Wesleyan University. When she first found out about Painter, Emily thought it was made for her. At that time, Emily was creating illustrations for magazines, including *Prevention*; for book companies, including MacMillan McGraw-Hill and Macdougal Littel Publishers; and for corporate organizations such as TIAA-CREF, in addition to various advertising agencies. Painter made working on projects for these companies faster, easier, and more fun.

Artwork found in Chapters 1, 7, and 8

ADAM SADIGURSKY
Phone: 415-321-7121
E-mail: adam308@ix.netcom.com

Adam was born and raised in Russia. He began sketching and drawing at the age of six. Later he graduated from the Russian Academy of Art. After emigrating from Russia, he lived in Western Europe before coming to the United States. During this period he was influenced by several artistic movements, but nevertheless, he kept his own Russian-inspired style.

Adam works in a variety of mediums, including acrylic, pastel pencil, charcoal, and ink. However, he favors painting in oil and has sold his oil paintings internationally. He has also branched into computer art. He won a second place in the Fractal Design international competition, Art Expo 1995. He resides in Palo Alto, California.

Artwork found in Chapters 5, 8, 9, and 15

JOHN STEPHANS
E-mail: elec pi@aol.com

John Stephens lives with his family on top of a large hill in rural Vermont. He divides his time between painting for his agent in California and working for New York publishing houses and ad agencies. He has been involved in software development and on occasion writes for computer magazines.

Artwork found in Chapters 11 and 14

JEREMY SUTTON
Phone: 650-325-3493
Fax: 650-325-3499
E-mail: jeremy@portrayals.com
Web site: http://www.portrayals.com

Jeremy Sutton, author of *Fractal Design Painter Creative Techniques*, published by Hayden Books, is an award-winning computer artist whose artwork has been exhibited and published internationally. Jeremy has taught computer painting at San Francisco State University and at the San Francisco Academy of Art College. He leads Painter workshops throughout the world and is currently teaching Painter online via his Web site. Jeremy has demonstrated Painter for MetaCreations (formerly Fractal Design) at many national and international industry trade shows. Besides creating digital fine art, illustration, and animation, Jeremy also performs live digital portraiture with Painter at special events. His clients have ranged from DreamWorks to Virgin Atlantic Airways.

Artwork found in Chapters 9 and 12

MARGARET SWEENEY
E-mail: marjak@gate.net

Margaret graduated from the University of Cincinnati with a degree in graphic design, and went on to work in advertising. Throughout her 20-odd years in this career, Margaret always painted in her spare time. Four years ago she decided to make the break and devote herself to painting full-time.

Several times throughout the year, Margaret travels to different locations, sketching scenery for paintings she'll later do on the computer. "I'm mostly a painter of small towns, simple pleasures, and back roads, because that's what means the most to me," she says. Margaret then exhibits her work in the galleries and shops near the locales she has visited and sells her work as limited edition prints. She prefers to make the prints herself to keep control over the process, perfectly duplicating what she sees on the screen by selectively shifting colors where necessary.

In 1995, Margaret was a finalist in Fractal Design Painter's Digital Art Contest, and in 1996, she was the contest's second-place winner.

To create her paintings, Margaret uses a PowerMac 7100 AV with 72MB of RAM, a 5GB hard drive, a 6 × 8-inch Wacom tablet, an Apple 14-inch color monitor, an Apple One scanner, a Tektronix 140 color printer, a LaserWriter Plus, and an Apple color printer. When she makes her prints, she uses the Cannon 850 color copier with a fiery interface, and then transfers that print to a 140-pound or 300-pound cold-pressed watercolor paper.

Artwork found in Chapters 8, 9, 11, 12, and 14

AYSE ULAY
Ulay + Ulay Communications
Phone: 626-796-4615
Fax: 626-577-2155
E-mail: ulay@wavenet.com
Web site: http://www.wavenet.com/~ulay

Traditionally trained at Art Center College of Design in Pasadena, California, Ayse Ulay has a BFA in Illustration and Graphic Design. In 1990, she formed a partnership with her husband and formed a design and illustration studio, Ulay & Ulay Communications.

Ayse's work has been exhibited nationwide. Some of her clients include A&M Records, California's Museum of Science & Technology, California Institute of Technology, and Letraset and FontHaus.

Artwork found in Chapter 15

PAT WATSON
Phone: 702-831-1314 extension 3107
E-mail: pwatson@sierranevada.edu or Watsonian@telis.org
Sierra Nevada College Visual & Performing Arts department Web site: http://www.sierranevad.edu/vpa/

Pat teaches and works in the Lake Tahoe area, near the Nevada/California border. Pat has had two solo shows of his digital pieces and has been a part of numerous group exhibits. He was a finalist in Fractal's Art Expo in 1996, and some of his artwork is on the packaging for Painter 4.0. An Assistant Professor at Sierra Nevada College, he teaches Graphic Design, Digital Design, and various other studio art courses. A graduate of California State University, Long Beach, Pat has an MA from California State University, Dominguez Hills.

Pat has been working with the Macintosh since 1988, and uses it for his instructional work as well as for freelance assignments. He taught high school art and photography for 11 years before working in commercial art for three years, prior to his current work at Sierra Nevada College. His current efforts are to integrate digital prints with traditional media for gallery exhibition in mixed media and assemblage pieces, to be shown at the Nevada Museum of Art in the summer of 1997.

Artwork found in Chapters 9, 11, and 14

HIROSHI YOSHII
E-mail: hiroshi@yoshii.com
Web site: http://www.yoshii

Hiroshi was born near Nagoya, Japan, in 1962. He graduated from the Nippon Designer Institute, Nagoya in 1983. After working as a graphic designer, in 1990 Hiroshi began work as a freelance illustrator. In 1995, Hiroshi wrote and published *Painter Wonderland*. Also in 1995, he received a third-place award from the Fractal Design Art Expo.

Artwork found in Chapter 15

INDEX

3D images
   creating patterns from 3D text, 146
   techniques for Russian Glasnost coin, 149
3D modeling
   for *The Owl and the Pussy Cat*, 119
   using Painter with applications for, 189–193
8-bit mask, 39

A

Abstract Background (Sammel), 175–176
Adjust Color command, 160
Adobe Illustrator
   importing and exporting shapes from, 53
   using with Painter, 189
Adobe Photoshop
   compatibility of plug-ins with Painter, 7
   compatibility with Painter, 189, 196–197
   Composite Methods compatible with, 60
   converting alpha channel layers into Painter, 41
   digitizing art in, 7
   importing Painter color images to, 9, 79, 196
   layer masks in, 58
   masking features of, 39, 40
Age of Reason, The (Crowe), 164
Ægypt (Campbell), 204
Ah (Yoshii), 215
Airbrush filters, 20
Alley Doors (Sweeney), 88
anchor points
   editing vector text by averaging points, 143–144
   selecting and adding, 142
Anguish (Campbell), 125
animation. *See* Web animation
Animation option (Save As dialog box), 83
Apples (Erickson), 97
Apply Surface Texture command
   creating chrome text, 145
   creating special effects with, 171–172
   making patterns from 3D text, 146
   raising type with, 144
Aquarius (Barbante), 198–199
Argon Zark! (Parker), 106–108, 130–134
art. *See* images; paintings; photographs; *and specific art listed by name*
Art Materials palette, 29–34
   Color palette, 29
   Grad palette, 30–32
   Paper palette, 29–30
   Patterns palette, 32–33
   Weaves palette, 34
artist index, 221–227
Artists filters, 21
Atzenhofer, Anton, 3, 48, 49, 99–100, 101, 196–197, 199, 212, 213, 221
August Flowers (Hopkins), 138
Auto Clone command, 154
Auto Select dialog box, 42
Auto Van Gogh command, 153–154
Automatic Transform command, 51–52
Average Points command, 143–144
AVI movies
   creating and editing, 183–184
   linking to PDF files, 84
   sending Painter output to, 83–84
Axis Pitcher Cover (Lockyer), 140, 141, 149–150
Axis Superheroes (Lockyer), 90

B

Back Alley Blues (Sweeney), 101
backgrounds
   adding depth to, 144
   compositing techniques for, 118–119
   creating, 118–119
   on Web pages, 181–183
Barbante, Ben, 46, 47, 48, 49, 186–187, 198–199, 206, 221
Baseball (Obar), 157
Beatles (LeVan), 205
Bell, Jay Paul, 109, 110, 111, 128–130, 221
benevolence (Mandel), 198
Berkla, Dennis, 73, 222
Bevel World dialog box, 62
Bevel World plug-in
   creating beveled type effects, 146–148
   creating buttons with, 181–182
Biker, The (Hopkins), 192–193
Birch (Berkla), 73
Black Lilies (Sammel), 162–163
Black Nose (Yoshii), 215
black-and-white images, converting to color, 158–160
blends
   effects with Composite Methods, 59–60
   gradations vs., 52
   in shapes, 52–53
Blessing, The (Watson), 114–115
Blinding Light of Truth, The (Lichty), 209
BLOCKSA (Dowlen), 191
Blue Flower Face (Yoshii), 215
Bodyclock (Faulkner), 39
borders, 118–119
Bouquet (Greenberg, A.D.), 80
Brady Bill (Johnson), 210
brightness values, 42
Broken Heart, 50
Brush filters, 21
Brush Look Designer, 17
Brush Tracking dialog box, adjusting settings in, 14
brushes
   adjusting strokes for stylus, 15
   brush variants for Image Hose brush, 67–69
   Cloners, 115, 157
   compositing images using photographs and, 111–114
   Controls palette for, 15
   creating mask from brush strokes, 42–44
   customizing and saving, 109
   editing masks with, 42
   eliminating brush variants, 43
   picking, 16
   using multiple, 89
   using New Paint Tools brush library, 87–88
   using Transparent Layer, 61
   Van Gogh 2, 155–156
   See also Image Hose brush
Brushes palette, 16–28
   photo examples of, 22–23, 24–25, 26–27, 28–29
   picking brushes, 16
   thumbnails for, 17–21, 23, 26, 28
Buddy System (Campbell), 196, 197
Burnham, Sheriann Ki-Sun, 102, 103, 136, 137, 170, 222
Burning Heart (Fritsch/Rucker Design Group), 173
Burning Leaves (Sweeney), 214
buttons, 181–182

C

cameras, digital, 7–8
Campbell, Steve, 104, 125, 171, 196, 197, 204, 222
canvas output, 75, 80
Capture Pattern dialog box, 32, 33
Cartoon Cell fill, 104–105
cartooning techniques, 106–108, 130–134
Carver (Clark), 177, 178
Cat Who Walked By Himself, The (Stedman), 93
Catch of the Day (Hopkins), 40
Cat's Pajamas (Phillips), 126, 127
CD-ROM
   contents and requirements for, 219–220
   Garden Hose, The, 73, 220
   interactive opener for, 182
   loading nozzle files from, 66
   movie on, 83
CEO Parody (Gore), 74, 75, 80–81
Ceremony (Crowe), 95
Chalk filters, 18
Chameleon (Phillips), 99
Chao Meng Fu (Krauter), 96
Charcoal filters, 18
Cherokee Mist (Crowe), 95
chrome text, 145
Cinepak option (Save As dialog box), 84
circular radiation styles, 31
Clairvoyant, The (Rosenberg), 211
Clark, Gary, 103–104, 177, 178, 200, 222
Clearing (Orlando), 213
Clone of Charlie Runs (Lockyer), 89
Cloners Brushes
   analyzing strokes of, 115
   using, 157
Cloners filters, 22–23
cloning
   creating composites with cloning brushes and, 114–120
   creating mosaic and, 176, 177
   used in *The Owl and the Pussy Cat*, 119–120
CMYK color, 78–79
Coffeehouse/Last Rites (Campbell), 125
color
   adding to a weave, 34
   converting black-and-white images to, 158–160
   correcting with Tonal Control command, 162
   creating selection from, 42
   matching output for, 78, 81
   out-of-gamut, 79
   Pantone, 36, 81
   removing from images, 160
   selecting, 29
   See also grayscale images; Kodak Color Management System; RGB color
Color palette, 29
Color Select dialog box, 42
color separations, 80
Color Set palette
   adding weaves to, 34
   using, 36
commands
   Apply Surface Texture, 144–145, 146, 171–172
   Auto Clone, 154
   Auto Van Gogh, 153–154
   Automatic Transform, 51
   Average Points, 143–144
   Convert to Selection, 155
   Create Drop Shadow, 144
   Grid, 155
   Make Mosaic, 151, 176
   mover, 14
   Place Elements, 70–71
   Raster Plugins, 7
   Select, 42
   Surface Control, 160
   Tonal Control, 160
   Tracing Paper, 156
Composite Methods, 59–60
composite techniques, 111–139
   about Cloner Brush variants, 115
   combining paintings and photos, 111–114
   compositing images with masks, 40
   using
      cloning and cloning brushes, 114–120
      floaters, 120–135
      selections and floaters, 137–139
      working with shapes, floaters, and selections, 135–136
Constrain File Size check box (Resize dialog box), 9–10
Controls palette
   adjusting the, 15–16
   controlling opacity of Image Hose brush with, 70
   thumbnails of Composite Methods in, 60
Convert to Selection command, 155
Copy (Atzenhofer), 196–197
copying
   device profiles, 79
   floaters, 45, 56
Cosmological Constant (Krauter), 125
Cowboy (Barbante), 206
Crab (Yoshii), 215
Crack, The (Crowe), 124
Cracker House (Sweeney), 87, 88
Crayons filters, 19
Create Drop Shadow command, 144
Crowe, Dan, 95, 104, 105, 123–124, 163–164, 170, 222
Cupid (Lockyer), 120–121
curves attached to straight line, 50
custom palettes, 36–37
customizing
   brushes, 109
   inking pens, 107
textures, 101–104
Cybervice (Barbante), 206
Cyborg (Hopper), 210

D

Dampiera Diversafolia (Erickson), 137
Day Dream Charlie (Lockyer), 190
Deck Chair (Noble), 123
default libraries, 14
Derry, John, 88–90, 172–174
Desperado (Sadigursky), 212
Deus ex Machina (Watson), 165
device profiles for KCMS, 79
digital cameras, 7–8
Digital Junk (Krauter), 64, 65, 72–73
Directional spray option (Image Hose brush), 67, 70
distortion
   distorting shapes, 52
   Glass Distortion filter, 169–170
Dog (Atzenhofer), 199
Dog Flight (Phillips), 126, 127
Donut Town (Greenblat), 194, 195
Dowlen, James, 75, 97–98, 105–106, 134–135, 191, 222–223
Draw Anywhere mask icon, 40–41, 42
Draw Outside mask icon, 41, 42
Droblas, Bea, 38, 39, 43–44, 223
drop shadows
   adding to image hose elements, 71
   adding to text, 144
dropping floaters, 59
Dutch Flowers, 153–154

E

Eastside#1 (Crowe), 170
editing
   floater masks, 58, 59
   paths, 50–51
   vector type effects, 141–144
Effects commands, development of, 172–174
8-bit mask, 39
enhancing images, 153–167
   adjusting original paintings and scanned photos, 163–167
   changing lighting, 160–162
   converting black-and-white images to color, 158–160
   painting
      with Auto Clone, 154
      with Auto Van Gogh, 153–154
      with Van Gogh 2 brush, 155–156
   tracing over digital images, 156
   using
      Cloners brushes, 157
      tonal control, 162–163
Ennis, John, 34, 123, 166–167, 178, 179, 200, 223

EPS file format, for prepress output, 80
Eraser filters, 17
Erickson, Dorothy "Pat," 97, 126, 137–138, 223
exporting
    files to other applications, 189
    shapes from Illustrator, 53
Extra Brushes folder, 94
Eye (Atzenhofer), 212
Eye (Sammel), 169–170

F

F/X filters, 24
Face (Atzenhofer), 3, 99, 100, 101
Face (Campbell), 171
Fairy (Droblas), 38, 39, 44
Family (Ulay), 202, 203, 207
Fashion Scents (Phillips), 86, 87, 98
Faulkner, Andrew, 39, 55, 223
Feast of Fools (Crowe), 123–124
Feldman, Simon, 3, 10–11, 223
Felt Pen filters, 19
files
    format for Web output, 82
    GIF, 82, 185, 187
    importing/exporting to other applications, 189
    JPEG, 82
    linking movies to PDF, 84
    previewing service bureau, 81
    saving files with floaters, 59
    for service bureaus or prepress output, 80
    sharing on networks, 36
    See also nozzle files
Fill command, 42
Finder's Fee (Krauter), 200–201
fine art print output, 80–81
Floater Adjuster tool, 144
Floater List palette
    adjusting floaters with, 59
    adjusting text with, 51
    using, 35
floater masks
    about, 57–58
    converting shapes to, 135
    editing, 58
floaters, 55–63
    about floater masks, 57–58
    adjusting, 59
    applying plug-in, 62–63
    blending effects of, 59–60
    composite techniques using, 120–136, 137–139
    converting shapes to, 47–48
    copying and pasting, 45, 56
    creating, 56–57
        composite image with, 116–117
        nozzle files with, 71–73
        transparent layers, 61

editing floater masks, 58
in movies, 184
using, 55–56
Flower Seller, The (Sweeney), 193
Flying Robot (Yoshii), 216
Fool (Atzenhofer), 99
French Bookstore (Sammel), 208
Fritsch, Beate, 173, 223
Full Frames AVI option (Save As dialog box), 83
Fun brushes, 94

G

Galaxie Drive-In (Watson), 159–160
gallery, 203–217
gamut warnings, 79
Garden Hose, The CD-ROM, 73, 220
Garden (Sammel), 72
Garden Within, The (LeVan), 94
General Preferences dialog box, 14
Get Set command, 34
Ghostdance (Crowe), 104, 105
GIF file format
    tips for movie files, 185, 187
    for Web output, 82
GifBuilder, 184, 187
Girl of My Heart (Greenberg), 47
Glass Distortion filter, 169–170
Glowing Buddhas (Lichty), 191–192
Gold, Jack, 3, 4, 223
Golden Statue (Greenberg, A. D.), 57
Gone off to Look for America (Clark), 200
Gooey filters, 25
Gore, Kenneth, 74, 75, 80–81, 136, 138, 155, 178–179, 224
Grad palette, 30–32
gradations
    blends vs., 52
    editing with Grad palette, 30–32
grayscale images
    converting color images to, 160
    editing floater masks as, 59
    viewing mask without image, 44
Green Nude (Lichty), 94
Greenberg, Adele Droblas, 47, 55, 57, 80, 156, 224
Greenberg, Seth, 55, 70, 224
Greenblat, Rodney Alan, 194–195, 205, 206, 224
Grid command, 155
grids
    for precision drawings, 49
    using, 139, 155
Groovy Back Button (Jenkins/Rucker Design Group), 174
Guardzilla (Watson), 160

H

halftones, 6
Halverson, Randy A., 210, 221
Have a Prozac Day (Lichty), 65, 66
Heart and Hand (Sammel), 208
Her Mother's Dress (Sammel), 168, 169, 176–177
Highland Secrets (Ennis), 178, 179
Hockey (Obar), 157
Homage to Constable (Bell), 109
Hopkins, Stacy A., 7, 40, 96, 138, 177–178, 192–193, 224
Hopper, Fred R., 210, 221

I

I Like Vino (Sadigursky), 56
I-Com logo (Lockyer), 149
Illustrator, 53, 189
Image Hose brush, 65–73
    adjusting Nozzle palette sliders, 70
    controlling
        nozzle elements with ranking system, 67
        opacity with Controls palette, 70
    loading nozzle files, 66
    nozzle files and, 65
    placing elements with, 70–71
    seeing contents of nozzle files, 66
    using
        brush variants, 67–69
        floaters as nozzle files, 71–73
    See also nozzle files
image resolution, 6–9, 10–11
    digital cameras and, 7–8
    for multimedia presentations, 9
    playing back script with high, 10–11
    resizing images to computer monitors, 9
    setting for output, 7
images
    calculating scaling factor, 9
    changing flat shapes to textured 3-D, 47
    combining paintings and photos, 111–114
    compositing, with masks, 40
    converting
        black-and-white to color, 158–160
        color images to grayscale, 160
    enhancing digital and painted, 153–167
    outputting to Web, 8
    posterizing, 164
    raising text out of, 146
    removing color from, 160
    resizing images, 9–10
    resolution of, 6–9, 10–11
    screen frequency, 6
    tracing over digital, 156
    using as cloning source, 114
    See also composite techniques; enhancing images
Imagine (Schuler), 21, 211
impasto effects, 171, 175

importing
  drawings into Painter, 114
  files from other applications, 189
  Illustrator files, 189
  Painter color images to Photoshop, 9, 79, 196
  shapes from Illustrator, 53
Impressionism (Berkla), 73
Incredible Sign (Dowlen), 75, 78
InfoDog Underwater (Greenblat), 195
InfoDog with Email (Greenblat), 195
Information Anxiety (Barbante), 46, 47, 48, 49
inking pens, 107
Insects, 65
interface design, 183–184
interviews
  with John Derry, 88–90, 172–174
  with Mark Zimmer, 4–6, 88–90, 204, 220
Invisible Dog Films Web page (Lockyer), 183
Island View (Orlando), 213

J

Jenkins, Mark, 173, 174, 224
Joe Williams (Sutton), 175
Johnson, Dennis, 210, 221
Journey of the Navigator (Dowlen), 134–135
JPEG file format, for Web output, 82

K

keyboard shortcuts for tools, 15
Kodak Color Management System (KCMS)
  color matching problems, 78
  preparing color separations, 80
  setting up settings for, 79
  using, 78–79
Kodak Photo CD images, 164
Kotlarz, Tina M., 211, 221
Krause, Dorothy Simpson, 75, 224
Krauter, George, 64, 65, 72–73, 96, 125, 188, 189, 200–201, 224

L

LA (Lichty), 209
Labor of Love, Gift of Health (Gore), 75, 76–77
Lagoon (Burnham), 170
Lamp (Noble), 122, 123
Landscape Fragment No. 3 (Bell), 129–130
Landscape (Stedman), 81
Lasso tool, creating selection with, 56
Layer filters, 28
layer masks vs. floater masks, 58
layers
  converting Photoshop alpha channel layers into Painter, 41
  creating transparent floaters, 61
  in Photoshop, 58
  See also floaters

Lengthy Consideration (Watson), 214
LeVan, Susan, 94–95, 205, 224
libraries
  loading and changing default, 14
  New Paint Tools brush, 87–88
  Nozzles, 72
  String, 94
Lichty, Patrick, 65, 66, 94, 139, 171–172, 191–192, 209, 225
Life is Good (Erickson), 138
lighting, 160–162
linear gradation style, 31
lines and curves, 50
Liquid filters, 20
Lit (Faulkner), 5
Literate Cowboy (Phillips), 127
Load Library option (Brushes pop-up menu), 24
loading
  default libraries, 14
  nozzle files, 66
  Pantone Colors into color set, 36
  selections, 41, 42
Lobster Buoy (Gold), 3, 4
locking palettes, 13
Lockyer, Doug, 89, 90, 104, 118–122, 148–150, 183, 190–191, 197, 203, 225
Look of Her, The (Halverson), 210
Looking Back (Krause), 75
luminance masks, 44–45

M

Macintosh platform
  copying device profiles onto, 79
  recording work sessions in script, 36
  running QuickTime movies and CD-ROM demo, 220
Magic Wand tool, extending selections with, 16
Maid... (Bell), 110, 111, 128, 129
Make Fractal Pattern dialog box, 33
Make Mosaic command, 151, 176
Mancala (Lockyer), 121
Mandel, Debi Lee, 180, 181, 185–186, 198, 212, 225
Marbling command, 172–174
mask drawing icons, 40
Mask List palette
  selecting masks for nozzle file in, 72
  using, 35–36
masks, 39–45
  combining floaters with, 55
  compositing images with, 40
  creating, 42–44
  defined, 39
  floater, 57–58, 135
  floaters and, 57–58
  luminance, 44–45
  saving and reloading selections, 41, 42

  selecting images for nozzle files using, 72
  text, 171
  turning off editing mode for, 44
  using Select menu with, 42
  using selections as masks, 40
  using the selection mask icons, 40–41
  viewing without image, 44
Melting Watch (Mark Jenkins/Rucker Design Group), 173
Memory Portrait (Faulkner), 115–116
Merlin (Dowlen), 134
mixed media techniques, 94–95
Moon & the Earth, The (Yoshii), 217
Mooney's Cottage (Sweeney), 16
Mosaic command, inspiration for, 172–174
Mosaic Tile (Gore), 178–179
mosaics
  creating, 176–179
  text-derived, 151
Mouse filters, 26
mover commands for palettes, 14
movies. *See* AVI movies; QuickTime movies
moving floaters, 56
multimedia and Web animation, 181–187
  buttons and backgrounds on Web pages, 181–183
  creating and editing movies, 183–184
  creating Web animation, 184–187
  image resolution for multimedia presentations, 9
  interface design, 183–184
  resizing images for, 9
multiple applications with Painter, 197–201
murals, 75, 76–77

N

naming scripts, 36
Nature brushes, 93, 94
nature scenes, 93
Near Future of Akihabara (Yoshii), 216
Network palette, 36
New Paint Tools filters
  painting techniques using, 87–88
  thumbnails of, 26
Night Garden (Sweeney), 152, 153, 160, 161
Night Street (Sweeney), 160–162
Noble, Richard, 122, 123, 225
Nocturne (Phillips), 128
Nomad (Burnham), 102, 103
North (Atzenhofer), 213
North Jetty (Sweeney), 102
Nostalgia (Watson), 111–112
Novarius IV (Krauter), 188, 189, 200–201
nozzle files
  adjusting Nozzle palette sliders, 70
  controlling elements with ranking, 67
  creating, 71–73
  on *Garden Hose, The* CD-ROM, 220
  Image Hose brush and, 65

loading and viewing contents of, 66
selecting images for, 72
See also Image Hose brush
Nozzle palette
   adjusting sliders on, 70
   opening, 66
Nozzles library, adding to, 72

O

Obar, David, 157, 225
Objects palette, 34–37
   Floater List palette, 35
   Mask List palette, 35–36
   Network palette, 36
   Plugin Floaters palette, 34–35
   Scripts palette, 36
Okada, Corinne, 205, 225
Old Fence (Sweeney), 162
opacity, controlling mask, 42–43
optimizing performance
   for downloading Web images, 82
   playing back scripts at high resolution, 10–11
Orientation Distort command, 52
Orlando, Dennis, 4, 5, 30, 91–92, 93, 213, 225
Otilio (Sadigursky), 103
Outlook (LeVan), 94, 95
output, 75–83
   on canvas, 75, 80
   for fine art prints, 80–81
   matching colors, 78
      to Pantone Color system, 81
      using Kodak Color Management System, 78–79
   options from Painter, 75–78
   preparing and saving color separations, 80
   for QuickTime or AVI movies, 83–84
   sending to Web, 8, 82
   setting screen frequency for, 7
Oval Selection tool, creating selection with, 56
Owl and the Pussy Cat, The (Lockyer), 118–120
Oyster Bay (Sweeney), 214

P

Painter 5
   compatibility with Photoshop plug-ins, 7
   creating paths, 48
   development of, 4–6, 88–90, 172–174, 204
   digitizing in, 7
   importing and exporting shapes with Illustrator, 53
   masks in, 39, 40
   with other applications, 189–201
      Photoshop, 196–197
      for 3D modeling, 189–193
      using multiple programs, 197–201
   output options for, 75–78

running tutorials and demos for, 219–220
sharing documents on network, 36
Painter Gallery, 203–217
painting techniques, 87–109
   for cartooning, 106–108, 130–134
   creating
      custom textures from photographs, 103–104
      superheros, 90
   customizing brushes, 109
   integrating sketches, 95
   for nature scenes, 93
   painting over pencil, 96
   pencil, chalk, and water color, 94
   simulating
      pen and ink work, 105–106
      wet and dry watercolors, 96–98
   traditional sketching approaches, 91–92
   on transparent layers, 61
   using
      Cartoon Cell fill, 104–105
      custom textures, 101–103
      mixed media, 94–95
      multiple brushes, 89
      New Paint Tools brush library, 87–88
      paper textures, 29–30, 42, 98–100
      textures, 104
   See also brushes
painting tools for type effects, 148–150
paintings
   adjusting original, 163–167
   combining with photos, 111–114
   converting photos to, 153–158
   restoring digitally, 163
palettes, 13–37
   Art Materials, 29–34
   Brushes, 16–28
   Color Set, 36
   Controls, 15–16
   creating custom, 36–37
   locking, 13
   mover commands for, 14
   Objects, 34–36
   Tool, 14–15
Pantone Colors
   loading into color set, 36
   using and matching, 81
Paper palette, 29–30
paper textures
   selecting, 29–30, 42
   using, 98–100
Parappa CD Cover (Greenblat), 205
Parappa Playstation Ride (Greenblat), 206
Parker, Charley, 106–108, 130–134, 226
pasting floaters, 56
paths
   creating in Painter, 48
   ending, continuing, and editing, 50–51
   selecting text with Shape Selection tool, 142
   vector type effects and, 141
patterns in digital images, 33

Patterns palette, 32–33
Peacock Alley #1 Poster (Gore), 155
Peacock Alley #2 Poster (Gore), 138
Pears (Greenberg, A.D.), 156
pen and ink work
   customizing inking pens, 107
   simulating, 105–106
   using Pens Scratchboard tool, 90
Pen filters, 19
Pen tool
   connecting curves with, 49–50
   creating shapes with, 48–50
pencil
   beginning image with, 91–92
   with chalk and water color, 94
   painting over, 96
Pencils filters
   Brushes palette for, 16
   thumbnail of, 17
Pens Scratchboard tool
   customizing inking pens, 107
   uses for, 90
Phillips, Chet, 86, 87, 98, 99, 126–128, 182–183, 193, 226
Philosopher (Watson), 193–194
Photo filters, 26–27
photographs
   combining with paintings, 111–114
   composites and scanned images, 115–116
   converting to paintings, 153–158
   creating custom textures from, 103–104
   enhancing scanned, 163–167
   halftones, 6
Photoshop. *See* Adobe Photoshop
Pink Rhody's (Orlando), 92, 93
pixels
   image resolution and, 6–9
   reducing image size and, 9–10
   setting image resolution, 6–9
Place Elements dialog box, 71
Placement slide (Advanced Controls Random palette), 70
Play with Light & Shadows, A (Orlando), 30
plug-in floaters
   applying, 62–63
   creating special effects with, 172–176
Plugin Floaters palette, 34–35
Points slider (Place Elements dialog box), 71
posterizing images, 164
Pressure spray option (Image Hose brush), 67, 70
printing
   for fine art prints, 80–81
   resizing images for, 9
   See also output
prophecy, 198
Puffy Saves the World (Greenblat), 206
Puppet Fall Down (Campbell), 104
Purple House (Sweeney), 16
Put Set command, 34

Q

Quick Warp command, 145
QuickTime movies
  on CD-ROM demo, 220
  creating and editing, 183–184
  creating link to PDF files, 84
  sending Painter output to, 83–84

R

Rabbi (Crowe), 163
radial gradation styles, 31
Raiders of the Lost Toys (Phillips), 98
Random spray option (Image Hose brush), 67, 70
ranking
  adjusting Nozzle palette sliders, 70
  controlling nozzle elements with, 67
  system of Image Hose, 67
Raster Plug-ins command, 7
Resize dialog box
  determining pixel resolution with, 8
  understanding options of, 9
resizing images, 9–10
resolution. *See* image resolution
RGB Canvas Mask eye icon, 44
RGB color
  converting to CMYK equivalents, 78
  importing Painter images to Photoshop, 9, 196
Robocasso (Hopkins), 192
Ronald the Dragon, 105–106
Rooster (Hopkins), 96
Root Cellar (Sweeney), 12, 13, 33
Rosenberg, Charles, 211, 221
rotating and distorting shapes, 52
Rucker Design Group, 172–174
Russian Glasnost coin (Lockyer), 149

S

Sadigursky, Adam, 56, 103, 135, 212, 226
Sammel, Chelsea, 54, 55, 61, 72, 162–163, 169–170, 175–177, 208, 226
saving
  brush variants, 109
  files with floaters, 59
  selections, 41, 42
scaling
  calculating factor for image, 9
  text, 51
scanned images
  composites and, 115–116
  reworking, 165–167
Schuler, Karen M., 211, 221
Scottish Magic (Ennis), 34
screen frequency
  determining, 6
  setting for output, 7
Script Options dialog box, 11
scripts
  playing back at high resolution, 10
  recording work sessions in, 36
Scripts palette, 36
Sea... (Bell), 128
Secret Donut Protector (Greenblat), 195
Select menu, 42
selection mask icons, 40–41
selections
  choosing patterns for filling, 32–33
  composite techniques using, 135–136, 137–139
  converting
    paths to, 48
    shapes to, 155
    text to, 146
  floater masks and, 56
  of masked images for nozzle files, 72
  saving and reloading, 41, 42
  selecting floaters, 59
  tips for using, 41–42
  transforming into paths, 42
  of type with Shape Selection tool, 142
  using as masks, 40
Sequential spray option (Image Hose brush), 67, 68
serigraphic style, 138
service bureaus
  for fine art print output, 80
  previewing files from, 81
Shape Selection tool, 142
shapes, 47–53
  combining curves and lines, 50
  composite techniques using floaters, selections and, 135–136
  converting
    to floaters, 47–48
    to selection, 155
  creating automatically, 51–52
  ending, continuing, and editing paths, 50–51
  importing and exporting from Illustrator, 53
  rotating and distorting, 52
  scaling text, 51
  tools for creating, 48
  using
    blends, 52–53
    Pen tool, 48–50
Shelf (Yoshii), 216
Shoreline at Same Lord's Castle (Orlando), 92, 93
Shortcut to New Brushes palette, loading F/X filters from, 24
Shubat Tulips (Erickson), 126
Silicon Gaming Face (Okada), 205
silk-screen effects, 61
Size slider (Brush Controls Size palette), 70
Sketchers (Sweeney), 214
sketching
  in Painter, 95, 107
  using multiple sketches, 95
  using traditional approaches to, 91–92
Skipping Stones (Sweeney), 174–175
Sky Dream (Sweeney), 124–125
Sledding (Kotlarz), 211
Small Luminance Cloner brush, 67, 68
Sonata (Burnham), 102
Song of Peace (Sutton), 116–117
Sonoma (Berkla), 73
Source spray option (Image Hose brush), 70
Space Tango (Burnham), 102
special effects, 169–179
  development of, 172–174
  with plug-in floaters, 172–176
  using Glass Distortion, 169–170
  using Painter with other applications, 189–201
  working with Apply Surface Texture, 171–172
  working with mosaics, 176–179
  See also multimedia and Web animation
spiral gradation styles, 32
Spirit of 'Inde'pendence (Phillips), 193
Spring Flood (Clark), 103
St. Joan of the Cross (Lichty), 139
Stedman, Emily, 3, 4, 5, 81, 82, 93, 226
Stephens, John, 158, 159, 196, 226
Still Life with Glass and Peaches (Feldman), 3, 10–11
Stocking Up (Sweeney), 101
Storm (Sweeney), 96
String Library, 94
strokes for Cloner brushes, 115
Studio Gecko (Lockyer), 148, 149
stylus brush strokes, 14
Suitable Salesman (Watson), 113–114
Summer Flowers Planter (Orlando), 4, 5
Summer Solstice (Ulay), 207
Sun Mule (Lockyer), 203
Super Cloners filters
  photo examples of, 28–29
  using, 28
superheros, 90
Surface Control commands, 160
Sushi (Greenberg), 70
Susquehanna (Clark), 104
Sustainable City (Ulay), 207
Sutton, Jeremy, 116–117, 175, 226
Sweeney, Margaret, 12, 13, 16, 33, 87–88, 96, 101–102, 124–125, 152–153, 160–162, 174–175, 193, 214, 227
Sword and Butterfly (Ennis), 123

T

Tall Chief (Ennis), 166–167
techniques
  cartooning, 106–108, 130–134

mixed media, 94–95
for water color, 96
See also composite techniques; painting techniques
Texas (Lichty), 171–172
text
  adding drop shadows to, 144
  creating
    chrome, 145
    paper texture from, 30
    shapes from text, 47
    special effects with, 51
    vector effects with, 141–144
  making patterns from 3D, 146
  manipulating with Automatic Transform command, 51–52
  raising out of digital image, 144, 146
  See also type effects
Text tool
  creating paper texture from text, 30
  manipulating text with, 51
textures
  creating from photographs, 103–104
  custom, 101–103
  paper, 29–30, 42, 98–100
  raising type with Apply Surface Texture command, 144
  using, 104
Therapist (Watson), 166
3D images
  creating patterns from 3D text, 146
  techniques for Russian Glasnost coin, 149
3D modeling
  for *The Owl and the Pussy Cat*, 119
  using Painter with applications for, 189–193
thumbnails
  for Brushes palette, 17–21, 23, 26, 28
  for Composite Methods, 60
  for Image Hose brush variants, 68–69
  of plug-in effects, 63
Tibetan Ceremony (Dowlen), 97, 98
Tibetan Girl at Yamdrak Tso (Dowlen), 97
Tied Hands, The (Stedman), 3, 5
tiling in *The Owl and the Pussy Cat*, 120
Tilt 'n' Tumble (Lockyer), 197
tonal control
  adjusting, 162–163
  converting color images to grayscale, 160
tools
  Controls palette for, 15–16
  creating selections for masks with, 40
  for creating shapes, 48
  keyboard shortcuts for, 15
  using type and painting tools for type effects, 148–150
  See also specific tools listed by name
Tools palette, 14–15
Touchstone Energy (Lockyer), 122
Tour Poster (Crowe), 164

Tourist (Watson), 113
Tracing Paper command, 156
Train (Atzenhofer), 48, 49
Transcendentalist, The (Burnham), 136, 137
Transitional Thought (Watson), 214
Transparent Layer brush, using, 61
Tree of Bird (Yoshii), 217
Trees (Hopkins), 177–178
Tri-Ominos for Kids (Lockyer), 197
tutorial images, 220
Twins (Yoshii), 217
twirled type, 52
type effects, 141–151
  beveled, 146–148
  chrome text, 145
  creating
    mask from text, 171
    mosaic from text, 151
  raising type, 144, 146
  twirled type, 52
  using painting tools for, 148–150
  vector, 141–144
  See also text

U

Ulay, Ayse, 202, 203, 207, 227
Ultimate Interactive Guide to Painter 5, The, 182, 183–184, 219–220
Un Monde Unis (Mandel), 212
Unicorn Girl (Ennis), 200

V

Van Gogh 2 brush, 155–156
Van Gogh Mural (Gore), 136
vector type effects, 141–144
Vivo (Sadigursky), 135

W

Waking Beauty (Ennis), 39, 40
Water Color filters, 23
water colors
  converting black-and-white images to color with, 158, 159
  with pencil and chalk effects, 94
  simulating wet and dry, 96–98
  techniques using Water Color brush, 96
Water filters, 18
Water Lily Flower (Hopkins), 7
Watson, Pat, 111–115, 159–160, 165–166, 193–194, 214, 227
Weaves palette, 34
Web animation, 184–187
  of cat, 180, 181, 185–186
  of CD-ROM graphic, 185
  of mouse, 186–187
  using floaters for, 184

Web pages
  creating animation for, 184–187
  creating interface for, 182–183
  for Invisible Dog Films, 183
  outputting art to, 8
  resizing images for, 9
  sending Painter output to, 8, 82
Wedding (Stedman), 3, 4
Welder, The, (Orlando), 91–92
Windows platform
  copying device profiles onto, 79
  running QuickTime movies and CD-ROM demo, 220
Wine Country (Stedman), 81, 82
Woman, Ship & Pearls (Stephens), 196
Wooden Home Button (Jenkins/Rucker Design Group), 174

Y

Yoshii, Hiroshi, 215–217, 227

Z

Zimmer, Mark, 4–6, 88–90, 204, 220

Publish

THE MAGAZINE FOR ELECTRONIC PUBLISHING PROFESSIONALS

FREE 101 Tips Book!

Pixel-Perfect Scans

Managing Color: Get Consistent Results From Start To Finish

The Next Generation of Publishing Software

Affordable Big-Screen Monitors

Top Products of the Year

Choose The Right Paper For Dramatic Effect

Can You Trust Onscreen Proofing?

To receive your FREE ISSUE and FREE *101 TIPS* book, simply detach this postcard and return it today. No purchase required.

1 FREE ISSUE AND A FREE BOOK
absolutely free

Yes, I'd like to sample 1 issue of *Publish*. I understand that I'll also receive 101 Best Electronic Publishing Tips FREE just for trying *Publish*. If I like my sample issue, I'll pay just $29.95 for 11 more issues (for a total of 12 issues). I'll save $29. That's 50%!– off the annual cover price.

If I don't choose to subscribe, I'll return your subscription bill marked "cancel" and owe nothing.

The FREE issue and 101 TIPS book will be mine to keep – free.

**Trial only.
Don't send money.
Just mail this card!**

Name

Title

Company

Address

City State Zip

E-mail

H80111

Just an hour a month with *Publish*

gives you the edge in mastering your electronic publishing tools— from design to → print → web screen → or CD-ROM!

With today's explosion of new electronic publishing technologies, you have more options than ever before. To keep up, you need the magazine that pioneered the digital publishing revolution... and still sets the pace for graphics professionals.

It's PUBLISH. Month after month, PUBLISH improves your skills at every step in the electronic publishing process.

PUBLISH provides the ongoing education you need to save time and money in today's competitive world of electronic publishing. Our experts not only discuss new digital technologies, they show you how to use design and imaging tools to achieve spectacular results.

Yours FREE for trying *Publish*!

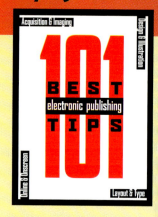

We're giving this free gift to catch your eye and call your attention to our no-risk, no-commitment offer of 1 FREE ISSUE.

The electronic publishing secrets in 101 Best Electronic Publishing Tips guarantee you'll ignite your creativity and shorten the learning curve for your favorite programs. They're FREE just for mailing the reply card. Do it today. Don't wait!

- Acquisition & Imaging Tips
- Design & Illustration Tips
- Layout & Type Tips
- Online & Onscreen Tips

Tips apply to the current versions of programs on both Macintosh and Windows platforms of -

- Fractal Design Painter
- Adobe Photoshop
- Adobe PageMaker
- QuarkXPress
- Macromedia FreeHand
- Adobe Illustrator
- Corel Draw
- And more!

NO POSTAGE NECESSARY IF MAILED IN THE UNITED STATES

BUSINESS REPLY MAIL
FIRST CLASS MAIL   PERMIT NO. 237   BRENTWOOD, TENNESSEE

POSTAGE WILL BE PAID BY ADDRESSEE

SUBSCRIPTION DEPARTMENT
P.O. BOX 5039
BRENTWOOD, TN 37024-9815

my2cents.idgbooks.com

Register This Book — And Win!

Visit **http://my2cents.idgbooks.com** to register this book and we'll automatically enter you in our fantastic monthly prize giveaway. It's also your opportunity to give us feedback: let us know what you thought of this book and how you would like to see other topics covered.

Discover IDG Books Online!

The IDG Books Online Web site is your online resource for tackling technology — at home and at the office. Frequently updated, the IDG Books Online Web site features exclusive software, insider information, online books, and live events!

10 Productive & Career-Enhancing Things You Can Do at www.idgbooks.com

- Nab source code for your own programming projects.
- Download software.
- Read Web exclusives: special articles and book excerpts by IDG Books Worldwide authors.
- Take advantage of resources to help you advance your career as a Novell or Microsoft professional.
- Buy IDG Books Worldwide titles or find a convenient bookstore that carries them.
- Register your book and win a prize.
- Chat live online with authors.
- Sign up for regular e-mail updates about our latest books.
- Suggest a book you'd like to read or write.
- Give us your 2¢ about our books and about our Web site.

You say you're not on the Web yet? It's easy to get started with IDG Books' *Discover the Internet,* available at local retailers everywhere.

ABOUT THE AUTHORS

Adele Droblas Greenberg is a New York-based artist, retoucher, and desktop/prepress multimedia consultant. She teaches Painter and Photoshop at the Pratt Institute. Adele is also the former training director of a New York City prepress house.

Seth Greenberg is a computer consultant, database/multimedia programmer, and freelance writer. He has also worked as a television producer and scriptwriter, and he has written articles on computer software for several magazines.

Adele and Seth are also the authors and publishers of the *The Ultimate Interactive Guide to Painter 5*. In addition to *Painter 5 Studio Secrets*, Adele and Seth co-authored *Illustrator for Dummies*, also for IDG Books Worldwide.

COLOPHON

This book was produced electronically in Foster City, California. Microsoft Word 7.0 was used for word processing; design and layout were produced with QuarkXPress 3.32 on a Power Macintosh 8500/120. The typeface families used are Myriad Multiple Master, Minion Multiple Master, and Trajan.

Acquisitions Editor: Michael Roney
Development Editors: Katharine Dvorak, Amy Thomas
Technical Editor: Ben Barbante
Copy Editor: Nate Holdread
Production Coordinator: Katy German
Book Design: Margery Cantor, Cátálin Dulfu, Kurt Krames
Graphics and Production Specialists: Renée Dunn, Andreas F. Schueller, Elsie Yim
Quality Control Specialists: Mick Arellano, Mark Schumann
Proofreader: David Wise
Indexer: Rebecca Plunkett
Cover Art: Adam Sadigursky
Back Cover Art: Ben Barbante, Chet Phillips, Margaret Sweeney

IDG BOOKS WORLDWIDE, INC. END-USER LICENSE AGREEMENT

READ THIS. You should carefully read these terms and conditions before opening the software packet(s) included with this book ("Book"). This is a license agreement ("Agreement") between you and IDG Books Worldwide, Inc. ("IDGB"). By opening the accompanying software packet(s), you acknowledge that you have read and accept the following terms and conditions. If you do not agree and do not want to be bound by such terms and conditions, promptly return the Book and the unopened software packet(s) to the place you obtained them for a full refund.

1. **License Grant.** IDGB grants to you (either an individual or entity) a nonexclusive license to use one copy of the enclosed software program(s) (collectively, the "Software") solely for your own personal or business purposes on a single computer (whether a standard computer or a workstation component of a multiuser network). The Software is in use on a computer when it is loaded into temporary memory (RAM) or installed into permanent memory (hard disk, CD-ROM, or other storage device). IDGB reserves all rights not expressly granted herein.

2. **Ownership.** IDGB is the owner of all right, title, and interest, including copyright, in and to the compilation of the Software recorded on the disk(s) or CD-ROM ("Software Media"). Copyright to the individual programs recorded on the Software Media is owned by the author or other authorized copyright owner of each program. Ownership of the Software and all proprietary rights relating thereto remain with IDGB and its licensers.

3. **Restrictions On Use and Transfer.**

(a) You may only (i) make one copy of the Software for backup or archival purposes, or (ii) transfer the Software to a single hard disk, provided that you keep the original for backup or archival purposes. You may not (i) rent or lease the Software, (ii) copy or reproduce the Software through a LAN or other network system or through any computer subscriber system or bulletin-board system, or (iii) modify, adapt, or create derivative works based on the Software.

(b) You may not reverse engineer, decompile, or disassemble the Software. You may transfer the Software and user documentation on a permanent basis, provided that the transferee agrees to accept the terms and conditions of this Agreement and you retain no copies. If the Software is an update or has been updated, any transfer must include the most recent update and all prior versions.

4. **Restrictions On Use of Individual Programs.** You must follow the individual requirements and restrictions detailed for each individual program in the "Using the CD-ROM" appendix of this Book. These limitations are also contained in the individual license agreements recorded on the Software Media. These limitations may include a requirement that

after using the program for a specified period of time, the user must pay a registration fee or discontinue use. By opening the Software packet(s), you will be agreeing to abide by the licenses and restrictions for these individual programs that are detailed in the "Using the CD-ROM" appendix and on the Software Media. None of the material on this Software Media or listed in this Book may ever be redistributed, in original or modified form, for commercial purposes.

5. **Limited Warranty.**

(a) IDGB warrants that the Software and Software Media are free from defects in materials and workmanship under normal use for a period of sixty (60) days from the date of purchase of this Book. If IDGB receives notification within the warranty period of defects in materials or workmanship, IDGB will replace the defective Software Media.

(b) IDGB AND THE AUTHORS OF THE BOOK DISCLAIM ALL OTHER WARRANTIES, EXPRESS OR IMPLIED, INCLUDING WITHOUT LIMITATION IMPLIED WARRANTIES OF MERCHANTABILITY AND FITNESS FOR A PARTICULAR PURPOSE, WITH RESPECT TO THE SOFTWARE, THE PROGRAMS, THE SOURCE CODE CONTAINED THEREIN, AND/OR THE TECHNIQUES DESCRIBED IN THIS BOOK. IDGB DOES NOT WARRANT THAT THE FUNCTIONS CONTAINED IN THE SOFTWARE WILL MEET YOUR REQUIREMENTS OR THAT THE OPERATION OF THE SOFTWARE WILL BE ERROR FREE.

(c) This limited warranty gives you specific legal rights, and you may have other rights that vary from jurisdiction to jurisdiction.

6. **Remedies.**

(a) IDGB's entire liability and your exclusive remedy for defects in materials and workmanship shall be limited to replacement of the Software Media, which may be returned to IDGB with a copy of your receipt at the following address: Software Media Fulfillment Department, Attn.: *Painter 5 Studio Secrets*, IDG Books Worldwide, Inc., 7260 Shadeland Station, Ste. 100, Indianapolis, IN 46256, or call 1-800-762-2974. Please allow three to four weeks for delivery. This Limited Warranty is void if failure of the Software Media has resulted from accident, abuse, or misapplication. Any replacement Software Media will be warranted for the remainder of the original warranty period or thirty (30) days, whichever is longer.

(b) In no event shall IDGB or the authors be liable for any damages whatsoever (including without limitation damages for loss of business profits, business interruption, loss of business information, or any other pecuniary loss) arising from the use of or inability to use the Book or the Software, even if IDGB has been advised of the possibility of such damages.

(c) Because some jurisdictions do not allow the exclusion or limitation of liability for consequential or incidental damages, the above limitation or exclusion may not apply to you.

7. U.S. Government Restricted Rights. Use, duplication, or disclosure of the Software by the U.S. Government is subject to restrictions stated in paragraph (c)(1)(ii) of the Rights in Technical Data and Computer Software clause of DFARS 252.227-7013, and in subparagraphs (a) through (d) of the Commercial Computer—Restricted Rights clause at FAR 52.227-19, and in similar clauses in the NASA FAR supplement, when applicable.

8. General. This Agreement constitutes the entire understanding of the parties and revokes and supersedes all prior agreements, oral or written, between them and may not be modified or amended except in a writing signed by both parties hereto that specifically refers to this Agreement. This Agreement shall take precedence over any other documents that may be in conflict herewith. If any one or more provisions contained in this Agreement are held by any court or tribunal to be invalid, illegal, or otherwise unenforceable, each and every other provision shall remain in full force and effect.